SUBJECT LESSONS

SUBJECT LESSONS
Life Histories as Reciprocal Empowerment

John Forrest

berghahn
NEW YORK · OXFORD
www.berghahnbooks.com

First published in 2024 by
Berghahn Books
www.berghahnbooks.com

© 2024 John Forrest

All rights reserved. Except for the quotation of short passages
for the purposes of criticism and review, no part of this book
may be reproduced in any form or by any means, electronic or
mechanical, including photocopying, recording, or any information
storage and retrieval system now known or to be invented,
without written permission of the publisher.

Library of Congress Cataloging-in-Publication Data

Names: Forrest, John, 1951- author.
Title: Subject lessons : life histories as reciprocal empowerment / John Forrest.
Other titles: Life histories as reciprocal empowerment
Description: New York : Berghahn, 2024. | Includes bibliographical references
and index.
Identifiers: LCCN 2024015777 (print) | LCCN 2024015778 (ebook) |
ISBN 9781805396543 (hardback) | ISBN 9781805396550 (e) |
ISBN 9781805396567 (web pdf)
Subjects: LCSH: Oral biography. | Oral biography—Study and teaching. |
Social sciences—Biographical methods.
Classification: LCC CT22 .F67 2024 (print) | LCC CT22 (ebook) |
DDC 920.0072—dc23/eng/20240603
LC record available at https://lccn.loc.gov/2024015777
LC ebook record available at https://lccn.loc.gov/2024015778

British Library Cataloguing in Publication Data

A catalogue record for this book is available from the British Library.

ISBN 978-1-80539-654-3 hardback
ISBN 978-1-80539-655-0 epub
ISBN 978-1-80539-656-7 web pdf

https://doi.org/10.3167/9781805396543

I dedicate this work to every single one of my students who developed qualitative fieldwork skills under my supervision. I am proud of you all.

CONTENTS

Preface	viii
Introduction	1
Chapter 1. Fieldwork Methods for Undergraduates	28
Chapter 2. Elisabeth Jackson	39
Chapter 3. Bonnie McCutcheon	63
Chapter 4. Michael Avrut	77
Chapter 5. Isadora Sahl	93
Chapter 6. Onalie Mesa Oakstar	135
Chapter 7. Janette Yarwood	150
Chapter 8. Andrea Pernstich	166
Conclusion	193
References	202
Index	207

PREFACE

I realize in reading and editing this book for the hundredth time that it serves multiple purposes simultaneously and they can sometimes feel discordant. Mea culpa, mea maxima culpa. The book is, to a small degree, a reflexive analysis of my experiences teaching life history methods to undergraduates, so that it weaves together epistemological and pedagogical foundations, methodological issues, and practical examples of life histories in a complex tapestry. The work spans thirty-five years of my career, so it is complex. No apologies.

If you teach field methods to undergraduates, you should find ideas here for use in the classroom; if you are taking field methods as a student, I hope you find inspiration in the projects presented here; and if you are a casual reader, I would like to believe that you will find passages of interest. Herein are the voices of forgotten people who deserve to be heard. Many of my students came to me as forgotten people as well, lost in a world that had largely abandoned them, yet optimistic enough to see a bachelor's degree as a way up and out of their current lives. Because of their secondary school backgrounds, they had trouble with the academic expectations of college and struggled to keep up. Three such students are represented in this volume. Life history documentation was a safe haven for them.

The critical aspect of recording life histories for all students, disadvantaged or not, is that the process does not require the conventional writing skills of the academy. Its centerpiece is recording and transcribing the authentic voices of narrators, and this job requires careful attention to ways of speaking and not ways of writing, and, therefore, does not penalize lapses in conventional grammar and word choice. Noting down life histories is thoroughly democratic.

The main issue that I want to highlight in this volume is my concept of reciprocal empowerment through the life history method. Both the narrator and the fieldworker empower each other in the process. As such, working with life histories shares some of the qualities of postcolonial field methods, such as engaged interviewing and reflexivity. But there is more to the method than that. It can be a truly life-changing experience for the fieldworker, as you will see.

As you read this work, my profound debt owed to my students will become self-evident. In particular I wish to acknowledge the vital help I received from Janette Yarwood in the final stages of manuscript preparation. I would also like to acknowledge the assistance I received from multiple anonymous reviewers who encouraged me to edit and edit, and then re-edit. The work is much improved in consequence.

Introduction

Life History Method

History as a general discipline has had its own long and convoluted history, with diverse topics of interest and reasons for pursuing them coming in and out of favor. At heart there is the question of *what* happened in the past, followed by an inquiry into *why* certain things happened. There can also be a question of the relative importance of certain events and their consequences, which depends on your reasons for inquiring in the first place. Thus, we have political history, economic history, social history, military history, and on and on. For centuries, history as a discipline concerned itself with matters that the elite members of cultures cared about because they were the ones with the ability to read and write, or had the resources to employ a class of people who could. We know about kings and queens of the past and their general exploits because they took the trouble to have them written down. Thus, we can speculate, to a degree, about the interests and exploits of Cyrus the Great or Richard the Lionheart because we have a few surviving documents to work with produced by scribes and priests. But if we want to know about the life of an English peasant in the tenth century CE or a Persian soldier of the sixth century BCE, we have to resort primarily to archeology, and even there we have precious little data.

Hundreds of thousands of Anglo-Saxon people lived, worked, and died in England, facing sorrows and hardships along with joys and delights, yet we know next to nothing about the particulars of their lives.

There are glimpses now and again when a scholar gives us a hint or two, but centuries drift by with—nothing. What did it feel like to spend the winter at Valley Forge with George Washington (who had a private house to hole up in), or to face down the French troops as a sick and exhausted bowman under Henry V at Agincourt? Our views are forever colored by drama, fiction, and ahistorical speculation. Even letters home, diaries, and poetic musings are specialized, and crafted, views. When Stephen Crane wanted to get the real feel of life on the battlefield during the American Civil War before writing the *Red Badge of Courage*, he sat around in the park in Port Jervis, New York, and talked to veterans of the war. Those are the real stories of everyday people, not the carefully polished ruminations of professional historians.

I am not trying to make the case that the people who lived through momentous times tell a story that is somehow better or more real than the story historians tell. But it is a *different* story—and it is different in critical ways. First and foremost, the first-person narrative of events can get inside the experience of the event—what it felt like to be there. For the most part, historians are not concerned with issues of lived experience, and they have precious little to go on even if they are. Social history, which exploded in importance in the second half of the twentieth century, made a valiant effort to come to grips with the daily lives of ordinary people but without much data to work with. Enter the ethnographer.

We cannot go back into the past beyond living memory and magically create primary documents that bring those times to life, but we can speak to people who are now in their nineties, which puts us back into the late 1930s, and all points from then until now. How did the Vietnam War change life in Australia ? (Yes Australian conscripts were sent to that war.) What was it like to live through the Pol Pot years in Cambodia? Where were you when the Twin Towers fell on 9/11? What was life like in Uganda under Idi Amin? . . . And on and on. Pick the time and place you want, and you can find an abundance of eyewitnesses whose recounting of history has a very different quality from official records.

An oral narrative about one's own lived experience is not like any other kind of history—it is in a genre by itself. While such a tale can be characterized as autobiography, it is a different animal from what is normally thought of as an autobiographical story. There are several key differences between the two types. First, an oral life history is spoken and not written. It is told in the narrator's own voice—what is sometimes (misleadingly) called "authentic voice"—suggesting that the tale is not artificially crafted in the way that written prose is. It is crafted, of course, but not in the same way that a written story is. An oral tale does not require skills in writing, or even literacy. Second, an oral narrative is told to another person rather than being a solo enterprise, and, therefore, the interaction between teller and listener is an essential component in the way the narrator shapes the tale, depending on the relationship between the two—which can be conceived of as a certain kind of partnership. How this relationship operates is a major theme of this book.

Back in the 1980s, teaching fieldwork methods to undergraduate anthropology majors was a rarity, and, indeed, there were many graduate programs that did not require such training. I went into the field for my doctoral fieldwork in 1978 with no training beyond the occasional hands-on project I had done for a term paper. I was expected to just sort of pick it up. Since then, things have changed radically. For example, H. Russell Bernard pioneered summer programs in fieldwork methods of diverse kinds for anthropologists at all stages of professional development and accompanied them with diverse publications (e.g., Bernard 1998 and 2005).

When I was asked to revise the requirements for anthropology majors at Purchase College, SUNY in 1988, I added a course in fieldwork methods to be undertaken in the fall semester of the junior year. The college had (and has) a senior thesis requirement, which for anthropology majors up to that point had usually consisted of library research. Having taken a methods course, the students could then contemplate conducting a limited field research project, which proved to be immensely successful. The star component of the methods course for most of the students was the life history project, which a great many of them found utterly transformative. From the first year in which I taught the course (1989), I was blown away by the quality of the life histories produced, and I even coauthored a paper with one of my students on her work (Forrest and Jackson 1990). She is also represented in this volume.

Thirty plus years later, expectations for undergraduate field research have changed dramatically, and methods courses are becoming the norm. There are, nonetheless, complex challenges when directing undergraduate field research despite its obvious benefits.

Undergraduates as Fieldworkers

In 1969, as part of a root-and-branch reexamination of anthropology, Dell Hymes made the following apocalyptic pronouncement:

> The future of anthropology in the United States is . . . a question of whether its present institutional context, especially the graduate department, will prove to have been chrysalis or coffin. If anthropology remains confined

> there, it may wax as an instrument of domination, wane into irrelevance, or—more likely—combine both fates. It is unlikely to contribute much to the liberation of mankind. (Hymes 1972a: 6–7)

Many in the profession might quietly affirm that this vision has proven extraordinarily prescient. The problems that Hymes was alluding to may reasonably be subsumed under the general rubric of professionalism; that is, a largely tacit, but all-consuming, function of graduate departments is to perpetuate themselves and to enhance the reputations of their members more than to increase our knowledge of humankind and to further the needs of its members, and their goals are fatally introverted.

The gilded path for the graduate student in a major department is something on the order of: coursework, exotic fieldwork, PhD, professorship at a major department leading to the training of other graduate students who perpetuate the cycle. Despite seemingly heartfelt appeals by successive generations of presidents of the American Anthropological Association to push anthropological insights into public consciousness, the development of numerous applied programs, the employment of anthropologists as congressional advisers, and so forth, there is still a strong sense within the profession that the gilded path is the way of the best and brightest and that these other courses are second best—at best. More usually, popularizers and activists are held up to subtle (and unsubtle) forms of ridicule and discrimination within the ranks of graduate faculty at elite research universities.

Teaching undergraduates is often perceived by the luminaries of graduate departments as an index of failure as a professional anthropologist. That is, PhDs who accept appointments at predominantly undergraduate institutions may be characterized as having had to settle for the low road, ultimately destined for obscurity and drudgery. Likewise, the task of instructing undergraduates at major research institutions is frequently seen as a necessary evil: it pays the bills and keeps the deans happy, but few graduate faculty relish the prospect. Introductory courses, commonly the only anthropology courses that undergraduates take and the mainstay of undergraduate programs, can be relegated to the care of graduate assistants—in part or in total. Furthermore, at some elite universities, a record of good undergraduate teaching is registered as a black mark on one's professional credentials. I was once interviewed for a position at one of the top anthropology departments in the United States, and a senior faculty member advised me beforehand not to mention my love of undergraduate teaching, or to even bring up the topic.

Compare the actual state of affairs nowadays with Hymes's hope for the future of the discipline:

Introduction　　　　　　　　　　　　　　　　　　　　　　　　　　　　　5

> The critical and scholarly role is indispensable . . . especially given the pres-
> ent disarray and inadequacy of relevant knowledge. Nevertheless, within
> the academy, a redistribution of attention and prestige from graduate to un-
> dergraduate training of anthropologists is important. Given the opportunity,
> undergraduates could be trained in anthropological work as well as graduate
> students, perhaps better; much graduate time is spent on activities required,
> not for training, but for induction into the hegemony of a particular de-
> partment and a prospective profession. . . . Undergraduates would be freer
> to acquire relevant training and do good work, having in mind long-range
> plans not under the control of their teachers. The greatest contribution of an-
> thropology departments might be to send into the world many lawyers, his-
> torians, activists, workers for various institutions and agencies, well trained
> in anthropological work. (Hymes 1972a: 56–57)

The agenda here is, in its broad outlines, disarmingly simple: allow
graduate departments to continue in their scholarly function, but pay
much greater attention and devote more resources to the training of
undergraduates, especially those whose ultimate professional goals are
outside the discipline. Thus, the broader professional and activist world
becomes leavened with the spirit of anthropology, and thus are spread
the knowledge, aims, and ideals of the discipline beyond the narrow
confines of academic circles. In principle, such redistribution of energy
and resources is perfectly practicable; all that is entailed is the will to do
it. But the will is tied to a rather thorny detail, namely, the ability (and
desire) to shift prestige from graduate to undergraduate training. This
cannot occur by an act of will alone; the training of undergraduates
must develop its own prestige.

The attraction and kudos of graduate training lie in its association
with creative scholarship. Graduate seminars keep faculty up to the
mark in the latest research developments in specialized fields and may
lead to publications by faculty and participants. Undergraduate training, by contrast, is routinely treated as drudgery—roughly equivalent
to conjugating verbs in French 1 or observing the effects of osmosis on
potato cells in a general bio lab. The task is often conceived as the duty
to convey a certain body of information and basic theory on the part of
the teacher and to memorize it sufficiently to pass a few examinations
on the student's part. But if this is all there is to undergraduate training,
then it should not be a matter of wonder that Hymes's ambitions for
it have not and will not ever be realized. It is hard to imagine prestige
accruing to such a minimal exercise, or much leavening of the general
public occurring as a consequence. More likely, all parties are equally
delighted when the semester ends and the experiences therein can be
forgotten.

For many decades there has been a certain level of disingenuousness hovering over introductory classes in anthropology. Look over the vast welter of textbooks on offer and you will see much the same substantive content packaged only marginally differently from decades gone by. Somewhere along the way you will encounter the Iroquois kinship system, potlatch, and the kula ring, as if these topics are part of an essential grounding in the field. Why? The fieldwork that such knowledge is based on is really old—at least one hundred years, or more—and a critical eye surveying these eternal verities of the field easily spots the fissures in what ought to be firm foundations for new research. Nor does eschewing the old ways for a radical postcolonial perspective help the cause sufficiently; instead, such an enterprise has to be tacked on to existing texts, written under old models, because a radically innovative textbook stripped of all the old and outdated theory and substance has not been written yet.[1] The simple fact is that intro courses in anthropology are largely obsolete methods of indoctrination into a field that no longer exists. This is not how to realize Hymes's model for undergraduate education in anthropology. We need to be more practical and get down into the weeds.

For undergraduate training to hold the same significance as graduate training, undergraduates must be taught to appreciate anthropology by practicing it, and they must be guided to produce worthy, original work. I have experimented with numerous methods over the years, but this book cannot delve into all of them (see Forrest 2022 for more). Rather, I will expound on one significant component (maybe the most significant) of my overarching teaching technique, that is, to introduce students at the earliest possible moment to field materials and to get them out doing their own fieldwork projects as quickly as is reasonable.

My purpose is straightforward. Without an appreciation of how field data are gathered and what they look like in the raw state, it is difficult to understand where ideas about cultural patterns and general social theory come from, and therefore all too easy to imagine that it is hocus pocus: one theory being as good as another (which is not awfully far from the truth). The notion of probing basic data personally is the justification for having new students of biology dissect frogs, or physics students stretch springs, or language students take a summer abroad. In introductory classes for freshmen and sophomores, I expose them to my own field data in the very first class, and periodically throughout the semester—unedited video footage, audio tapes, transcriptions of interviews, slides—sometimes so fresh that I have barely had time to catalog, let alone reflect on, them myself. My students see both the richness of

Introduction **7**

fieldwork and also all of my mistakes, bumbling maneuvers, and errors of judgment. Together we explore—through discussion—patterns and meanings latent in the materials, as well as the advantages and pitfalls of classic methods. I also give all of these students the opportunity to design and implement small, supervised fieldwork projects of their own, such as collecting kinship data from their families or photodocumenting a familiar ritual. First-semester-junior majors begin on their own more extensive field investigations in the course I created, and senior majors design, execute, and write up a complete ethnographic project of their own devising over the course of an academic year.

I have only one basic directive that I expect my undergraduates to follow in all of their projects: they must *care* about what they are doing. They must demonstrate to me that they have some purpose for the task beyond handing in an assignment or getting a grade. My goal with this directive is twofold. My first concern is ethical. I do not want my students engaging with the lives of others without a strong sense that people matter. When a student in a lab plunks zinc into a beaker of sulfuric acid to produce hydrogen, there is little need to be concerned about the feelings of the zinc or the morality of the act. But interviewing people about their lives can always be touchy. Doing it without thinking or feeling is always morally wrong. Secondly, when my students misguidedly ignore this directive, their work is always trivial and uninteresting; when they follow it, their work always contains valuable nuggets.

It is not enough simply to give the order that they must care about what they are doing, however. To do no more than that is as alienating as saying "you must all get As" or "you must not miss any classes," and likely to be as productive. The process has to start by showing them what it means to care, and how to work on caring as an intrinsic part of the methodological process. One step in the right direction is to show them by example that I care about what I am doing. This approach, however, may appear as no more than vanity, or eccentricity, or worse if unsupported by other conditions. What seems to turn the trick more often than not is the students' encounters with people in the field who care about what they are doing. In such cases it is the person being questioned, rather than the fieldworker, who provides the motivation and justification for doing the fieldwork, that is, empowers the fieldworker. Thus, finding someone who cares deeply about their work can be a kind of conversion experience for new fieldworkers. The symptoms are usually clear: a glow of success, a babble of talk about how exciting the project was, and a write-up that is reams longer than required. The sense of fieldwork being a collaboration between student and interlocuter, with both of them empowering the enterprise, begins at this point.

Good work of the sort produced by my best and most caring undergraduate fieldworkers deserves to be published, but the justification for publishing it is not quite the same as for the work of graduate students and other professionals in the field (see Spradley and McCurdy 1972; Jenike 2005; Lancy 2003). As has been noted several times by such scholars engaged with undergraduate researchers, undergraduate fieldwork is strongest in producing rich data, and often rather less successful when it comes to the sophistication of analysis. I do not find this state of affairs troubling, limiting, or even surprising. Why would we expect an undergraduate of traditional college age to produce a nuanced appraisal of field data that is as profound as that of a seasoned scholar? Their competence as fieldworkers lies less in their encyclopedic knowledge of anthropological theory and practice and more in their energy and devotion to their interviewees. In fact, their limitations in theoretical depth and rigor may be a virtue in that they may be more inclined to gather data without a strong sense that they are championing a specific ideological cause. They may, thereby, discover hitherto untapped narrative resources.

Because of this relatively low level of interest in professional concerns, and career advancement, via fieldwork, undergraduate relationships with people in the field are special, and I will discuss this issue at greater length in due course. For the moment I will note simply that the projects represented in this volume are not of the same type and quality as those created by postgraduate researchers. For example, these life histories quite often act as the vehicles for the presentation of authentic voices that are seldom, if ever, heard in professional circles or even in mainstream media. Neither are these voices dressed up in flamboyant theory nor otherwise laden with interpretation. Rather, they are allowed to speak for themselves; their theoretical stances latent within them.

Whether or not such work can attract to it the prestige that is currently attached to the more usual types of postgraduate professional research is not for me to decide or legislate. What I might say instead is that the notion of the shifting (or redistributing) of "prestige," as such, is unlikely to occur for all manner of reasons associated with professionalism; but if we replace "prestige" with "value," then some kind of reorientation of interest may happen. The discipline may not have the capacity or desire to bestow prestige on the works presented in this book; but these projects do, nonetheless, have value for the discipline, and may be used by it. Although this semantic difference may seem meager or unimportant at first, the implications of seeing genuine value in undergraduate fieldwork are weighty. Not least of these is the recognition that undergraduates can be much more than the passive recipients

Introduction   **9**

of an education (if passive receiving can be honored with the name "education"). They can be our collaborators, as an intrinsic part of the process of universal learning: we can learn from them as well as vice versa. The appropriate trope for this kind of education is, therefore, "sharing" rather than "instructing," and suggests ways in which learning in the social sciences might act as an example for other disciplines.

Related curricular initiatives have been garnering much attention in higher education circles for some time under a variety of rubrics such as "collaborative learning" and "cooperative learning," and, indeed, such pedagogic concepts have an exceedingly long and distinguished history (see, for example, Rau and Heyl 1990; Slavin 1989; and Totten et al. 1991). But my goal is much greater than simply to create a learning environment that motivates undergraduates to do good work for me. I am encouraging students to produce work that has intrinsic interest for professionals within the discipline as a whole. I am aiming to make my students my professional colleagues in certain well-defined ways, and to make their research *matter* outside the classroom and the college.

It seems to me to be profoundly contradictory and ultimately self-defeating for us to preach humanism but teach tyrannically. Valuing undergraduate contributions to the discipline does not arise from a desire to have it so, however, any more than endowing them with prestige does. Part of the function of this book, therefore, is to make it clear through both direct presentation and through a measure of interpretive analysis where the value in this work lies.

Undergraduate fieldwork at its best is so good—as Hymes suggests—because students' care for their data can, and does, take precedence over all other personal and vocational interests. My students have no need to act as my academic shock troops, as graduate students frequently act for their advisers (the reward being a strong job reference). Nor are they in the service of any particular ideology or theoretical stance. Most of the time they are innocent of such drives so that they are potentially more humanistic than further advanced scholars; and we can all learn from their devotion to the work itself as opposed to how it looks to others, or where it will get them professionally.

The materials represented here were all gathered and written up by undergraduates, although all have long since graduated. Only one of them continued to pursue postgraduate training in anthropology, my colleague and consultant Janette Yarwood (who vacillated for many years between medicine and anthropology). All the others are employed as social workers, activists, and professionals of various stripes. But all retain a strong sense of the anthropological method, and they often refer back to their fieldwork classes as turning points in their understanding of key concepts: how to listen well, how to attend to authentic voice, how to situate meaning in cultural context, and so forth. They are the realization of the vision that Hymes had over fifty years ago; they are also the personification of my own hopes and aspirations for the field, and of a series of individually rewarding relationships.

For the sake of fairness I should point out that the engagement of undergraduates in ethnographic research has had its problems, and there is an ongoing, though now largely muted, debate within the discipline concerning the advisability of having undergraduates participating in fieldwork (see Ingold 1991; Middleton 2018; Piot 2016; Sharma 1989 and 1991; Sharma and Wright 1989; Thorn and Wright 1990; Watson 1995). Many social and cultural anthropology programs in Britain and America in the 1980s and 1990s embraced undergraduate fieldwork as a core curricular component, but this trend met with loud resistance from some quarters. The chief objections to undergraduate fieldwork are that the positive benefits are limited and do not outweigh the harm that can be caused by inexpert researchers both to themselves and to those they are working with. Without getting knee-deep into this debate, I would simply say that adequate advanced preparation and constant supervision by trained faculty mitigate the potential dangers that can arise and, in my experience, the value of undergraduate projects has been immense. If it were not, I would not be writing this work. Not least, I believe that training in field research methods, contrary to some critiques, is a solid marketable skill upon graduation, and many of my students have been hired from college by research firms as fieldworkers.

(Anti-)Objectivism in Anthropology

Caring deeply about people with whom one is engaged as a fieldworker makes it completely impossible to record and interpret their behavior in objective fashion. The critique of objectivity in anthropology was well under way at the time that the essays in Hymes's collection *Reinventing Anthropology* (Hymes 1972b) were being developed, and the last two sections of this anthology focus on several different facets of this critique (see especially Jay 1972; Scholte 1972; and Diamond 1972). Since then, the forces of philosophical opposition to objectivity in anthropology have shaped into well-known main currents in the discipline, such as the movements toward reflexivity and humanism (see, e.g., Clifford and Marcus 1986; Dwyer 1999; Geertz 1990; Kumoll 2010; Marcus 1998; Richardson 1990; Scotford 2012).

Introduction

The critique of objectivity in the social sciences has taken many forms. What I would like to examine here, though, is less the notion that the materials of life history—as represented in this volume—are *unobjective*, or incapable of being made objective, than the idea that they are quite deliberately *anti*-objective: they stand in conscious *opposition* to objectifiable data. No doubt parts of life histories may be objectified when it comes to certain kinds of facts, but that is not their point. Personal meanings are inscribed deeply within them, and these are not matters of objectifiable fact at all but, rather, what certain incidents or events *mean* to the individual in question (see Linde 1993; Rosenwald and Ochberg 1992). Such meanings cannot, by their very nature, be made "objective," and any desire to do so is misguided or muddled.

What I am given to wonder, however, is whether this anti-objective approach to field data does not always require some kind of conversion experience mediated by people in the field. Robert Jay hints at such a possibility (Jay 1972), and the experiences of my students, plus my own time doing field research, seem to support such a claim. I have reported at greater length elsewhere how my friends in the field in Tidewater, North Carolina, helped me move away from attempting to objectify the data that constituted their daily lives, but it was a hard-fought battle for a while (Forrest 1988; and Forrest and Blincoe 1995).

The following exchange took place in my very first interview in the town where I conducted my doctoral fieldwork in 1978. I was sitting in FI's[2] living room, and she had a quilt on her lap that was a prized family heirloom. Because I was eagerly intent on getting the facts I asked:

JF: So when was it made?
FI: Well let me see . . . it was made by Lizzy Brown, my daddy's grand-daddy's second wife when they were first married. I think he was around 42 or 3 at the time. Now he died when I was five and he was 93, and I was born in 1902, so you work it out.
JF: OK, He must have died in 1907 at the age of 93, so he was born in 1814, which would have made him 42 in 1856. That means it's about 120 years old.
FI: Uh-huh.

It took me well over six years of listening to this and other interviews again and again before the penny dropped, and I realized the degree to which FI and I were pursuing radically different agendas. It is perfectly possible to objectify certain facts about the quilt, such as its date of manufacture (or its age), but such objective facts are outside FI's value system in relation to it. Two responses in FI's discourse make this clear. The first is the command, "so you work it out," which could be expanded to something of the following order (which she would never have dreamed of saying directly to anyone): "I will tell you what I know about the quilt's chronology in terms that matter to me, or are significant to me, and you can convert them into your value system if you want to—I don't want to and am not going to." Having then finished that part of our conversion, and being proud of my mental skills, and, indeed, beginning to see the "value" of the quilt in *my* terms (i.e., "my gosh, 120 years old"), FI brushed aside my interest with the noncommittal "Uh-huh," which stops short of being impolite but could be translated as "if you say so, but so what?" Her value terms in relation to the quilt are:

1. the maker's *name*
2. her *affinal* relationship to the maker
3. her *consanguineal* relationship to the maker's husband
4. chronological information associated with rites of passage
    a. the maker's husband's age at *marriage*
    b. the maker's husband's age at *death*
    c. FI's age at the maker's husband's *death*
    d. FI's year of *birth*

From this we may further learn that in this community, affines get *named* when discussing them, but consanguineal kin are referred to almost exclusively by *kin terms*. Furthermore, even though an affine made the quilt, its history is linked to the chronological details of a blood relative. Having made this discovery, I could then to go back to other interviews with FI and note that she always said, "my daddy made . . ." or "my mama did . . ." but never "my husband worked . . ."; always "Lem worked . . ." (and also important to see that both the kin terms and the names used are affectionate diminutives).

I was too far removed from the value system of the community at the time of these interviews to be able to be instructed in anything other than a kind of objectified way. It was not just a simple matter of me being a foreigner geographically (born in Argentina, raised in Australia and England); I was a cognitive stranger as well. The sad truth is that I would have related to them in their own terms a lot quicker than I did if I had never studied anthropology, because the discipline had inclined me to *study* them rather than to *learn* from them. They tried their best to include me in their value system, but my training resolutely resisted their efforts. I get it now—too late, of course. What is critically important to understand, though, is that no matter how bad a pupil I was, our

Introduction **13**

interviews always had an instructional purpose, and that what I thought I was trying to discover was less important in the minds of the people in the community than what they thought I ought to know.

This last point brings us directly to consider the nature and purpose of life histories as social documents. A life history, meaning a particular subset or species of oral history—a personal narrative recounted orally to someone else—is, strictly, neither autobiography nor biography. It is autobiographical in the sense that it is a person's self-construction (and derives meaning and power from this fact). But it is told *to* someone and not simply created as a general work for universal consumption. Often the narrative would not exist in any preservable form were it not for the person that it is told to; and who that person is vitally important in the construction of the narrative.

If the person recording the life history acts as a representative of a generalized "other" (that is, the tale teller sees the listener as an outsider), then the tale may well be relatively "objectified" or neutral, in both its overall construction and in specific details (inasmuch as this is possible). Much of my early fieldwork in life histories in Tidewater, North Carolina, was of this sort. My "other"-ness often forced the discourse into modes of communicating that my interviewees thought I would understand or were what I wanted. And, the kinds of questions I asked, and the kinds of responses I gave to their narratives, reinforced their (largely unconscious) moves in that direction.

If the teller has some direct and obvious affinity for, or some clear cultural connection with, the fieldworker, however, the life story may well take on more personalized meanings. The fieldworker may be co-opted as a kind of apprentice or novice, for example, to be taught the powerful components of the teller's life—and to pass them on in turn. The samples represented in this work are of this type, although the variations on the basic theme are myriad and of extreme importance in understanding the material so produced.

In addition, the fieldworker has the capacity to shape the narrative in the same way that a biographer would, but is shaping the direct transcription of the words of the teller rather than the more comprehensively objectifiable components of data that go to make up a conventional biography. The fieldworker is channeled and directed (perhaps even limited) by the interviewee's words and constructions. So, the fieldworker may use a number of editorial devices and decisions to augment or amplify the oral text, but he or she almost invariably uses the patterns and meanings evoked by the narrator as foundational (whereas the classic biographer, as essentially *external* to the data—i.e., "objective" observer—characteristically sees the job of biography as finding or creating the pattern and meaning in the materials—or, perhaps of weighing alternative patterns). As such, life history, unlike biography, is a *collaboration* between narrator and fieldworker.

In addition, it is vitally important to remember that life histories, while written and edited, are still essentially *oral* documents. Such oral documents have a long history. The oldest known so-called autobiography in English, for example—*The Book of Margery Kempe* (Windeatt 1985)—is really an oral life history, since Margery Kempe could not read or write, and, therefore, had to enlist the aid of a lettered priest to record and edit her oral narrative sometime around 1436. This text stands as a good example of the type in that it reveals several qualities that are unique to, and diagnostic of, the oral life history. These are elaborated more fully in the following section, but, in brief, they include the twin features of *authentic voice* and *personally constructed meaning*. A life history is never simply a neutral description of a life course (even when recounted to a completely indifferent transcriber) but always contains critically personalized elements.

The way in which a narrator constructs meaning in a life history is strongly influenced by the relationship between the teller and listener, and within this collaboration, the issue of who has initiated the narration (teller or listener) has a profound impact on the structure of meaning within the narrative. Conventionally within the social sciences, it is the fieldworker who initiates the sessions because of a desire to gather information. But, as in the case of Margery Kempe, some life histories have an inner compulsion built into them by their narrators—an Ancient Mariner effect, as it were—that governs their structure and meaning. The tale teller feels constantly obligated to seek out listeners and retell the life tale. Yet, whether the act of recounting a life history is initiated by teller or listener, these texts are rarely, if ever, records of the objective facts of a person's life: they serve specific personal purposes.

It is because life histories are recounted in personalized terms—and not in spite of this fact—that they are critical documents for social scientists. They record lived experience in a singular manner. It is precisely their lack of objectivity that makes them so important: they are testimonies of the subjective felt sense of experience in a particular period—the essence of what German social scientists, such as Wilhelm Dilthey and Max Weber, called *Verstehen*, "empathic insight," emanating from the actors of history themselves.

Dilthey places a high value on historical documents that exhibit subjective *understanding* rather than objectified *knowledge*, and among these he sees autobiography as key cultural data from which to generate theory:

Introduction

> Autobiography is the highest and most instructive form in which the under-standing [*Verstehen*] of life confronts us. Here is the outward phenomenal course of a life which forms the basis for understanding what has produced it within a certain environment. The man who understands it is the same as the one who created it. A particular intimacy of understanding results from this. The person who seeks the connecting threads in the history of his life has already, from different points of view, created a coherence in that life which he is now putting into words. He has created it by experiencing values and realizing purposes in his life . . . (Dilthey 1961: 85–86)

But the autobiography that Dilthey so values is of the literary type: Augustine, Rousseau, and Goethe. Oral life history, because it exists within oral tradition, goes several steps further than these in that it is both *immediate* and *democratic*. The autobiographies that Dilthey analyzes are all literary forms; meticulously crafted products of highly educated minds, bent on certain kinds of reflexive thought. They are composed by being written, and are written in order to be read. Oral life histories are crafted and reflexive also, it is true, but they are destined to be told and retold—bearing all of the hallmarks of a folk form versus a literary one (the delimiting points of these two types being the sum and substance of folklore scholarship).

Thus, the oral life history has a degree of spontaneity and malleability (absent from the literary autobiography) because it is generated afresh each time it is told. Furthermore, it is democratic in the sense that it requires neither literary training nor access to publishing resources (nor an identifiable capital market) to disseminate it—coupled with the inherent limitation of all oral forms, namely, its dissemination must occupy a meager compass.

To some extent the invention of the tape and digital recorder (along with the development of mass-produced, cheap equipment), has cut into previous limitations of the oral life history, making the ephemeral potentially permanent and more widely distributable. But this fact brings another person into the picture: the fieldworker. The fieldworker acts as the broker between the world of the narrator and a wider audience by recording, transcribing, and editing the life history; and to a great degree, the voice recorder has also democratized this process. Prior to the invention of cheap, portable tape recorders that could record several hours of material at a time (with occasional pauses to change tapes), one would have had to have been an extremely facile stenographer to record a life history verbatim while allowing the narrator to talk in a natural manner. Such skills are not easily acquired, and the use of them would have fundamentally narrowed the potential for personal interaction between teller and recorder—unless the steno were the human equivalent of a tape recorder hired by the fieldworker, at considerable expense.

That life histories, as subjectively legitimate understandings of life and culture, are fundamentally valuable social documents is becoming increasingly evident in anthropology and the social sciences in general. Certain of these documents—e.g., *Black Elk Speaks* (Neihardt 1932), *Crashing Thunder* (Radin 1920), *Sun Chief* (Simmons 1942), *Son of Old Man Hat* (Dyk 1938)—have already achieved a kind of classic status within the discipline. But there are also many more that are being solicited in order to broaden and deepen our understanding of social systems from the individual's point of view (see, e.g., Behar 1993; Crane 1987 and 1999; Freeman 1979; Hurston 2018; Rosengarten 1974; Rosenwald and Ochberg 1992).

Beyond the employment of life histories in social science, there is also developing a body of theoretical insight into the nature of oral life histories themselves (Angrosino 1989; Behar, 1990; Bertaux 1981; Chamberlayne et al. 2000; Jolly 2001; Hertz 1997; Linde 1993; Ochs and Capps 1996; Peacock and Holland 1993; Riessman 1990; Urban 1989), as a significant component of the general interest in reflexivity, metacommunication, and meaning that has evolved out of the postmodern critique of the fundamental materials of social science (Berg 2006; Clifford and Marcus 1986; Davies 1999; Ellis and Bochner 1996; Goodall 2000; Sanjek 1990). As part of this general reevaluation of the agenda of social enquiry, attention is being devoted to the very methods of collecting and transcribing life histories as a concern related to, yet also significantly distinct from, general interview technique (see, e.g., Crane and Angrosino 1984: 75–87; Crapanzano 1984; Forrest 2022; Ives 1974; Langness 1965; Langness and Frank 1981; Mishler 1991 and 1995; Riessman 1993).

What still needs to be better explored is the nature of the individual and subjective *relationship* between fieldworker and life history narrator, and how a life history emerges out of such a partnership: that is, the prime subject of the present work (see, for example, Casagrande 1960; Kratz 2001; Riessman 1987 and 1993; Shostak 1981). The bond between interlocutor and fieldworker is delicate yet strong; a bond that we have all experienced but not always adequately analyzed or understood. It is the cornerstone of everything we do in the field and everything we become in our disciplines; it limits, colors, and shades our insights; it empowers us. Such empowerment can and should be mutual and reciprocal.

Reciprocal Empowerment

It is easy for a fieldworker to feel enriched by the life stories of key interlocuters; to see them as a gift or as something to be taken away in a personal economy of subtraction. You had a life story to give, and you gave it to me—it is now mine. This trope of narrative as (precious) commodity, albeit a commodity that may be refashioned and given out anew, seems to me to miss the point of life history telling altogether. *Giving* may be an important component of the act, but the narrator may be *receiving* a great deal as well.

The strength of the life history method is that it allows us to build historical, or ethnographic, or biographical images from multiple subjective points of view, and such images are inherently more faceted than an analysis that seeks the objective truth from the single point of view of the academic observer. As such, we may tease out certain kinds of motivations that underlie the telling of a life history, each of which *empowers* the narrator in some obvious way.

By definition, a life history is *personal* history. Sometimes life histories relate directly to events that the academic or popular worlds deem "important"—the Holocaust, say, from the perspective of a concentration camp survivor. But regardless of the "importance" of the broader framework of the narrative, the stock in trade of the narrative is the personal detail. The importance of the details is governed strictly by their personal value within the meaning system of the narrator. Thus, an entire generation of US citizens asks, "What were you doing when you heard the news of Kennedy's assassination?" They do not ask, "Did it matter?" or, "Were you upset?" Not only are the answers to these questions obvious, but they are also implicit in the first question. What the answers to the first question reveal is the kaleidoscopically rich world that the event burst in upon. And the fact that everyone can give an immediate (well-structured) answer is adequate testimony to the power of the event—in microscopically personal terms. It is banal to assert *that* the event was important, or even to suggest reasons *why* it was important; life history mines the riches of *how* it was important, one person's experience at a time.

Similarly, we may see life history as *alternate* cultural viewpoint. Typically, it does not present the meanings of events in terms of an elite or hegemonic frame of reference—although this state of affairs is greatly colored by the status of the narrator (see Frisch 1990). Inasmuch as such meanings are habitually couched in personal terms, they may modify, augment, or even flatly contradict prevailing interpretations in the academy (or in popular consciousness). This is not to suggest that life history is somehow "better" or more "real" than conventional academic analysis but only that it can provide a different lens through which to perceive the world.

Within the domain of life history as personal or alternate point of view, we may perceive certain general motives for the telling (and recording) of oral narratives, and, again, fieldworkers are active agents here insofar as they act as both immediate audience and as mediators to wider audiences. The two most obvious, and more or less related, motivations for the telling of life history narratives are as part of personal *therapy*, and as general *testimony*. These are linked to a third possibility, namely, life history as *exhortation* or *social instruction*.

The "talking cure" is a well-known component of Freudian, and derivative, modalities of psychotherapy. Perhaps less well-known is the particular use to which life histories are put within "twelve-step" programs—initiated by the founders of Alcoholics Anonymous (AA). One of Bill W.'s great insights into the recovery process was that alcoholics do not like to be lectured to concerning their problems or told what to do. What really got through to them was hearing *someone else's* story of decline and revival. The telling of the alcoholic's life history is a two-way therapeutic process, however, helping the listener and the teller. The teller needs an audience for his/her story, but he/she is really telling it reflexively to himself/herself as a form of reinforcement of the rightness of his/her actions. The (alcoholic) listener vicariously identifies with components of the teller's story and is able to use it as a model without feeling directly instructed.

What began as an almost accidental discovery became quickly integrated into the formal structure of AA. At every meeting, attendees relate fragments of their life history as part of the group process, but each is expected at some point in recovery—usually well into it— to present a formal life history narrative to the group. These follow a well-worn path: how I started drinking, the slippery slope, hitting bottom, finding AA, and so on. But for all the formulas, each tale is unique and rich in personal detail, and what is clear from hearing a number of such narratives is that their purpose is to frame a life in such a way that its linear structure reveals the more global meaning latent within it. Furthermore, the AA type of life history allows for a realignment of meaning. Wrecking a car, losing a job, losing a family, etc., are the kinds of life events that are generally categorized as "bad" in Western culture, but the AA brand of life history frequently reassesses such events as "good," inasmuch as they are the components of hitting bottom where recovery can begin.[3]

Introduction

Outside the structures of formal modes of recovery and analysis, the life history may perform similar therapeutic functions to those within them, although the process may not be as self-conscious or as formulaic. That is, what AA does as part of its system may be achieved by fieldworkers who provide both the necessary audience and the overarching framework within which narrators may work through their life problems by discovering latent meaning. It is important to understand, though, that the fieldworker is not a therapist, and a professional therapeutic relationship is not a desired outcome of the method, or one to be encouraged. But some components of the traditional "talking cure" may emerge spontaneously and unconsciously as part of the process of gathering a life history.

Related to this power of life history as a therapeutic tool is the notion that telling one's story may serve as *testimony* (see, e.g., Peacock and Tyson 1989, Titon 1988 for extended accounts). Obviously, the commonest context of such narratives is Christian evangelism, within which the structure and vocabulary may be as stylized and formulaic as within AA. But the motivations for telling a life history as testimony are importantly different from the therapeutic. In particular, the talking cure is fundamentally reflexive, whereas a testimonial usage serves essentially to send a message outward. Certain kinds of events—such as the public life histories of AA—may share both purposes, and one might argue that all life histories participate in both to some degree. Thus, therapy versus testimony is not so much a dichotomy as different ways to perceive a complex whole.

As already implied, such narratives may also serve the function of indirectly exhorting listeners to action of a certain sort. This is as true of AA narratives as of evangelical testimony. The teller may be relating a very particular life course, but the purpose is more than the simple passing on or dissemination of information. The teller is also implicitly saying "this is the life path for you too if you are in similar circumstances." Such life histories, thus, serve as *exemplars* that instruct.

Complementing the notion that life histories are personal narratives with personal motivations is the simple fact that they are told in a uniquely personal *voice*. The preservation and admiration of such distinct voices— often characterized as inferior by hegemonic institutions—are critical ways in which the fieldworker may empower an individual. Countless commentators have extolled the power of narrative voice and have shown over and again that "ways of saying" contribute mightily to the meaning and reception of literature. Convincingly simple in this regard is George Orwell's paraphrase of a famous passage in Ecclesiastes—"I returned, and saw under the sun, that the race is not to the swift, nor the battle to the strong, neither yet bread to the wise, nor yet riches to men of understanding, nor yet favour to men of skill; but time and chance happeneth to them all"—from the standard to the voice of a modern academic: "Objective consideration of contemporary phenomena compels the conclusion that success or failure in competitive activities exhibits no tendency to be commensurate with innate capacity, but that a considerable element of the unpredictable must invariably be taken into account" (Orwell 1946)." Likewise, the ethnopoetics and sociolinguistics agendas advanced by Dell Hymes and others, have repeatedly indicated the poetic and stylistic complexities of oral texts—all of which may be lost if a narrative is not transcribed verbatim (see, for example, Bauman and Sherzer 1974; Giglioli 1972; Gumperz and Hymes 1972; Hymes 1974 and 1981). It is superfluous to rehearse the principles of these schools of thought here. It is important to say, though, that even neophyte fieldworkers are capable of appreciating the complexities and subtleties of authentic voice, and by using even relatively rudimentary recording equipment, they may create verbatim transcriptions that maintain many of the essentials of that voice. A fieldworker's most basic service to the narrator, therefore, is to empower that voice by valuing it, and preserving it intact.

The central issue here is that a life history is not the same kind of narrative as a literary autobiography, nor is it simply a justification or exposition of a particular life course. Many of its meanings emerge because of the voice in which it is told. As with all linguistic phenomena, meanings and values are expressed on many different levels—cognitive, affective, aesthetic, and so forth. The fieldworker's principal task here is to transcribe the recorded material in such a way that the written material is fluently readable, yet the essential qualities of the narrator's voice are maintained for the average reader to pick out (see Frisch 1996).

Such a rehearsal, which is admittedly no more than a series of signposts to the general academic literature, serves to outline some ways in which life histories advance the needs and interests of narrators. What has yet to be fully acknowledged is the degree to which the method empowers the fieldworker. We all understand at some level that anthropologists may become powerful in their own circles by being in command of powerful data, but it is an actively debated question whether the power of the data derives more from the ability of the fieldworker to garner (and construe) it or from its intrinsically powerful properties to begin with. Again, such straightforward dichotomizing is potentially unrewarding in that all fieldwork when seen as collaboration is empowered by all parties to its practice, and if any imbalance needs to be redressed, it is in granting greater significance to the role of the storyteller in furthering the agendas of the fieldworker.

Introduction **21**

The picture is rather different for undergraduate fieldworkers from that of postgraduate researchers and other professionals in the field, however. It is my general experience that undergraduates, because they are not normally driven by personal desire for professional advancement in the field or by the correlate need to attack or defend high-profile theoretical stances, have a greater (and perhaps more humane) desire to *identify* with their interviewees rather than to *distance* themselves from them; or, in my terms above, to *learn* from them rather than to *study* them. Such identification is the cornerstone of their empowerment by their fieldwork partners.[4]

All of the life history segments presented in this volume are clear examples of the strong identification of the student fieldworkers with their interlocuters because of some shared social or cultural value, and in almost every case the fieldworkers were inspired to accomplish the work because of vicarious pride in the achievements of the people they interviewed and a desire to emulate them in their life course. Generally, this means that fieldworker and interviewee are perceived by the larger culture as co-members of negatively stereotyped social categories—welfare mother, gay man, poor immigrant, disabled worker, African American slum dweller—and, therefore, the process of recording each life history becomes one of collaboration to erect models of the members of those categories that counteract the negative stereotyping.

Some kind of vicarious identification with one's interlocuters may be the norm, certainly commonplace, for anthropological fieldworkers. But in the case of these undergraduates the identification is scarcely vicarious, and there is less a sense of the fieldworker looking at another culture through the eyes of one of these "other" people and more a sense of direct bonding between a senior and a junior member of the *same* social group.

The process of taking down the life history, thus, may become a form of cultural instruction for the fieldworker, learning the strength and power of the positive components of their shared social experience and also learning appropriate symbols of pride, revised social history, and so on. As such, this kind of fieldwork is really kin to traditional modes of learning rather than an intrusion into them; and where traditional transmission of culture has been obstructed or disrupted somehow, fieldwork may function as an agent of cultural (re)construction.

Such cultural learning is clearly marked in Michael Avrut's piece (chapter 4), for example, indicating a timeless dilemma for gays and lesbians; namely, that, unlike almost all other social groups, they cannot learn appropriate in-group behavior from their families—the crucible of culture for virtually everyone else—because their families are not gay or lesbian (except under rare circumstances). They must acquire their culture elsewhere, and at a more advanced age than other children (see Blincoe and Forrest 1993).

When a life history interview replicates traditional modes of learning from elders, certain inherent problems of the power relationship between fieldworker and interviewee are automatically diminished, allowing for a greater reciprocity between the two. In classic fieldwork situations of the early twentieth century, the fieldworker came from a powerful culture, with all the tools and paraphernalia of that culture, and came to a culture that was commonly economically and politically subordinate to the fieldworker's culture. Power relations in that situation were obviously asymmetric, and it was hard, if not impossible, to create a balance. But such is not the case with my students. They are working within their own cultures (in the role of younger members of those cultures), and they are coming more obviously in the role of learners to be instructed than as representatives of a dominant culture. Thus, interviewees can perceive their own roles as being more powerful than in more traditional fieldwork settings because they are instructing junior members in the ways of their own culture, as well as possibly helping them to succeed in the hegemonic world of the university. Proof of the latter feeling comes when, as is commonplace, the interviewee wants to know if the student fieldworker got a good grade for the project.

A vital element of this kind of cultural instruction, as outlined above, is the use of authentic voice. But it is not just a matter of the narrator using or even teaching the fieldworker a way of speaking by example. Even within the most liberal of educational institutions, certain ways of speaking are classified as substandard (i.e., "ungrammatical" or "illiterate" or "wrong") when used as a written form of English. So there remains the implicit message that, while certain ways of *speaking* may have in-group power, the forces of hegemony still control the *written* word. Transcription of authentic voices of narrators allows an escape route from this trap. Transcription turns ways of speaking into ways of writing, allowing authentic voice to exist as a literary form, and allowing both interviewee *and* fieldworker to share in the power of that voice as a written form.

Specific Methods

All of the life histories presented here grew out of work for a single course, *Fieldwork: Qualitative Methods*, which is a core component in the curriculum for undergraduate social sciences majors at Purchase College, SUNY. It is a requirement for all anthropology majors, and for those majoring in the interdisciplinary social sciences and the arts program. These programs are committed to teaching fieldwork methods to undergraduates on the grounds that concentrated, hands-on experience in gathering data—along with collateral activities, such as, preparing a research design, professional data presentation and the like—provides students with a better understanding of the empirical aspects of the social sciences and of the process of generating theory from field materials than a comparable period of time spent in the library. The course may also satisfy requirements in sociology, and a few stray students from photography and film making ask to join now and again.

The course as I originally organized it was divided into seven discrete projects; or, roughly one every two weeks over a single semester. In brief these were as follows:

1. *Self study*: An essay in which the students analyze their motives for wanting to engage in fieldwork and assess their strengths and weaknesses.

2. *Proxemics*: One or two hour-long periods of observation in public spaces in which the students document how people use spatial relations (between each other, or between themselves and objects in the environment) in socially meaningful ways.

3. *Mapping*: Students draw several scale maps that demonstrate social aspects of space.

4. *Process documentation*: Students each pick a skilled artisan, and through a combination of observation and interviewing, document a skilled process in its sociocultural, psychological, or personal contexts. Photography or videography may be used here.

5. *Participant observation*: Students each choose a public function (ritual, ceremony, entertainment) that is unfamiliar to them, at which they act as both active participants and observers.

6. *Sensory documentation*: Students either conduct a second participant observation study or document some other activity, focusing on only *one* of the senses (and they must choose one other than sight).

7. *Life history*: Students conduct two one-hour taped interview sessions (one directed the other undirected), concerning a selected person's life history. The students then select portions for detailed transcription.

This course has several general objectives. It is designed to sensitize students to different methods, which in larger research projects may be used together, but which in this course are treated as discrete units so that the students can appreciate the merits and functions of each in isolation. The course is also structured to lead the students slowly into deeper and deeper methods, beginning with those that require observation at a distance and concluding with those that are more intimate or intrusive. There is also a sense in which the later projects build on the skills of the earlier (participant observation, for example, may incorporate proxemics or mapping).

As I taught it, each two week unit was divided into five parts:

1. *Description*: Students prepare by reading a chapter in a methods text. I described each method in detail, and indicated my expectations for the project.
2. *Practicum*: I set up an experimental situation in the classroom that the students can use as a practice session to learn the pitfalls of each method before embarking on their own projects. This practicum could take several forms: sometimes I showed videotapes of other students at work on similar projects, or I used myself as a guinea pig. The idea was for the situation to be controllable and open to constant reflexive commentary.
3. *Discussion*: Students brought problems to class that they had encountered in designing or carrying out their individual projects, for group discussion and resolution. We could also discuss problems encountered in the practicum session if they were germane.
4. *Presentation*: Two or three students presented their projects to the entire class (on a rotating basis, so that everyone presented at least once), for peer critique.
5. *Critique*: After reviewing the class's work as a whole for each project I gave a summary critique. In conjunction with this exercise the students read selected sections of each other's finished projects.

Thus, the life history project may be seen as the capstone of an extremely intense program of activities, and for many of the students in the class this project marks the turning point in their understanding of social investigation. My directives to them for the project are relatively simple:

- find someone to recount part of a life history
- record a one hour undirected narrative
- record a one hour directed narrative
- transcribe about 45 minutes of narrative

Introduction 25

Working through the various projects over the course of the semester supposedly prepares the students for this kind of intensive one-to-one activity, but they are, nonetheless, frequently intimidated by the scope and the intimacy of the life history method.

Finding the right narrator is easy for some, next to impossible for others. From the very beginning of the semester, when I review the sweep of the course, students are aware that the life history is lurking on the horizon, and many ponder deeply from the outset whom to choose. Others find the right person in the course of other projects (the process documentation, for example), or stumble on an appropriate choice, having been sensitized to the power of the method in the class (samples of previous projects are available for them to review). Yet others come to the class already aware of potential narrators, having been warned by more advanced students at the college of what lies ahead for them.

I request that they do two interviews for a number of reasons. Not least is the lesson of redundancy: two interviews act as an insurance policy against the failure of one (recorder malfunctions, broken appointments, unexpected interruptions). But, the primary methodological purpose is to have them understand the importance of listening intently and reflecting on what they have heard. Thus, the first interview is expressly aimed at encouraging them to keep their mouths shut and their ears open. I ask them to initiate the interview with the broadest of openings; such as, "tell me about your personal history," or the like, and to remain silent subsequently, unless silence would be uncomfortably awkward, or in some other way socially inappropriate (I do allow them to use general phatic utterances to keep a sense of connectedness).

The next step is to listen to the recording—several times if possible. The goals here are many: to index the recording, to review technique, and to get a deeper sense of the substance of the narrative—voice, content, structure, and so forth. Not uncommonly, this act of listening is an eye opener. Students find out that while they believed they were as silent as tombs during the interviews, the recorder tells them otherwise; or they discover that they have completely misunderstood whole chunks of the narrative, or failed to hear key passages at the time of the interview. Armed with these insights they pick a passage of the first interview that they feel could use explication or elaboration and return for a second—still trying to keep in the background, but also attempting to keep the narrative within certain predetermined bounds.

As with the first recording, I expect them to listen to the second with the same general goals in mind. The point is to help them understand that the method is endlessly dialectical—listening poses questions, and the responses to these questions pose new questions—and that, therefore, listening is far from a passive act. They may then begin transcribing.

I ask them to pick two 20 minute segments (ideally one from each tape) for verbatim transcription, basing their decision on their own interest in the content of those segments. I recommend that they use one of two related transcription methods, namely, that they use no punctuation, but, rather, listen for the pauses in the narrator's speech and indicate them by a dash or by starting a new line at every pause. Part of my purpose here is to keep the process as simple as possible, but it is also to get them to concentrate on the strictly oral voice and its natural rhythms—without the added complications and distraction of having to translate these voices into a literary form.

Even without any concern for the potentially Byzantine convolutions of advanced transcription techniques, the students are always amazed at what a grind it is to get an interview down on paper. They average a transcription ratio of around 9:1, that is, one hour of tape takes about nine hours to transcribe. Yet, despite the dogged effort involved, it is often during this process that much of what I have been trying to stress over the course of the semester falls into place. Verbatim transcription is itself a form of intense and detailed listening: *really listening*. They hear the same phrases over and over, strain to catch nuances of diction, puzzle over unusual terms and turns of phrase, anguish over pauses and phrase length, so that by the end of it all they know their transcription better than any other text they have encountered in their education.

Their pride of accomplishment is outstripped, however, by the insight they have gained into the nature of data collection and into what is required of a good listener. These are precisely the kinds of life skills that training in anthropological method can teach anyone, and which can be turned to good usage in all walks of life. That is, Hymes' ambitions for anthropology in the larger world might well most consistently be achieved by teaching field methods as intensively as theory.

Study Questions

1. This chapter mentions the difference between *studying* a group of people and *learning* from them as a fieldwork method? What do you think the difference is? Are there different benefits and pitfalls to each method?
2. How is the notion of studying people versus learning from them related to the idea that education can be a form of sharing rather than instructing?

3. What are your career goals at this point? How do you imagine training in oral history and fieldwork will enrich that career—if at all?

Notes

1. My son and I are working on it.
2. FI is her code name in my system of note taking. All interlocutors' names in this work are codes or pseudonyms
3. See Bill Wilson's *Alcoholics Anonymous* for further details on life history as a method within AA.
4. To some extent my goals here fall under the general aims of the pedagogic theory commonly called "action research" (see Berg 2006, Kemmis and McTaggert 1988, McCutcheon and Jurg 1990, and McKernan 1991). There is also an element of constructivist learning theory involved (see Brooks and Brooks 1993, Crotty 1998, Kukla 2000, and Prawat and Floden 1994) which has a venerable history from Vygotsky and Piaget to Gregory Bateson and beyond.

1
Fieldwork Methods for Undergraduates

The purpose of this chapter is primarily to probe a little more deeply into the classroom methods that I use as part of the process of developing capable fieldworkers, but also to get an initial sense of the kinds of motivations that my students bring to my fieldwork class—to understand what it is that I and they are working with to produce the life histories represented here. I would like to add the key warning at the beginning that I am mistrustful of the phrase "classroom methods" meaning "tricks of the trade" or "things to try when you are at a loss" or "proven strategies for success." That is not what I am offering here. Very little that I do seems to work well twice, and absolutely everything is old by the third time around. If I am not excited by what I am doing, my students never are; and I cannot be excited by old material no matter how good its track record is. Furthermore, as the culture changes, my students change. What resonated with them ten years ago may have little relevance today. I am changing too. What resonated with me ten years ago may be passé today. So, rather than presenting you with my "ten secrets to a better experience in the classroom," I am offering what one critic has described as a "life history" of my fieldwork class. Like any such document, it is not meant to be complete, it is deliberately personal, and it sees everything that has gone on in the class from my point of view alone.

It is also unreasonable for me to go through the methods I employ in the entire class. That is a book of its own (see Forrest 2022). What I am going to do instead is focus on the life history. As noted in the

Fieldwork Methods for Undergraduates

previous chapter, in a fifteen-week semester on field methods, I assign seven projects (roughly one every two weeks) with the life history being the last project of the semester. I drop little hints along the road that the life history is coming and will be demanding. I suggest as they carry out other projects, such as participant observation or photographing a skilled worker, that they keep the life history in the back of their minds. I advise them to be on the lookout for likely people all the time—giving them very broad ideas of what they will have to accomplish. But I do not get into real detail until we have finished our other projects.

The first concern I raise with them, when going over my expectations, is the time commitment that the life history involves. I emphasize right up front that both interviewing and transcribing are monumentally time consuming and cannot be rushed. To relieve any fears they have about getting it done along with finals and term papers all due at the same time, I reassure them that if they have finished their other projects, I will not mind giving them an incomplete so that they are less rushed with the life history. Generally an incomplete gives them about four weeks beyond the regular due date for them to finish. Normally about two-thirds of the class takes advantage of this offer.

I talk first about selecting a suitable person, but I do not make a big issue out of this. My main directive is that they must pick someone whose life history is of interest to them. I tell them that they will understand as I describe the project in more detail just how important it is to have a genuine interest in the person's narrative: the whole thing will absorb so much effort that without the initial commitment it will be hard for them to get through to the end.

I try not to make too much of this part—despite its critical importance—because there is little I can say of a general nature about choosing someone except to find a person who matters to them. Usually if they get stuck at this juncture I am better off helping them on an individual basis. Besides, a few of them have picked their interviewee already (and in rare cases students come to the class knowing about the life history project and have a person picked from the very beginning). My main focus, therefore, is on the mechanics of interviewing and transcribing.

On the day I first describe the project, I normally take one of my portable recorders to class. If possible, we set up the chairs in the classroom to imitate a living room. I show them my preferences for sitting with an interviewee and where to place the recorder, and then also show them possible variations that may suit them as well. It is always my preference to sit facing my interviewee with the recorder at the interviewee's elbow. I can then make eye contact easily, and the recorder is not directly in our line of vision. I can see it at a glance to make sure it is going (my various models usually have a signal light to indicate that the machine is recording, and therefore I know if it is not set up right or if it has stopped recording for some reason). The interviewee, however, cannot easily see it and so may not be self-conscious about its presence.

We play around with different setups—say, sitting side by side holding the recorder, or putting the recorder behind the interviewee—and I let them figure out what placements suit them. I also do sound checks to indicate the aural advantages of different recorder placements. For example, I put the recorder behind me and set it to record. Then in a normal speaking voice I say, "The recorder is behind me now . . ." and then add a few sentences. I do this for various placements and then play the whole thing back so they can hear what differences in quality that the placement makes.

In addition I give them the most basic of reminders about principles of labeling and the like (much of which repeats material from earlier projects). If using a digital recorder, make a backup copy immediately and label both copies with the narrator's name along with the time, date, and place of the interview.

Then we talk a little about the nature of the interviews. I suggest to them that they do two hour-long interviews separated by at least several days. The first interview is meant to be as undirected as possible. Their goal is to set the recorder going and then ask the most general of open-ended questions—"Tell me about your life as a soldier" or "What do you remember of your childhood?" or "Tell me how you first came to America." It is their job to let the interviewee do all the talking and to speak only when absolutely necessary. If things come to a halt they should ask another open-ended question, and so on. After an hour they should stop the formal interview process.

I recommend that they index the first recording as soon as it is convenient after the interview. This entails playing the entire interview through and listening to it at least once from beginning to end. They should set the recorder's timer to 0:00 and then start the recording. On a blank sheet of paper they should put 0:00 in a column on the left and write a short description of the first topic of the interview beside it. They should keep listening, and every time the subject changes, or something of interest comes up, they should note what the timer is reading and write down the new topic.

This exercise is useful in itself, but it also serves as a tool for close listening. They cannot listen on automatic pilot; they must *really listen*. So, apart from indexing, they are also beginning a critique of their own method, and beginning to analyze the substance of the interview. They

Fieldwork Methods for Undergraduates

hear more than they heard when conducting the interview because they are not burdened with all the minutiae and stress of interviewing. They can concentrate strictly on the words themselves. I ask them to note any points that they would like clarified or extended, and to pay attention to breaks in the narrative or other indicators that the narrator would have said more about a certain subject if the topic had not changed (for whatever reason).

Armed with the questions developed in this way, I ask them to conduct a second hour-long interview. They may be more direct in their questioning because they are responding to the first interview, yet I tell them to still be as open-ended as possible and to let the interviewee do most of the talking. They are then to index this tape as well.

All of this technical stuff is enough to digest for one class, so I leave it to the next class, the practicum, before I get into transcribing and other issues of presentation of the data they have collected. For the practicum class I bring in a variety of samples of work that I and my former students have done. We may watch excerpts of videotapes of interviews—stopping them periodically to conduct a class critique of method—or we may listen to field recordings and do the same thing with them.

Transcription Methods

For the next step I show them examples of transcriptions. The method is meant to be simple and direct. All the students need to do is transcribe the interview material word for word, including all repeats, false starts, stumbles, and the like, without any intrusions of punctuation. Instead of using punctuation, I ask them to do no more than mark the pauses that the narrator makes (that is, the kinds of pauses that in prose are marked with punctuation) using a dash, or two hyphens, to indicate the pause. This preserves the essential rhythm of the speech, so that someone reading the transcript out loud can replicate the flow of the voice reasonably well.

If my students desire to do more with the transcription later for some other reason, they may wish to convert the raw transcript with dashes into a smoother-looking prose format that comes closer to replicating normal prose. But for the moment I feel that a more basic style of transcription is hard enough and time-consuming enough for them. I ask that they transcribe between forty minutes and an hour's worth of interview material, and that they try to pick two or three long segments of narrative rather than lots of short passages.

32   *Subject Lessons*

Here is a small sample taken from the original transcription of the life history recorded by Andrea Pernstich (chapter 8), showing some of the possibilities for transcription method. The first transcription example is the basic raw transcription that my students routinely produce first time around. Every time the speaker pauses to take a breath or think, the transcriber records two hyphens (or an em dash). Otherwise there is no punctuation of any kind. Everything is transcribed, including repeats, phatic remarks, stammers, and the like. Only proper nouns are capitalized. Following this raw transcription are three other methods using the same sample.

Pauses with Dashes

everybody had a number— I was number 79— and my cell number was 89— and— at one point they put me again in a single cell— which was 69— they put me in a single cell— because at one point— ahm— I was underage— and there was a problem what to do with me— and— they decided that they would have to— release me— and— ahm— so right before I got out— a week or five days before I got out— they put me into this single cell— because they didn't want me— it was also before they told me that I am going to— go— because— ah— they didn't want me to carry any information or anything somehow out— so they put me— without me knowing about it— one day they just came in— said like OK five minutes to pack all your stuff— come with us— so— and— then I just took all my belongings— said goodbye— and they put me into a single cell— and then soon after— I heard that— ahm— they release me from prison— which was at my point— in my situation— I was not happy about it at all— because in a way I felt comfort in there— because I knew that everybody else in there— was in the same boat— everybody was thinking the same way— it is probably kind of silly— but sometimes like at night— we would just scream— things like— I hate this country—which of course you couldn't do outside— there is no way— I mean people were thrown into prison for saying things like that

Scholars sometimes use a similar transcription process but use a line break to mark pauses in the original in place of the dashes or hyphens. The result, quite deliberately, has a poetic look to it. Certain speakers' verbal styles when transcribed this way show a reasonably regular pattern of rhythm and meter that can even be broken into stanzas (see Forrest 1988: 175–80, 247–50). Numbering the lines makes it easier to refer to sections of the narrative. Despite the changes in presentation format, this is still a totally verbatim transcription without punctuation, omissions, or editing of any kind.

Fieldwork Methods for Undergraduates

Numbered Lines with Breaks

1. everybody had a number
2. I was number 79
3. and my cell number was 89
4. and
5. at one point they put me again in a single cell
6. which was 69
7. they put me in a single cell
8. because at one point
9. ahm
10. I was underage
11. and there was a problem what to do with me
12. and
13. they decided that they would have to
14. release me
15. and
16. ahm
17. so right before I got out
18. a week or five days before I got out
19. they put me into this single cell
20. because they didn't want me
21. it was also before they told me that I am going to
22. go
23. because
24. ah
25. they didn't want me to carry any information or anything somehow out
26. so they put me
27. without me knowing about it
28. one day they just came in
29. said like OK five minutes to pack all your stuff
30. come with us
31. so
32. and
33. then I just took all my belongings
34. said goodbye
35. and they put me into a single cell
36. and then soon after
37. I heard that
38. ahm
39. they release me from prison

40. which was at my point
41. in my situation
42. I was not happy about it at all
43. because in a way I felt comfort in there
44. because I knew that everybody else in there
45. was in the same boat
46. everybody was thinking the same way
47. it is probably kind of silly
48. but sometimes like at night
49. we would just scream
50. things like
51. I hate this country
52. which of course you couldn't do outside
53. there is no way
54. I mean people were thrown into prison for saying things like that

Each of the first two methods of transcription can be burdensome to read, especially if the speaker stumbles and backtracks to the point where the written version is not at all smooth and readily comprehensible. The next level of transcription is, therefore, to preserve the verbatim text as much as is possible, but to clean the text up in several ways. First, the pause dashes or line breaks become regular prose punctuation, with a comma marking a short pause and a period marking a longer pause or the end of an idea. Some pauses are left unmarked if a speaker would not normally pause at that spot in the narrative. Even with punctuation, the prose produced may still be awkward in places. Second, some "ers" and other pause words are silently edited out, as are repeated words and false starts. The text becomes a little easier to read, but this ease comes at the expense of strict accuracy of transcription, with a concomitant loss of information concerning the verbal style and quirks of the speaker.

Simple Edit—Basic Punctuation and Tidying

Everybody had a number. I was number 79, and my cell number was 89. And at one point they put me again in a single cell, which was 69. They put me in a single cell because at one point I was underage, and there was a problem what to do with me. And they decided that they would have to release me, and so right before I got out—a week or five days before I got out—they put me into this single cell because they didn't want me . . . It was also before they told me that I am going to go because they didn't want me to carry any information or anything somehow out. So they put me without me knowing about it. One day they just came in, said like, "OK five minutes

Fieldwork Methods for Undergraduates

to pack all your stuff. Come with us." Then I just took all my belongings, said goodbye, and they put me into a single cell. And then soon after I heard that they release me from prison, which was at my point, in my situation . . . I was not happy about it at all, because in a way I felt comfort in there, because I knew that everybody else in there was in the same boat. Everybody was thinking the same way. It is probably kind of silly, but sometimes, like at night, we would just scream things like "I hate this country," which of course you couldn't do outside. There is no way. I mean people were thrown into prison for saying things like that.

At the farthest end of the spectrum is a transcription that seeks to present the life history in language that is as close to grammatical prose as possible while still maintaining as much of the verbatim narrative as is consistent with producing readable text. Words other than basic "ers" or stumbles are omitted if by so doing the narrative is smoother. Likewise, words can be inserted in square brackets to indicate that the speaker did not say them, but with their addition the speech becomes clearer. In the process the text is closer to a literary form, and therefore some of the authentic voice is lost.

Complex Edit with Omissions and Full Punctuation

Everybody had a number. I was number 79, and my cell number was 89. And at one point they put me again in a single cell, which was 69. They put me in a single cell because at one point I was underage, and there was a problem what to do with me. They decided that they would have to release me, and so right before I got out—a week or five days before I got out—they put me into this single cell. It was also before they told me that I am going to go because they didn't want me to carry any information or anything out. So they put me without me knowing about it. One day they just came in, said, "OK Five minutes to pack all your stuff. Come with us." Then I just took all my belongings, said goodbye, and they put me into a single cell. Soon after I heard that they [would] release me from prison. I was not happy about it at all, because in a way I felt comfort in there; I knew that everybody else in there was in the same boat. Everybody was thinking the same way. It is probably kind of silly, but sometimes at night we would just scream things like "I hate this country," which of course you couldn't do outside. There is no way. I mean people were thrown into prison for saying things like that.

I generally prefer the first method of transcription for basic reporting of the life history interviews because it is simple, easy to learn, and preserves authentic voice well. Sometimes students will ask if they may use the second method for their own personal reasons. Given that it is a variant of the first method, preserving much the same data, I am happy to acquiesce. The third and fourth methods are not useful for straight reportage of data. They may, however, work better for some means of dissemination, such as theses or research reports where short transcripts are interspersed with analysis. In these cases, where sometimes content and readability are more important than voice and narrative style, a little editing can be useful. Nonetheless, I insist that a more verbatim transcription accompany the piece as an appendix to act as a balance.

When I first wrote this book, all the interviews conformed, more or less, to style 1—breath pauses marked by an em dash, with no other punctuation, because that is how my students had presented them to me originally. As they considered their work over time, and we discussed publication, some of them decided to edit the interviews themselves, to make them more accessible to a lay audience, while others were content to let the originals remain. Through various exigencies, the originals got whittled down one by one, until now only one remains—Michael Avrut's piece (chapter 4). He really wanted to preserve the voice of his interviewee as much as possible, and in the chapter I have made some suggestions concerning how to read the interview.

The discussion period in the lesson following the practicum usually begins with a number of picky technical questions concerning transcription. "Should I include every 'um' and 'er'?" "Do I capitalize proper nouns?" Almost invariably someone raises the issue of spelling for people who have heavy accents or speak in dialect. I make the point that English as written is not phonetic so that when you transcribe your own speech you do not attempt to capture actual pronunciation. For example, all English speakers drop the "g" in participles when speakin' casually. Even though we might say "He was runnin' for the bus," we will always transcribe our own speech as "He was running for the bus." If we do this for ourselves, we must do it for our interviewees also—otherwise we are setting ourselves up as more "standard" in our speech than we really are, and creating a larger gap between our voices and those of our interlocutors than really exists.

This issue often leads to a discussion of the power relationship that exists between fieldworker and narrator. I certainly want them to understand that as fieldworkers they inevitably have a great deal of control over the situation. They ask the questions, select the portions for transcription, and so forth. I need them to be aware of this state of affairs, but then I also need to help them understand how they can soften the situation—and how reciprocal empowerment can grow naturally and organically out of what may start as an asymmetrical relationship. Depending on how the class has evolved over the course of the semester, I may point out that a similar adjustment of power has occurred between me and them.

On more than one occasion I have adjusted my teaching style because my students have instructed me. For example, the desks in the classrooms where I taught were always laid out in rows, and it did not occur to me that this configuration was problematic in any way. It was what I was used to. About ten years into teaching the course, I was just finishing up my beginning remarks on power dynamics in the first class of the semester when a student asked me, "If your goal is for a more egalitarian and empowering learning experience, why don't we sit in a circle?" Good question. Why don't we? We moved the desks into a circle and the whole dynamic of the class was radically altered (I sat in the circle as well).

As a matter of some methodological importance, I do not believe that the relationships represented in the body of this book were ever as asymmetric as many relationships between professional anthropologists and the people under study, for obvious reasons. These are undergraduates after all, and their access to the power of publication and other rewards to be offered to their interviewees is slim. Often narrators grant interviews because they think by so doing they can help out these poor struggling students trying to better themselves. The interview is sometimes a sort of act of mercy, with the narrator feeling more in control than the fieldworker. And, of course, as I noted in the previous chapter, many of these interviews take the form of elders instructing their juniors in the ways of a culture they both share. Again, the power is more in the hands of the narrator than the fieldworker. This state of affairs makes the undergraduate-generated life history invaluable and, in some cases, unique.

Once the fieldworkers get back to the university, though, the locus of power can shift as they begin the general transcription and editing process. The more they smooth and manipulate and trim, the more of themselves they are injecting into the product. I mitigate this as much as possible through the transcription method I have adopted, but frequently students use the life history data in other papers, and even in their senior theses (it is good, hard earned data after all). If I am their thesis director, I allow a great deal of leeway in editing and shaping the text as long as the original interviews appear in unedited and unabridged form in an appendix to the thesis, so that the interested reader can go back and see the context of the edited material.

There is always an important check on the transcription stage, too, in that I ask my students to take a copy of the final document for their interviewees to read. If there are any problems, they can be negotiated with the interviewee, although in eighteen years of teaching the course I have heard of only one difficulty, which was relatively simple to resolve. Taking the document back to the interviewee also ensures that the interview process is not hit and run. The interviewee has a sense of continuing engagement with the fieldworker (as frequently manifested in the relationships described in the following chapters) and has the document itself as a touchstone of the relationship.

Returning a copy to the interviewee may also be a bonus because they can save it and give it to family members and heirs. Sometimes family members are not willing or able to hear a life history from an elder. But with it preserved in written form it becomes available to read when the time and circumstances are right, and therefore to cherish. The interviewee may, thus, feel that they have given a lasting gift to their loved ones. In the case of the life history recorded by Janette Yarwood (chapter 7), the woman she interviewed was estranged from her children, but Janette was able to give the woman her story in written form for all of them to read and absorb, and in so doing was able to broker a reconciliation between them. Isadora Sahl's life history (chapter 5) had a rather unexpected benefit when she gave a typed version to her interviewee. Her interviewee claimed that the promises she made in her life history—to secure better employment, buy a house, and so on—became irrevocable because they were now in print. She forced herself to follow through.

I cannot say that every life history I receive is of great interest to me, and it would be utopian to imagine that I could teach the course in such a way that every student would live up to my highest expectations. But I will say that I have never received a life history that did not have some merit, and I would much sooner read the average life history than a pile of final papers on dialectical materialism or the arts of the Yoruba. Every life history I read embodies something fresh and new to me, and in every year, one or two grip me. I always look forward to the end of the semester because of the promise of these life histories. When I anticipate end-of-semester grading with pleasure, I know I am doing something right.

Study Questions

1. Choose a segment from the transcription in the following chapter or one of the other chapters that uses a plain transcription method. Edit it in different ways (as in the sample above). What problems arise in the process of editing? What advantages and disadvantages do you find?
2. Do you have a person in mind you would like to interview? Why? What attracts you about that person's life history?
3. Do you have any concerns about interviewing? If so, what are they and how will you deal with them?

2

Elisabeth Jackson

It is important to me to start the substantive chapters of this book with the work of Liz Jackson,[1] because she was really the catalyst that started this whole enterprise in the first place. To understand her vital contribution, you have to begin by picturing the scene in my first fieldwork class in 1989. The anthropology program at Purchase College, at my urging, had just instituted the policy that all undergraduate majors must take a fieldwork class as a requirement for graduation. In those days this move was considered radical. Almost no undergraduate departments in the United States expected any kind of fieldwork from its students, and at the time I was not aware of any undergraduate program with a core requirement of a qualitative methods class. In fact, only around one-third of doctoral programs had a formal requirement of a qualitative methods class before budding professionals took off for the field. It was not required in my own doctoral program in the early 1970s, although one year's intensive fieldwork was mandated for the dissertation.

A major component of my department's reluctant agreement to the requirement, from my perspective, was that I would teach the class. I had certain goals for the course based on my own fieldwork experiences. I had been drawn to anthropology as a graduate student because of my own intellectual interests, but then (as is true of so many people in the field) my life had been transformed by my doctoral fieldwork. It was important to me to give my own students some sense of the power of fieldwork, so that they could understand the discipline better. It seemed to me that juggling other people's data and learning the theoretical paradigms of the great men and women of anthropology was only a partial education. The real work was in the field, and they had a right to know about it firsthand. At the same time that I was interested in teaching field methods to undergraduates, I was also concerned to use the class as a place to refine field methodology in general. My aim was to use the students in my classes as junior assistants, helping me experiment with new ideas to put some rigor into data collecting.

In retrospect I realize that my ambitions for the class and for the students were less well-defined than they might have been, and that I had placed an extraordinarily heavy load on their shoulders. Most of the students in the class were overwhelmed by what I was expecting of them, especially by the notion that I wanted them to *care* about what they were doing. I suspect that most of them had never been asked to care about their work in their entire school careers, and so they were not prepared for this precondition. The majority of them responded by doing what they did in most classes, namely, finding topics that they thought I, the professor, would find interesting whether or not they cared about these topics themselves. Liz was different.

Right from the start she threw herself wholeheartedly into all the projects and really did care about each and every one. Truth to tell, I was a little caught off guard myself by her involvement and commitment. I had asked for real caring and then was not quite sure what to do with it when I was given it! It turned out that Liz really made *me* work in class, a good deal harder than I was used to. For one thing, she challenged and worried my ideas during discussion sessions. I could not simply outline a project and let it be. She wanted everything spelled out, and she wanted me to clarify all the details I had left vague. She also wanted to make sure that for every project she was on the right track and that I approved of her agendas.

When she observed fellow students in the class offering what she deemed lackluster effort or when they appeared uncaring about their results, she gave them a hard time—and I mean a really hard time. Periodically she reminded all of them of the difference between coming from a White middle-class background and a poor African American one, and what that meant in terms of the ease or difficulty of acquiring an education. Her constant theme was that if you have to struggle, your education means more to you and you put more into it, with me in the background silently cheering her on for saying the things that I am usually too reserved to say to students.

But none of this was as challenging as her statements about her personal situation. The class met two days per week in the fall semester from 3 to 4:30 p.m. Barely two weeks into the semester, though, Liz started leaving a few minutes early. This small irritant was quickly resolved for me when she explained that she lived in the projects in Brooklyn, and the particular street where she lived was dangerous after dark. To make the point absolutely clear to me, she explained that her boyfriend (and father of her only son) was killed by being shot ten times in the chest right outside the entrance to her building. So, if it was all right with me, she would like to leave a little earlier each week. It was all right with me. But I was also beginning to feel out of my depth.

With Liz I had come face to face with real social issues and with someone truly willing to come to terms with those issues, and I was not sure I had the intellectual and emotional resources to handle the situation. Take the day that Liz called me up at home in a panic about her first interview for a class project, for example. Many students get nervous about their first interview, but their problems are trivial in comparison with Liz's. She called me because she had set up an appointment for the interview that morning, but while she was sleeping, a crack addict burglar had entered her apartment via her bedroom window and terrorized her and her son before leaving. She wanted to know if she should still keep the interview appointment even though her stress level was through the roof. This is not the kind of student problem I was used to handling. Helping Liz through the semester taught me a great deal about my own limitations.

Certainly, if caring about the work was the sole criterion of success, Liz was a model student. Everything she did for me was creative, well-thought-out, and closely related to the social problems that she faced on a daily basis. The one key issue was that she did not write like a White middle-class student. She wrote like a poor, disadvantaged, African American woman. I did not want to make a huge deal out of this one thing from an academic standpoint because I was looking more for good data collecting and research design than for lucid prose style. But two problems persisted for me. While I recognized the possibility that her writing style represented her authentic voice, I was afraid that if I accepted it uncritically, I might disadvantage her should she go on to do graduate work (a fear that proved abundantly justified). Second, and perhaps more basic, I did not understand everything that she was writing in this voice that was largely foreign to me (even though I understood her spoken language perfectly well). So we struggled throughout the semester to find some middle ground between her voice and mine.

Then at the end of the semester, she came to me asking for an incomplete because she was struggling with the life history (before this was my normal practice for the class). I granted the incomplete, but I was worried that she was crumbling under the pressure of work. This was about the most serious misunderstanding of a student I have made in over thirty years of teaching. When she finally presented her project to me it was a masterpiece: I could not believe what she had accomplished in such a short time. What I received was an eighty-page verbatim transcription of the experiences of an inmate of Attica Correctional Facility during the 1971 rebellion who was incarcerated in the cell block that was at the center of the rioting.

The text was absolutely riveting in itself, and I found it impossible to put it down until I had read it all through. But equally important, the entire narrative was in the authentic voice of a poor, disadvantaged African American, and that was all right. In fact it was more than all right; it was the only voice that was suitable for that particular narrative. So in the end, Liz had won the day. She had found a legitimate way to present an authentic voice like her own, and through it she was able to voice vicariously the concerns that she herself had.

I was so impressed by the paper that I determined on the spot to find a way to publish segments of it (see Forrest and Jackson 1990). I had begun to shape in my head the notion of reciprocal empowerment, so clearly evident in her case; but I was also beginning to see something similar developing between her and me. She was providing me with fresh insights into fieldwork (and pedagogic) methods, just as much as I was teaching her. The classic cliché of the student teaching the professor as much as the professor teaches the student was playing itself out, but with one critical difference from the usual scenario. Typically that old chestnut is trotted out to pour approbation on exceptionally gifted students. Liz was an exceptional student all right, but not in the classic sense. She was not a "good" student by the standards of the college, her GPA hovered around the danger mark, her prose style, spelling, and grammar were cause for concern, and she was far from diffident or deferential to the faculty. This unpromising student was teaching me more than all my other students combined.

I never taught Liz again in another class, but we saw a fair bit of each other in her remaining semester at Purchase because I wanted to get her life history in print, and there was a deal of work to be done on it to get it in shape. Although her plan was to go on and get an MSW (possibly a PhD) and move into politically active social work, she had been inspired by the life history project and wanted to do more. So, she determined to keep working with her interviewee, Danny, to get a complete book-length oral narrative from him that could be published. The transcription here represents a small piece of that larger work, the part that deals with Danny's family background in South Carolina.

She also saw the life history method as a potent tool in the continuing struggle for recognition of the strengths of African American culture and its leaders. At one point (before all of his legal and personal problems developed), she contacted Mike Tyson to see if he would be interested in having his life history taken down and actually flew out to Indiana to spend a weekend with him to discuss her ideas. A story for another time.

I have kept in reasonably close contact with Liz through all of her plans for life histories (as well as through her trials and tribulations in graduate school), and the process of reciprocal empowerment between the two of us has continued. She also used to return to Purchase College on a regular basis and occasionally sat in on a class, bringing back old memories because she continued to speak her mind largely without filter. She often brought her mother with her on her visits, and our discussions had a very complex three-way flow to them, each of us bouncing ideas off the others in a process of mutual learning based on mutual respect.

I did not imagine when I first planned the fieldwork course that over three decades later I would still have a close personal attachment to one of my first students and her family. Nor did I expect that such a relationship would continue to be fruitful for both sides, but it has been. The products of this volume are in large part the outcome of that friendship. Because Liz taught me what really good work could look like, I am always on the alert for more of the same. I expect the highest of my students now because of what Liz taught me; and because I expect the best from them, they often give it to me, and, in return, I offer my best to them.

The segment I have chosen to excerpt here, from newer tapes Liz had made with Danny after her work in the class, focuses on issues concerning African American families and the role they play in socializing children. Liz's senior thesis at Purchase College concerned the cultural problems entailed in placing Black children for adoption in White families. Since that time, she has trained and worked as a social worker, gaining an MSW and a PhD in social work, with a particular concern for family structure, and her abiding interest concerns the functions and dysfunctions of African American families.

Danny here is teaching her about the cultural differences between African American culture and Euro-American culture by using his own family background as an example. He is also showing how his own descent into crime was facilitated by the family structure he was raised in and became accustomed to. You can see the ways in which Liz is grasping at a reconstruction of the history of African peoples in America while interviewing Danny. This portion of Danny's life history is mostly unedited, but it is only a small portion of hours of recordings. The transcription is not exactly as Liz did it. She used simple em dashes to show the breath pauses in order to evoke precise nature of his authentic voice. I have replaced them with punctuation marks, to make the piece easier to read, but I have not edited the material in any other way. Most of the breath pauses are now commas, but a few are periods. The original pauses are the same length. *Oral presentation is not written prose.* There are a couple of points marked with ellipses—[. . .]—which indicate places where the tape ended and Liz had to put a new tape in, that is, back in the days when tape cassette recorders were the best tools for this type of work.

Life History

L: Where you was born?

D: Wherever I came from and all that shit?

L: Yeah.

D: Well as far as I know, I can go back to my so-called birthplace, Camden South Carolina. I know my mother's father and mother, I know my father's mother and father, and of course, my mother's peoples was so-called like, general mixture of white peoples. And my father's peoples was a general mixture of Indians and Africans, and, on my father's side they was root doctors and shit and on my mother's side they was very religious Christians. And uh, my grandfather on my father's side was never a sharecropper not that I know of he always owned his own land. And on my, mother's side they was always sharecroppers, or, [inaudible] in the boondocks, and go to church every Sunday and spread the, Christianity religion the white man taught them. Was a mix of French, French and African, some other European, Caucasian

L: What was your mother's last name?

D: Evleigh, that's a name that very few people can spell

L: How do you spell it?

D: [spelling] E V L E I G H, Evleigh, that's French [inaudible] but anyway my father's people's name on my grandmother's side was Swapshy, it was either Navajo Arapaho Arapaho or Blackfoots. They was some kind of Indians, they was Indians, they was Indians

L: so these was, Evleighs, French from France

D: right

L: right

D: right right

L: OK so that's where

D: [inaudible] the white mans are from France. There was very few, very few. Well, you know, not as now. There was very few black, French, slaves, OK, but Anglo-Saxons, whoa, they had all kinds of slaves right? Like why do you think most of the black Americans, so called, what do they call it? the miracle million? All names is Brown, Johnson, Jones, Jefferson, Smith, you know. English names, so-called, English names, English, English supposedly meaning Anglo-Saxon

L: so how did you get your last name as Jefferson?

D: well, up through my father peoples, though they weren't slaves per se, but they came as slaves OK? My great-grandfather on my father's side name was Jo Jefferson. He was a, witch doctor, and, he, came up with a formula for gonorrhea, that was, so-called, that was a European disease OK?

L: uh-huh

D: Gonorrhea. Indians never heard of gonorrhea, Africans never heard of gonorrhea. Gonorrhea came direct from Europe, you know. I mean, it's what they call a, we call it a sexual disease Anyway, it's a disease from copulation, and, uh, my uncle, I mean, I'm sorry, my great-great, my great-grandfather, uh, as a African, as a African witch doctor, he, knew of, a root and a bark in a tree that make the cure, the so-called gono-cortical germ, or the gono-cortical, uh, virus. Because, see, when you got gonorrhea, that's a, virus, OK? Like a cold, you got a strepto-cortical, gono-cortical, is, uh, viruses, and they grow, and they start out little-bitty and next thing you know you got a little worm running, ass is running, whatever the deal is. But anyway my great-grandfather could cure it, and his name was Jo Jefferson. He, he cured so many white peoples, of this, gono-cortical germ, because . . . OK, I don't want to get, I don't want to get off the topic, but, ninety, percent of all diseases, that came to America, OK? are, post, the Conquistadores, or let's say, uh, any, uh, Columbia, came from Europe, they came, that's how they killed Indians, they did kill more Indians with disease than they ever killed with guns, cause, see, these peoples, like in Africa, same thing, they brought disease out of German, I mean, out of Europe, Europe was infested with diseases, OK? because they was some filthy peoples

L: like the bubonic plague

D: the black, plague

L: which was the bubonic plague

D: no no, there was two different

L: really?

D: there was a black plague, uh, matter of fact if I, if I can quote you here. The black plague, came, in, fourteen, I'm sorry, thirteen something, and the bubonic plague came in fourteen something. Now that's when all the Europeans started to spreading out trying to find new lands to live, OK, and all this comes from the fact that they had diseases in Europe like you couldn't fucking believe, OK? And I mean they're stupid diseases, and these diseases didn't exist in, uh, so-called, uh, the Amazon, or, uh, so-called forest peoples, or, uh, so-called nomadic peoples from the, uh, Kalahari or the Sahara or even the peoples that was in the so-called lost places, lost continents of Americas. The Indians, shit, ain't know nothing about measles mumps chicken pox gonorrhea syphilis. They never got none of this shit, but, uh, these diseases, that they had, that was infested in Europe, uh, like I said, in the thirteen hundreds and the fifteen hundreds, uh, fourteen hundreds, they wiped out, uh, something like a hundred and twenty five million, a hundred and twenty five million people. And uh, anyway, my grandfather could cure this so-called, this uh, what do you call it? We got a name for it when you, when you, when you have a sexually transmitted disease, we call it a

L: STD?

D: No, no, I won't say LTDs either, OK?

L: venereal disease

D: right, OK, thank you, a venereal disease, OK? And my great-grandfather could cure this shit with some bark of a so-called my father says sycamore tree. See, take the uh, the bark off the north side of a sycamore tree I really don't know what the fuck I'm talking about, on this right here. Take the bark off the north side of a sycamore tree in the, morning, dew, when the moss is growing on the same side, and mix it with ontonconca root which I never knew what an onconca root was, and stir it up in the same proportions. You drink this shit and it would dry your penis up from leaking, so-called gono, gono-cortical germ, or, uh, as we call it today, claps, OK? Right, well anyway, my parents, my great-grandfather could cure it, so they was classified as doctors, not to a black man but to a white man

L: oh

D: OK? And? Somehow, way, my great-grandfather, uh, got his freedom from that, from curing white peoples of the European diseases, and, uh, I mean I'm not trying to get away from my mother's family

L: but it, but I'm not understanding where the original name

D: Jefferson?

L: the, the, the Indian name

D: oh, Swapshy

L: Swapshy

D: oh, well, well, well, my great-grandfather was acquired by an Anglo-Saxon, called Jefferson, OK? And I don't know if it was president Jefferson [laughs] you know, one on the two dollar bill or not, I wish it was the son of a bitch, give me some of them bills [laughs], anyway, uh, he was a pure African, my great-grandfather was pure African. He was a witch doctor on that, from the Ivory Coast, uh, they called it, uh, uh, North West Africa, OK? Most slaves come out the Ivory Coast anyway, a place called Nigeria, anyway, uh . . . He came here, he had these, well, to the white man, European white man, phenomenal powers, that he could cure a European disease. That wasn't the onliest ones he could cure, 'cept that was the major one—cure that gonorrhea—and long before penicillin ever came about, or ampicillin. Forget about that, medicine. Didn't know anything about that. I'm talking about well before penicillin was ever invented. My great, grandfather, had a cure for the European disease called gonorrhea, or the gono-cortical germ, OK? And uh, and the proof of the pudding is in the taste because my grandfather wind up with the so-called trade, cause he really didn't apply. I don't know my great-grandfather but I heard about him. His name was Jo Jefferson, and my grandfather's name was Thomas Jefferson, believe it or not. Not the one on the two dollar bill either. But anyway, he had nothing but white custom. Black people didn't trust him at all. My mother was petrified of him. Used to say "root doctor Oh my God, [scared voice] ooooo, make roots on me make roots on me." But my father was kind of afraid of him too because my father didn't understand shit, and plus my grandfather didn't play shit. And uh, somehow we, my great-grandfather acquired a lot of land. Now when I say a lot, for black peoples at that time, you know you're going back, you're going back before Abraham Lincoln. My grandfather, my great-grandfather, was, a man, before Abraham Lincoln was ever born. Talk about emancipation, proclamation. They ain't never heard of such a white person, or, free the slaves, OK? But anyway my great-grandfather was a so-called African witch doctor, and he acquired somewhere in the neighborhood of five six hundred acres of land. And my grandfather, being one of the sons and one of the crazy ones, and supposed to have acquired the knowledge of, you know, working with these, as uh, Europeans would call them, witch doctors, or, quackery, but that quackery shit worked, OK? And he wound up taking a big piece of land, somewhere down around . . . He had three, three brothers and two sisters but he took the bulk of the land, my father swore because he was a son of a bitch, like his father was a son of a bitch, like my father was a son of a bitch, OK? And don't you say your father was a son of a bitch, but anyway, they were all a bunch of son of a bitch. So he took the bulk of the land. He took all the land on one side of the road, and left the rest for the family to split, brother's side. He said I tell you, fuck me, and then he acquired all of his father's customers, all white. I ain't never seen a black, person that's in pain, or sickness, or illness, come to my grandfather, my father's father, for a cure. But we used to see, we used to call them "up the road license plates," we used to see license plates coming from . . . You see anything in South Carolina we'd know [snaps fingers] that plate right around. But when we see them plates like, blue plates, and, yellow plates, and orange plates, we used to call them "up the road plates" And they was all up the road white peoples and they was coming from, way, way out of town as far as I could, recall, come to see my grandfather, on a Sunday. Sometimes he'd have five and six cars sitting in his yard, all white, and everybody in the church, you know, the Sunday, be patting "Oh Lordy help me Lord Oh save me God" and shit, and my grandfather'd be down there working roots on them fucking white people. But he was repaid, and always carried a gun. He always drank a lot of liquor and always smoked a pipe. First man I ever seen by the way I don't want to get off the topic, but that was the first man I ever seen take a, hundred dollar bill, first time I've ever seen a hundred dollar bill in my life, took it and stuck it in the fire place and lit his pipe with it, understand? And this was back in the forties, uh, he lit his, uh, a hundred dollar bill, uh, back in the forties would be like a thousand dollar bill today, and my grandfather lit his pipe with it and throwed the rest of it into the fireplace, [inaudible]. He didn't give a fuck because he had money, he'd always had money that's how he got killed. When he got killed he had a pocket full of money, liquor and a big gun in his belt, front of his belt, but anyway . . .

L: how did he get killed?

D: a woman killed him, uh, because of the roots. She said he was working roots on her, and his land was next door to her, you know, next. Their border, their land bordered each other, and he had a fence and she said her cow, his cows was on her land, 'bout five thirty in the morning just before the break of dawn, and called him out of his bed, told him to come up there get your cows off my land and blowed his heart out with a shotgun. But anyway, my grandfather, he was, uh, he was pure African, and he, married, my grandfa . . . My grandmother's name, was, Ha, uh, Hannah Swapshy, and she was, half, Cherokee Indian, and her mother's name was Swapshy. And she married a man that was a Swapshy, they was both Indians or half Indians, but anyway, my grandmother's maiden name was, Hannah Swapshy, and my grandfather's maiden name we never knew. All his name was Jefferson because, you know, whoever his father's name was, was, was, you know, Jefferson. Bought nigger, you know what

I mean? And once Jefferson buy a nigger his name's Jefferson from then on, you know what I mean? Let there be no mistake about it, this is Jefferson's nigger, understand? This is Jefferson's nigger. My recollection coming to me when I was about I guess, about two and a half three years old, but we didn't live on my father's land, my grandfather's land, my father. I think he was scared of my grandfather too, everybody was scared of my grandfather,

L: what year did your grandfather die?

D: oh shit, nineteen, forty, nineteen fifty, nineteen fifty, let me see I was about, eight years old, yeah, yeah, nineteen fifty, uh, he didn't die he got his fucking heart blown out, you know

L: was murdered

D: yeah, he was murdered, right, and the woman that murdered him, white man paid her, uh, fifty thousand dollars. No, white man paid her, taxes on her land for five years, and, after she'd murdered my grandfather they gave her a fifty thousand dollar bill, and that was stupid money back in them days. If it . . . that was like, uh, like a million dollars today, or maybe better. Fifty thousand dollars was a lot of money back then, and the white man got out on bail in [snaps fingers] three days. And that's when my daddy broke camp. He came to New York, and left us down there, me and my brother and my mother, you understand? And he came to New York. But anyway, as a kid I did have some childhood down there, you know. My father he lived from one place to another, mainly, we never lived too far away from my, not my mother's mother and father, but my father's mother and father 'cause they the ones that had the money and they all, if you got uptight you could always go there and say "yo," drop this vittles in the sack. And we used to run up the road with coke sacks full of food, cause my daddy, you know, he was a uptight nigger just like everybody. And, uh, and then he started moving away, further and further from his father, uh, first we was only like, uh, stone's throw away, but didn't live on his land. Live on somebody else's land. And my grandfather never trusted my father because my father didn't step in his footsteps. But my grandmother trusted my father to death, and any time my grandfather go to sleep or left home or went out to the woods to dig roots she get my father anything he want. And my father, my father did very good, 'cause, he didn't farm, until he left that place, next to my grandmother and grandfather on his side. Then he moved a little further, so-called sharecropping position, and that didn't last long either. Him and some tall cracker got into it about, about, my oldest brother and, one of his animals, his mules, plowing his mules. They had a standoff toe to toe, and the white man put him off his farm. And my grandfather figured he'd come home, but he didn't come home he went further away. Went to another farming cracker, but this cracker didn't want no share cropping. He just wanted the nigger to pay some bills. And my father was out working at sawmill, loading trucks, and, cut wood. Cutting down trees and all that shit. But anyway, moving on, we all went to school at the same time, me and my brothers. There was only three brothers, well there was three of us altogether, me and my two brothers. We had a, a backwood life, a country life, But it was a good life because first of all my daddy was a hell of a man. But not because he was so hellified as that his, father's, father's, you know, his peoples such hellified people, you know? They, like, he didn't have to take a lot of shit. uh, that's why this first sharecropping cracker that he was with, uh, uh. When there was a big, confrontation that was about, the mule, the white man mule dragging my oldest brother. My, my father was drinking water and, my, my father told my brother to hold, the, lines, till he finished drinking the water. And the mules just pulled off, and my brother said "whoa whoa, whoa-whoa-whoa." Them mules just drug him on across the fucking woods, along when my father caught up to the mule, he grabbed the mule and knocked the fucking mule down. I mean, you see, you see, my father was nearly six foot four. That motherfucker used to weigh about two hundred and thirty five pounds and all of it was muscle, you know, and he didn't give one good fuck about nothing. So when he figured, he see my brother's face, you know it was drug all in the mud and shit, you know, and the lines was wrapped round his arms, and the mules just drug him. When he caught the mule he just grabbed the mule and unbri-, unbridled my brother and said "God damn it," you know like my father act like the mule had sense like him. I guess he had mule sense. He says "hey what the fuck are you doing to my son," you know, [fist into hand] he hit the mule, and, the white man were looking. White man came and say "yo man what you doing hitting my goddamn animal?" and my father say "what the fuck your animal doing pulling my son?" He say "well look I ain't got nothing to do with your son so who told you let your son hold the rein? But you won't hit my fucking animal." My father pulled his hat off and threw it on the ground and said "now listen" says "you'd die and go to hell for your animal, and I know you love him, I'd die and go to hell for my son, cause I love him too, so now what we got to do?" My mama was standing there shitting a brick, [inaudible], but my daddy never been afraid of shit, not in a real sense, because I mean he was a good working man. But he don't take nothing, like, like myself, [laughs] understand? But anyway, that led on up till, he got himself driving a tractor and, bought his own. We had our own refrigerator, we had, what you call it, Victrola? We could play our own records, we had a couch that turned into a bed, oh we was high, we was shitting in high cotton down there. We was, I mean for poor niggers, we was shitting in pretty high cotton. Well then when his father got killed my, father panicked. Then once he saw what the white people did, they paid the woman to kill his father, and then when they saw what the white people did to bail the woman out, I tell you, for killing his father, and he figured he was the oldest son, he figured he should break camp—and, I'm skipping a lot of shit but—he wound up here in New York City, in around nineteen fifty, or maybe nineteen, yeah nineteen fifty nineteen fifty one, and I was about eight years old, maybe, yeah seven eight years old. And he left me, my two brothers, of course we had a brother down there, in, in South Carolina, on that first man's property that died, named Sherman. uh, we was all born by midwives. I was born by midwife, my oldest brother born by midwife, my other brother born by, the one that died was born by a white man and that motherfucker. The white man just cut his dick damn off, cause he circumcised him, ran himself to death running back and forwards to the doctor's office. So he never lived, over a month, you know what I'm saying? But anyway, uh, after his father got killed, my father broke camp, and he left my mother, my mother, left me, my two brothers, and of course the other brother was dead. I had no sisters at that time, and uh, he came to New York because he was afraid, that he was going to be the next on the agenda because the Jeffersons was, root doctors, and they was evil doers, uh, no, they was, non cracker fearers. You don't fear the white man you shouldn't live, because how can you live in those Carolinas back in those days in the forties, and don't fear white peoples? And my father says "shit," his daddy, his daddy got his heart blowed out, my daddy figured he didn't fear them so he figured he'd get his heart blowed out too so he broke camp, you understand? He broke camp, and my mama she stayed but she didn't stay long, we left a car refrigerator Victrolas hideaway beds and corn liquor. I never forget that shit, OK? And most peoples down South didn't have cars, my father kept a car, kept a car, and ain't kept an old car, you know, not a brand new car but, one that, you could drive it anywhere you want to drive. And my mama she'd drive. She was, she was a bad driver, wouldn't want to drive her ass. And could shoot her ass off too. My daddy was a shooting son of a bitch too. All of us was shooters, every, everybody was shooters in the family. and matter of fact little bitty babies could

shoot. My daddy, make it, put a setup, and shoot, when we pull the trigger it'd knock us down. He say "all right get up and shoot it again." Because he made sure we knowed how to shoot. Everybody knowed how to shoot in the family. I never learned because, it hit me too young. Anyway, uh, he came to New York with his brother, and uh, he stayed in Harlem, got a job at a filling station some shit, I don't know, and left my mama there, and my mama she stayed with us, for about six months and she broke camp too, then she split us up, two, me and my other brother. Me and my brother that's alive today, went to one of my, one of her sisters, cause there was eighteen in her family. And then my oldest brother he went to, one of her other sisters, and we stayed there about a year, and mama used to send us clothes down for Easter. And every Christmas we always got, not every Christmas, we were down there about a year, mama sent and got us [clicks fingers] right away, well not right away but boy I was so glad. It seemed like a lifetime, cause I was only there a year, after she left but it felt like, cause I was down there with my, old, you know, peoples back, way back in the woods, plowing mules and shit. And get a little half a cigarette. We was all smoking, they were smoking cigarettes and shit, [inaudible]. My mama gave my uncle the first car he ever had, cause he never had nothing but wagons. That's how far we was back in the woods. They ain't never had light bulbs. They had candles, I mean, not candles, I'm sorry, uh, uh, kerosene lamps. And we, we had electric lights and shit, you know, like I say, relatively be, poor niggers, we, had a little something, you know. We didn't have shit but, cause if the shit hit the fan my daddy could always, revert back to his family, cause they had something, you know what I mean? My grandaddy, like I told you that motherfucker a hundred, lit his, pipe with a hundred dollar bill, and very few motherfuckers'll light, anything with a hundred dollar bill today, and this motherfucker did it back in the forties, you know what I mean? You know, talking, and everybody say, mister, uh, mister Andrew, you light, ah shut the fuck up. He just lit the fucking pipe and [sucking sounds], and took the stub and throwed it in the fucking fireplace, hundred dollar. I ain't never seen that, I ain't seen that lately. I mean I ain't never seen that in my life, you know what I mean, not since, so, you know, so they had some bucks, you know what I mean? My grandfather, my daddy had shit, but he knowed he could always revert to his mama, because them mamas always take on them sons, you know, mamas always take on sorry assed motherfucking sons, but that's what my mama called my daddy—sorry motherfucker. Anyway, and uh, after my father was gone for a year, less than a year, about six months my mother she broke camp, she split us up, and uh, she came here, she left us for about a year, OK? And then she say I got to have my three boys, you know, and somehow we, uh, that thing ain't stopped has it? She says, uh . . .

L: uh-uh

D: OK well, anyway she says I got to have my three boys, and I don't know how they did it, but they sent down, South, and got all of us the same time. We ain't come one at a time, we all three of us came together, my uncle would've came down, the same one brought my father to his brother's up here, and, we started living on Houston street and Seventh avenue over there,

L: y'all moved from, they left Harlem and everyone moved to Brooklyn?

D: moved to Brooklyn, yeah, thought they could have new places there. See my uncle, we didn't have enough room, they didn't have enough room for mama and daddy, my uncle didn't have enough room for nobody but daddy, but when mama got here they was squeezing, but when we came [laughs], we was a little packed, we was a little packed, we was a little packed. So when we got here we had to go live with some more aunts, my mother's peoples over there. Aunt Esther, over there on Houston and Seventh avenue. But we stayed over in Harlem, on hundred forty fifth street and Eighth avenue for a couple of days, not longer. Get on, we left, he says you motherfuckers got to leave here, say you don't have to go home but you can't stay here. I brought you here but you can't stay here. I understand that, so anyway, my daddy broke camp my mama broke camp, we all broke camp, came to Brooklyn, and I've been in Brooklyn ever since, anyway, [pause] I was a pretty bright fellow myself, schoolwise. Know why I was bright? well not bright I ain't never been bright. I don't want to sound pedantic or anything. But see, when my mama was kicking my brothers' asses about Alice and Jane and Dick and Jerry, and Ruth and Rumplestil, stump, Ruth and Rumplestiltskin, uh, when I seen the way my mama was kicking their asses making them to remember, Alice and Jane and Dick and Jerry and shit, and you know, how Ruth and Rumplestiltskin stuck his foot in the ground, and they couldn't remember it tomorrow night she stomped they ass. So when it come time for me to go to school, I say "oh Alice Dick and Jane and Jerry Ruth and Rumplestiltskin" [laughs], cause I was the youngest, you know, so by them getting their ass kicked by not learning, I was learning, you understand? And you know, you don't have to wait to kick a six year old son in school, cause that goes to show you, I'm living proof of that, you know? When I went to first grade, well, uh, they skipped me, after I finished the first grade, I

54   *Subject Lessons*

knowed so much about Alice Dick and Jane and, and, Ruth and Rumplestiltskin, until they put me right into third [snaps fingers], because they said "how could this motherfucking kid be so smart?" But I got tired of seeing my mama stomp my brothers about Alice Dick and Jane and Jerry and Ruth and Rumplestiltskin right? So I really moved, when I went to school. Oh I was singing this shit, say this boy what he know, cause this was, this was the homework they was giving my brothers, you know? Alice Dick and Jane and Jerry, you know?, and Ruth and Rumplestiltskin. So, so, and mama said boy you remember how to spell Alice? My brother say " A, C, I, E." My mama say you dumb motherfucker, she'd jump on his ass. I said oh my God I feel so sorry for my brother, so boy I said damn I wouldn't, I bet she'll never kick my ass like that, cause, because if she asked me about it, how do you spell Alice?, all right, [fast] A-L-I-C-E, Jerry? [fast] J-E-R-R-Y, you know? I was singing it, squirrel, S, cat C-A-T, you know I was singing this shit, so when I went to school, they say oh this motherfucker he's brilliant, but I wasn't brilliant, it's just I didn't want my ass kicked you understand? So I already knowed this shit so when I went to first grade they skipped me to third...

L: what age was you when you went to

D: to first grade? Sixth grade, you know [disgusted] sixth grade, six years, six years of age

L: so you was on time

D: I, I, started on time, but they say I was ahead of my time because, I know all about Alice Dick and Jane and Jerry and how to spell and shit, because I seen how my mama was kicking my brothers' asses about not being able to spell

L: but it had to be later because you said you was like eight when your grandfather

D: oh now I'm talking about, when I went to school down South

L: oh you went to school down South

D: yeah, oh I went to school down South, yeah, I didn't come here till I was about nine years old

L: oh OK

D: you understand? but when I came here to school I started here with PS 25 over there on K, well I should use the proper terminology, that's Kosciusko Street, we call it Kos-ki-ass-ko

L: [laughs] that's true, I didn't know it was what you just said

D: that's Kosiusko, that's Kosiusko

    [. . .]

D: well anyway, I started off in school, over here, in New York, in Brooklyn, uh, they say, I was in the fourth grade already, and they put me

Elisabeth Jackson 55

in the fourth grade, I think I was eight years old, eight or nine years, I was nine years old or somewhere there, and I was supposed to be in, the, fifth, but they said, "come from down South you're not that smart" so they put me back one, so I know, I gained one down South lost one in New York [laughs], uh, listen I need to take a rest

L: uh OK

D: stop this shit
   [tape stops]

D: you playing?

L: all right

D: OK, I went to school over there, on Kos, Koski-ass-ko, Koscisuko Street, Kosciusko Street is on down there, and uh, I went to school about six months then I, goed there, I could, shine shoes, I started shining shoes in front of a bank, on the corner of DeKalb Avenue and I was shining shoes like a motherfucker because the bank was opened up from nine o'clock in the morning, until one in the afternoon, and uh, and I used to shine shoes for a dime, a dime a shine, and I used to shine shoes

L: you needed to? you needed to work? the family didn't have . . .

D: no, because see where I come from everybody fucking worked, nobody gets away without working. We worked down South, OK? And, anybody that didn't work, my mama said . . . she was working when she had us, she said dropped us out her ass and whacked us off and cut the biblical cord and wrapped us up in a little manger or whatever the fuck it is they did Jesus Christ, and kept on working, you know, and had our birth date checked by a midwife, because I telled you I wasn't born in no hospital or no doctor's office I was born in a cotton field, or some kind of field, I don't know what fucking field, I know I was born in a field somewhere, and all my brothers was born in a field, all my sisters and shit was born in a hospital and shit, but uh, mama said that was a crock of shit, but anyway, she was a tough old lady, but anyway, uh, uh, I always thought I had to work, I ain't never thought that anybody that's, well bodied, should work, I think working is, a part of, life, because if you don't thrive in life, there is no life . . .
   [. . .]

D: . . . . God's creation, you see because earth is always working, see everybody think everything is just, stagnating standing still, everything's working, can't you see the oceans working? Can't you see, uh, everything's working everything's working. I mean like, the ants is working, cows is working eating and shitting and milking right?, uh, everything's working right? Everything's working everything's busy, you know? The bees is working, uh, the lions is working, you know? The lion he don't do much but he, he fuck, he procreate, he working, then he [roars] growl and shit right? So he let the motherfuckers know this my territory, this my procreation place, you know, procreation's work, like, like, people say "hey fucking is a pleasure," no fucking is a job, [laughs], if you look at it from an animal point of view, cause animals don't fuck for pleasure they fuck to procreate right? They, they they they, copulate to procreate, that's a mild way of putting it, [inaudible], that's kinda hard, but it's the same shit, they copulate to procreate, and matter of fact you cannot copulate unless you win a battle. Matter of fact it's the strong will copulate, and see what the procreation will be, cause this way, the strongest will do the copulation, and if the copulation, uh, uh, come up right, like, like the animal's got it figured. I guess God give them the [inaudible], then, there will be some of the species survive, cause weak shouldn't copulate. But man ain't got that much sense. Man figures he's fuck for pleasure, "yo yo baby I just want to keep in practice" [laughs], you know what I'm saying? But anyway animals do it to procreate the, the species, all right? Anyway, uh, as I was saying, uh, I learned to work. I always went to work, working was a part of the deal. I mean, hell, you didn't work motherfucker you didn't live, and uh, I felt like I, I felt like working. I couldn't sit around the house and look in my mother's face, you know what I mean? You know sit around the house, cause we didn't have no TV, hell no we didn't have no TV back then. We didn't get a TV till nineteen fifty four, and I was in New York in nineteen fifty one, fifty one, sixty one, seventy one, eighty one, ninety one. That be forty years in a couple of years right? And so you know, well yeah, a couple of years right, so you know working was a part of the deal, you have to work, working is not something that you volunteer to do working is something motherfucker, you have to do, unless you're ill. If you ill then, then everybody do work, look out for you, cause we came not from a— a— a— a— a how do you call it? We had our only, own socialistic system, you know what I'm saying? We didn't have no welfare, we didn't know where, as my daddy said, "well the fare was," we didn't know where that was, we had, like, Aunt Beulah, Aunt, you know, and Inez and that stuff, we all chipped in to help out the ones who needed it, but everybody be busy, and if one was sick or afflicted in some kind of way like got a gimp leg or a gimp arm you know or [growl] dingbat, then everybody help that dingbat out. But otherwise if weren't nothing wrong with your motherass you get busy. I told you my mother was picking cotton and picking corn and dropped baby out her ass, and, wiped them off herself and, clean them up and said call me miss josie mahey, said tell them I just dropped one, and wrapped them up in a little, sack there, then went on back to work. That's the way she had her babies, she she never go to the doctor's and talk about laying up for three or four days. She said shit you lost three days of work, you lost three days of work. Anyway, uh, she was a strong lady, and most, most, that's the way she learned like that, cause that's the way it was back then. So I had working on my mind when I got here, I had working on my mind all my, all my life. Working was something I had to do, I had to work, for . . . I didn't have to work, I mean, you know but, but I wouldn't be a human being if I didn't work. To me I would be less than a human being, just because I went to school doesn't mean I wasn't working. Now kids go to school, "oh well I go to school what the fuck I don't like work," you understand? But no, but you see, no, you you you, you do you schooling, go on home do your homework, and [inaudible] make a couple of quarters before you you know? call it a night. So, you know, working was meant, it was, it was a prerequisite. It was understood that, if you had any gump or any salt or any balls if you want to call it nuts, you worked, you know? And not because you had to supply, your your your, food or anything. My daddy worked during the day and my mama had a job too, but it was just that you be proud to come home with, uh, seventy five cents, you say here mama here's fifty cents, you say I made seventy five cents today, she say that's nice boy, you know, because a subway token only cost five cent right? You know how much seventy five cent would get her to work for two to three weeks, see? That seventy five cent would get her to work. I mean, it wouldn't buy her lunch and everything but it would get her to work, that's a lot of money, you know, and you be proud, and then when you want to go to a movie on a Saturday, shit, you deserve it, you done sit there and work for three weeks, so she give you a fucking quarter [laughs], she give you a quarter, she give you a quarter at the drop of a hat, but anyway, I'd shine the shoes, and I'd shine shoes so good, I got good at it, I was strong, you know, I was a country boy, I was real strong, and I could shine the motherfucking shoes you know, I used to start all this [popping sounds], and I ain't never shined a nigger's shoes cause very few niggers, very few niggers want a shoe shine, nigger say, "ten cent, what the fuck are you crazy?" White man, he come into the bank, on a Saturday, cause I couldn't shine shoes on Monday Tuesday Wednesday Thursday Friday, because the bank was closed by the time I got out of school and got my shine box. But on a Saturday, bank don't, uh, open half a day, between nine and one, and boy I cleaned up. I used to clean up, and the white peoples come in, yo boy when they go in there and make their bank transactions. I'd be standing out there, "shine sir shine sir?" and I'd have and I'd have a big smile on my face like a big old chickadee country assed motherfucker I was "shine sir?" so "sure"—and then I got real slick, I went and bought me a little, I didn't go buy it, I found in-in-in the alley, old broken down church chair, the chair that uh, church people sit in, and it were broke, and I went and wired that motherfucker up, and set there, and now let the white folks sit down and get a shine, and oh boy I started cleaning up. I started cleaning up. I said goddamn, you know? See it's just like, it's like business, when they got to stand up and get a shine, you know? you know? They're very impatient, hurry up there buddy. When I let them sit down, they'd just sit there [inaudible] counting motherfucking money. I'd be [popping sounds], when they'd look down their shoes like glass. I used to get quarters. I'd get a whole fucking quarter, sometimes they'd give me like two quarters, that was stupid fucking money for a, five minute shoe shine. My daddy didn't make that kind of money, fifty cent for a for a for a, fifteen minute shine, my daddy was shining fucking cars and he didn't make a dollar in the whole fucking hour, you understand? White people say "holy shit, I was get, I was getting ready to throw these shoes away, look what these, [inaudible] . . ." I had a stick of wash, I used to wash, I used to wash the leather. I had a thing called wash, had brown and black wash, and you could wash the leather, and it, reinvigorated leather, and I know, I know how to shine the fuck out of a pair of shoes, and I used to make stupid money. And after they'd leave me I would take my shine box and run home and give my mother the money, and run right back to Daldbaum's. "Miss can I carry packages? Miss can I carry packages? Miss can I carry packages?" Oh shit, I started carrying packages, I got so busy, until I couldn't carry all the packages in my arms, cause I was only nine, ten years old, nine years old. I had to get me a carriage, cause the packages were so big, they'd say "where's my boy? where's my boy?" understand? Where's my boy? You know? I was their boy, you know? I was everybody's boy cause I used to carry their packages. I'd have, when I had my carriage, I used to load the fucking carriage up, and put two in my arms, and push my carriage with my belly, and guide it with my elbows. I was, I was a determined motherfucker to work, I, I loved work, but I, I hate it now. I can't stand it I hate fucking work, but in the, but I thought it was my job, and they used to give me stupid money too. Like the average package, let's say a two block trip, from the supermarket to two blocks away, that was about, uh, twenty cent or a quarter, but the way I carried them, I used to get thirty cent. I used to make money, I used to make money, I used, I used to make sometimes on, Saturday, between the shine box and the, and the, and the, Daldbaum's, I used to make like, fifteen dollars, eighteen dollars. My father didn't, make, but that much after tax was tooken out, in like a whole week, on his job, that's serious. He was making forty dollars a week, and they'd tax him right? He'd come home with like thirty four, I used to bring home sometimes twenty twenty five, for one day, you understand? I was a working motherfucker, but that's from tips, and then the boys in the neighborhood started robbing me, you know—yo man, yo yo homeboy, yo country boy, come here, I know you making all the money man, I saw you with the box over there in front of the bank, I saw you with the carriage man, give me an old nickel, I was dumb enough to reach in my pocket, I had so much motherfucking change I didn't know where to get it. I had both pockets full of change, I'd be down there looking for a, looking for a nickel, [strikes table], stepping on me, and take it all,

L: oh they'd just slap your hand to make you . . . ?

D: yeah, yeah, I'd be dumb enough to be down there looking, trying to find a nickel, I'd have quarters and dimes and shit, I'd give them two or three nickels, cause I had a handful, I'd be standing back, they used to say, "yo yo" [strikes table] they'd hit my hand like that, and they'd go [shhh sound], like that, "yo Mick get that change" and everybody'd be scrambling, and I'd say "whoa wait that's my money," and they'd just get it and run off and say "ah fuck you," you know, and I'd say "oh shit." Then I started telling my mom about them taking my money. She said "boy I don't tell you to be no fighter, but I cannot shine shoes with you, I will not carry packages with you." Said, "if you can't, if you can't handle it, then you don't have to go out and shine the shoes, and you don't have to carry packages, but I'm not going with you, and if you're going to get your ass whipped, and get your money took, stay home, cause when Monday come, we're going to send you to school. But we're not going, I'm not going with you, to carry your, loaded shine box, and I'm not going to push your fucking, package cart, and watch your money. I don't have the time, you know, if you can't do that, leave it alone." So I said "I ain't going to leave this alone, I'm going to get straight," and I got straight. I took a lady, I told a lady about it, a lady lived on Lewis Avenue, and Kosciusko Street, uh, uh, she said "why are you so nervous?" I said "because them boys are going to get me." She said "what boys? You mean the ones that hang on the corner of DeKalb in the summer?"

She said "look, you don't fight them?" I said "no because, I don't know" I told her I was from the country and shit. She said "I don't give a shit where you come from." She said "you fight them son of a bitches, you got a right to work, you got every goddamn right in the world to work." And I said "but there's a whole bunch of them" and she said "well I don't give a shit" said "you try to avoid them" she said "let me give you something" said "I'm going to give you a quarter, bring your, bring your cart in my gate." I put the cart in the gate, she said "take that." I had a, a throw board, she said "pick it up," you know the mat for the baby, mattress and all, she said "pick that shit up." I picked up a big old sack. She said "put these bottles down in there." She said "I'm not paying you in bottles" she said "I'm paying you in fighting material" she said "they ask you for a goddamned quarter or a penny or a nickel or a dime" said "you just get down up under this board and get busy" said "cause you got a right to work," said "now if you've got to leave and stop early" said "you stop early" but throw these fucking bottles" said "I'm not giving you . . ." Cause back in them days, a bottle was, a penny for a little bottle and, three cents for a big bottle, something like that, yeah yeah, penny for a little bottle, penny for a small bottle, and, three cents for a big bottle, like beer bottle was three cents. She says "I'm not telling you, you take these bottles and take them to the store" she gave me about twenty five bottles, she said "when you see them approaching you," said "don't you budge until they get within firing range" [laughs], she said "when they come" said "you know what they coming for" said "how many times?" I said "I don't know so many times I'm ready to quit" she said "don't you quit" said "keep working" said "when they come to you" said "you just reach down in front of this, when they say, when they get close enough to say 'yo man, give me an old nickel'" said "you say 'I've got it right up under here'" said "you reach up under there with both hands" said "when you come out don't aim, just throw" and I said "damn" you know? "If I do this they're going to kill me" right? "If I hit somebody in the head with a bottle, when they see me next week, I'm going to be dead, this woman's telling me how to get killed." She says "I'm, I'm telling you how to survive boy" said "now you go, don't go back," said "now, look" said "I be late" she always come in the store late, like about six thirty seven o'clock, that'd be about dark. She said "this time you go home anyway" said "now when I finish you off you don't go back to, Somers Avenue, go down Lewis" she said "but they'll be looking for you, they'll cut you off at the pass" and she was right on the money. She said "but when they get within range of you, when they say 'yo yo my man, let me have a nickel,' say 'oh oh I've got it up under here'" said "when you come out" said "that one in the front, do the best you can, blast" And I was a country boy I could throw a rock. She said "well now you can throw a bottle you're in New York now motherfucker" and goddamn it I did just what that woman said, and you know what them motherfuckers told me? I was scared to go back to work, right? Cause I figured man all them motherfuckers. I fired them motherfucking bottles, I lit their ass up with them bottles, right? And I said "oh shit" I went home and told my mama about it, and she said "well you got all your money" I had pockets full of change, she said "well you got all your money." But I was, and still had several bottles left, when I got change, I cashed the bottles in. I had more money, you understand? She said "well, look, you want to quit, quit, are you scared?" I stayed off next week. I had plenty of money, and I was scared too, and I asked my brother to go. He said "well, you want us to fight for you?" I said "no, I don't want you to fight for me man" said "I want you to watch my back" said "man I ain't watching your motherfucking back, cause you'll come home you'll give to mama you won't give us none" so I said, I said "well I guess that ain't going to work" and I was, and when I would go to school I used to watch my back, but you know how I found out, that they weren't going to fuck with me no more? They said "there's homeboy, hey homey" and I'm going to school, I thought they were going to whip my ass, "yo man how you licked them jive mother-fuckers up that night" "huh huh?" I thought I had to run, I had my books, you understand? I had a little old pocket knife, mama didn't allow us to carry knives to school, but I had me one cause I figured they're going to kick my ass for throwing them bottles. I didn't know who I hit cause I was throwing bottles, I just had my head down, I was throwing them motherfucking bottles, I didn't give a fuck, like that woman said "who the fuck you hit, if you're innocent you shouldn't be there, and what are you doing asking me for money?" I was throwing them motherfuckers, "yeah" I said "I got it up under here," when I come, when I come up, I was throwing, I was throw-ing, "yo what the fuck is this, he's crazy [laughs]" I was throwing bottles with both fucking hands, I threw bottles with both hands right? shit, I see them niggers I said "oh shit" they're going to kick my ass now, "man that's my homeboy that dude don't take no shit, fucking homeboy don't fuck with my man, yo man cool" and I know I don't have no money. I'm as nervous as a mother. I figure they're going to gang, kick my ass, said "yo man, you cool man, talk to them motherfuckers" said "man, tell them you don't fuck around Jack, and listen, my name is Mo" you understand? "And you tell them mother-fuckers you fuck with you, man, tell them you know Mo" said "man, you cool man, look man you got balls, you know them guys over there got twenty five stitches" I said "yeah" I'm scared to death, said "man, be cool man, fuck them motherfuckers up there on mother-fucking, uh, DeKalb Avenue, man they ain't nothing but pussies" I said "pussies? Who are these pussies?" I thought I was a bigger pussy than they was "yeah they ain't but pussies man" said "I hear you fired their ass up man, I hear one of them motherfuckers got five stitches in his head." I didn't, I didn't, I didn't know I hit nobody. I just started throwing bottles, I was throwing the motherfucking bottles right? so I became a natural, now I had juice. I could walk down there, matter of fact, if you were to push up by, push your cart, I'd say "bro, you're working today," they called me, they called me Country BoJack, "Country BoJack says it's all right man, work today," and I, then I became a gangster, I said "why should I push a cart, I'm a gangster?" yo man I decided who worked, you know, I decided who worked, my mama said "boy you ain't working no more?" I said "I got money" cause I was taking it, I was doing the same thing they was doing. So they started me off in my career . . .

Study Questions

1. What is your first reaction to the way Danny speaks? Does it help or hinder the storytelling process in your opinion?
2. If you were put in charge of publishing Danny's whole life history, how would you transcribe and edit it? Explain your choices.
3. What do you think Liz was learning from Danny that would empower her in her career and life going forward?

Notes

1. I am going to use my familiar names for my students throughout to indicate the general familiarity of our relationships.

3

Bonnie McCutcheon

Bonnie McCutcheon was a younger contemporary of Liz Jackson's and took the fieldwork class a year or two later. But unlike Liz, I already knew Bonnie before she did her fieldwork projects because she had taken several classes with me before enrolling in fieldwork methods, and she was a declared anthropology major. She had first come to my attention because she seemed to be such a curious mixture of opposites. She was at one and the same time painfully shy and extremely ambitious for herself in her program of study. I was not aware until I had known her for some time that she was legally blind. She was not immediately forthcoming with the information, and despite the dark glasses that should have been a giveaway, she did not manifest any obvious signs to me of visual impairment. Basically, she did an excellent job of negotiating the world without hanging a sign around her neck that said "HANDICAPPED."

This does not mean that she completely hid her situation from everyone. She was quite comfortable telling me once she got to know me a little. She just did not feel the need to display everything about herself to the impersonal world at large. As it happens, I got to know Bonnie rather better than many other students, and she remained a close friend after graduation. Our relationship strengthened because she worked as an editorial intern for *New York Folklore* when my late wife, Deborah Blincoe, and I were co-editors. She was an invaluable assistant on the journal, and she also came out to stay with us at our house on several occasions to help with fieldwork projects that my wife was working on.

So, right from the start, our engagement as student and teacher was rather closer than usual, and the sense of reciprocal empowerment between us manifested earlier in the fieldwork class than was usual. In fact, every one of her projects was highly creative, and several used her blindness as a strength. For example, the third project in the course requires the students to produce a map that records some kind of social or human information in a graphic way. Bonnie produced a map of a room that was entirely tactile—you "read" it with your fingertips—and she enclosed it in a box so that you could not see it at all, and had to feel it "blind" to find your way about it. Not only did she complete the project in a creative way for someone legally blind, but she was also able to give the other students in the class an idea of what it means to have to rely on senses other than sight.

When it came to doing the life history, Bonnie chose her father. She did this at first simply because she was too shy to ask anyone else. But there were other reasons lurking in the background. She, like a great many students in the class over the years, saw this formal project as an opportunity to ask her father about his life and his heritage, so that she could have a better sense of her own lineage. Getting a coherent narrative from him about who he was and where he came from was a way that she could begin to construct the narrative of her own identity.

This process of constructing a conscious self-image was made more poignant by the fact that Bonnie's father had lost half of his right arm as a youth. He was, thus, also technically "disabled," but he was adamantly opposed to being so labeled and did everything in his power to live a normal life. His own struggle to avoid the stigmas of being handicapped had had a profound effect on Bonnie as she was growing up. Essentially, she was left with a deep ambivalence in her attitude to her own visual impairment. Should she follow her father's lead and generally try to give the world the impression that she was normally sighted? Or should she try to avail herself of avenues of assistance for the disabled and seek assistance both from individuals and from the bureaucratic system? The life history interview was a way for her to probe her father's motivations so that she could understand them more clearly. As such, she could decide whether to follow his path, because she understood it better, or use her understanding of his motivations to help comprehend and focus her own motivations better.

The chief thread that runs through her interview with her father, therefore, concerns his employment history and how his sense of self was determined in large measure by the status of his jobs. Her father very carefully emphasizes his qualifications and his progressive advancement. He is also careful to point out that despite all the problems he faced (physically and socially) he was able to not only stay employed but also actually advance himself during some of the toughest economic times of the twentieth century.

It is important to note that Bonnie's father rarely mentions the loss of his arm, and he rejects any notion that he was favored in hiring because of his circumstances. His point of view is that it was irrelevant or a disadvantage to be overcome. But, on the other hand, it is also evident that not having two strong arms saved him from following his own father down the coal mines or working as a common laborer. That is, he was enabled to rise from the laboring class to professional status *because* of his disability. Losing an arm was the spur he needed to move away from manual labor as a vocation. The one ambivalence that this situation seems to have established in his own mind is that to become a professional he had to do what he considers "women's work" and call primarily women his colleagues. Hence, there was an abiding desire to make it clear that he was still capable of "man's work." This was achieved ultimately by fulfilling one of his own father's dreams.

His father had desired to leave coal mining to become a farmer—still a labor-intensive occupation but a considerable rise in status, in part because of the independence of farming one's own land as opposed to digging someone else's coal from the ground. When he was financially able, Bonnie's father bought a farm of his own, although it was never a money-making enterprise but more a matter of personal pride. Of course, he had to face the challenge of farming with one arm—but because he was not economically tied to farming as a way to make a living, he was able to take on the tasks on his own terms.

Beyond the personal motivations explored in this life history, there is also an undercurrent created from Bonnie's father's own lineage. He was born and raised in an Irish Presbyterian environment characterized by a strong commitment to Puritan values as they relate to work and self-worth. This, in turn, is also Bonnie's heritage, which she is anxious to claim for herself even while at the same time she wants to distance herself from part of its ethos. She wants to have a family history, certainly, and her lack of direct connection with it is engendered by the fact that her father moved away from the family home in Pennsylvania (and is not on good terms with his siblings) and because there is a family history of wide gaps between generations. Bonnie's father was in his fifties when she was born, and he was born to a mother in her forties.

But she also feels an aversion to the Puritan spirit of the family. This is the ethos that holds so much stock in hard work and professional status as a measure of one's worth. Without her blindness she might find such an ethos oppressive, but with her blindness added to it she sometimes finds it overwhelming. Her father used that ethos to overcome his own disability, but Bonnie is ambivalent about following in his footsteps. Thus, Bonnie has told me bluntly that she cannot easily resonate with her father's need to reiterate his employment history and recount his eminent qualifications for his various positions. Yet underneath this friction is ambivalence on her part because his repetition of these issues in this interview is often prompted by her direct questioning. He wants to show her where the Protestant ethic can lead you—even with a disability—and she is not sure whether to accept or reject his viewpoint.

This ambivalence may also be driven by her current social status. Thus, she understands the importance of the farm to her father, but it does not have the same importance for her because she is not the child of a laboring family. Being a generation removed from that ethos, she considers the farm more of a burden than a symbol of social mobility. Her father has effected the move upward for her, and so she has less need of the symbols of that move than he does because she is more secure in her position. Therefore, she does not feel the need for particular jobs or qualifications as indices of her social position.

Even now, after years of friendship, Bonnie is not much of a talker. She used to come to visit my wife and me occasionally in our home in the Catskills where she was comfortable, and during one of those visits I got more information from her about her life history. Subsequent to the initial presentation of her father's life history to me, Bonnie transformed the transcription into more fluid prose by replacing the pause dashes with conventional punctuation. I have chosen to present this version rather than the original transcription for the sake of showing the effects of different transcription methods.

Life History

[B = Bonnie; F = Bonnie's father]

B: Tell me about your family.

F: Well, my father's name was William Irvine McCutcheon, which he later changed to William I. McCutcheon because he didn't like Irvine. He was mostly a laborer. He always wanted to be a farmer, he had ten acres at one time, but he never got around to farming it. When I knew him he worked in a coal mine. He was a miner, but when he got too old for that work they gave him a job driving a team of horses. And I enjoyed that because I would go over beyond [my] school and ride with him. He hauled cinders from the Union Railroad to the coal mines. The coal mines were operated by Hartman Brothers. And the cinders that he hauled were used to build up the roads for the tracks into the mine.

B: And where was this?

F: This was in Monroeville, Pennsylvania. Beyond the school it was a mile or so to walk. It was a big thing for me to walk over there and ride with him. I guess he worked in the mines more than anything else that I remember because there was a coal mine right down at the bottom of our hill. In those days it was called a slope mine. They just dug into the side of a hill and they would go under the slate where the coal was. The coal was there because it had been compressed by the glaciers. And many times the men had to work on their knees and turn sideways and dig with a pick so that they could break the coal loose and then they gathered it up. And then of course they kept working into the mine until they got to the place where they had to use posts to support the roof. And then they would lay track and had little cars. Mules would pull the cars. So they would work their way back into the mine. Then they would open up rooms where they would work. Then they would have to have stumps to support the roofs. But they just used posts to support where they worked. Then sometimes they worked back outwards towards the entrance. So if the roof did fall in it was all right because they had finished that work. They had the plans worked out so that they could take out the coal from the farthest point and work back towards the entrance where they began.

It was interesting some of the things. Sometimes the mules had to be pretty smart. Sometimes the mule would pull the cart out of the mine, and they got to the place where they had to dump the coal down the chute. So the wagons and the horses would pick up the coal and haul it away. Some of the mules had to be smart enough to jump out of the way in time that the cart would not come by and crush them. And they got pretty smart—mules are smart. If you treat them right they'll work, and if they're stubborn they just won't move.

B: So where'd your father come from?

F: Well, he came from McDonald, PA, which was west of Pittsburgh, still within Allegheny County. McDonald was named for the McDonald clan, because the McCutcheons belonged to the McDonalds. His people came from Northern Ireland. They were Scotch people who had gone over there just because there was more land available, and they were a little more venturesome than some of the other people I suppose. My dad's name was Will. His father was married twice.

He was of the second marriage. He had older brothers and sisters—half brothers and sisters—but he never talked much about them. He didn't seem to know much about them. But he had three sisters, Belle and Annie and Sadie. I never did get to know Sadie that well. Belle and Annie were seamstresses. They lived in Wilkinsburg and they made their living by sewing. And they may have kept boarders now and then too. Will lived with them until he met Maggie who was my mother—Margaret Meyers. She lived near Monroeville.

B: Do you know where they met?

F: They met in Wilkinsburg and what the occasion was I don't know. They weren't particularly young I don't suppose. Maggie must have been 34. She was born in 1870. She was 43 when I was born. I guess she was married when she was around 35 or 36. Maggie had friends in Wilkinsburg. She had an older sister there; they called her Sissy.

B: So your parents were both Presbyterian, right?

F: They were both Presbyterians, of course. Crossroads church is where they attended. Mother's father was Eli Meyers and he was raised on the McMasters' farm. I remember the McMasters were an old wealthy family. They were progressive farmers. I guess Eli was adopted by them. How Eli got there, I don't know. His father supposedly drowned or disappeared along the Allegheny river, and I don't know much about his family. Apparently he was picked up as an adopted son because he could work on the farm. Maggie's mother's name was McElroy. So that gave us another Mac. So, possibly I'm three-fourths Scotch; and the Meyers name could have been German.

B: You had brothers, right? Chester and Ralph?

F: Chester's the oldest. Chester was born October 30, 1907. Ralph was born October 16, 1910. And I was born October 26, 1913. All three years apart and the same month. The funny thing about . . . When I lost my arm—should I talk about that?

B: Yes, you can talk about that.

F: Let me see. That was when the Gasses had moved into our place. Mr. and Mrs. Gass. And they had a son, a baby boy, born in our house. They rented one of our rooms because they needed the place and we could use the money. And his son was born—Russell—and they gave him my middle name. And we had their baby cart one day. I got in the baby cart and Chester was pulling me around the lilac bush. I was afraid that if he went around to the left I would flip over to the right and something would happen. So I tipped it over to the left. But I twisted my arm and broke both the bones and split the blood vessels. It was a mistake; I blame myself for poor judgment. So we called Dr. Hoffman and he came out with his car and took me to

Bonnie McCutcheon

Columbia Hospital. He was quite a guy, Dr Hoffman. He had a heart. They had to remove the arm—cut right above the elbow. They didn't have any antibiotics, so they cut slits in the arm and used tubes and salt water to purify it: to get rid of as much of the blood poisoning as they could. I guess I was lucky to survive.

B: How old were you?

F: I must have been about seven. The thing I remember was going back to grade school: to third grade. And I didn't get back right away in September. The funny thing about that was when I got to teaching in the same school. The second year I was made principal, and I dated the third grade teacher for thirteen years. I often thought about that . . . the same room, although they added five more rooms between the time I graduated from there and the time I went back and started to teach there. That's something I always remember; going back to third grade. 1921. I was seven years old. Monroeville was just a little country town. Church on one end of town, a school on the other. Down the road now and then we had a country store. Several people operated it. They would get into business and then give up. Mrs. France, an English lady, operated the store there for a long time; about as long as I can remember.

[. . .] . . . . .

F: When I graduated from high school Sy Maynard, our neighbor, made it possible for me to get the Rotary Club Scholarship. It was one hundred dollars. That was a lot of money in those days. I wrote him a thank you note. John Lyle who had come into my life by that time—he helped me write him a thank you note.

We decided that if we got one hundred more dollars, then I could go to Pitt. John was already going to Pitt, so he could give me a ride. He had a little '28 Chevy his father had bought 1him. So Chester arranged to loan me a little bit of money. With a scholarship they'll only give you fifty dollars the first semester, fifty dollars the second semester. So that was smart, you see, to make it necessary for you to try harder. So we managed to get the money somehow. Ten dollars a credit, one hundred fifty dollars a semester it cost us. In fact Pitt's tuition rates stayed that way for a long time. I'm sure that even when I was doing some of my graduate work it was the same. I graduated in 1935. And then you had to take summer courses. So I didn't get my master's in Ed. until 1946. One summer I couldn't afford to go, then other things happened. Then they asked me to teach vocational science. There were certain vocational credits I would have to take, they would pay the tuition. All I'd have to pay was five dollars. One was an undergraduate course which I had to take, and by taking that course I lost time on my master's. They had to add one hundred a year to your salary if you got your master's degree.

B: When did you get your first job?

F: In 1935 I signed a contract to teach on my birthday, Saturday October 26, 1935. So I went to work the following Monday. That Thursday was the end of the month. The other teacher stayed with me that long. Then I was on my own November first. First year I had sixth grade. I had forty-eight kids. The school was eight rooms and we often averaged four hundred kids. That's fifty kids a room. I remember one time when Esma, the third grade teacher, my girlfriend—she had as many as fifty-three kids. The janitor would just have to come up, sit a chair in place and put screws in the floor to hold it in. The first year I was hired I started working the first of November. Then the next year we got a new supervising principal. Some of the teachers decided they were afraid of things, so they got other jobs. So I was the only man on staff and had been there longer. So he appointed me the principal. I had a bachelor's degree. Most of the teachers were only required to take two years of education to teach—certified to teach elementary. I took the bachelor's because I wanted high school. They had to pay you more money. So I got ten dollars a month more for ringing the bell and taking the hell, as I used to say. But, you know, it was fortunate in a way to be appointed principal the second year. Some of the teachers who didn't leave—they were older people. Evelyn Trayer had been a neighbor, she lived right down the road. She'd been teaching a couple years. Esma's sister was a teacher there, and for a while they didn't want to have two from the same family. And her father Tipper—some people were jealous of him. He probably had a little more money than the rest of us. He just operated a coal mine, that's all. He had a lot of land and they just stripped coal. He didn't want to get too large; just large enough to get by.

B: How long did you teach at that school?

F: I taught there for four years, and then they built the new Junior High. By then the new supervisor who had come in wanted me to go over there. They would've been grades seven, eight, and nine. I wasn't certified to teach there even though they hired me on an emergency certificate. There were other people qualified, but I wasn't. The politicians decided I should get the job.

B: You were a man?

F: Because I was a local boy. There were a hundred people after that job, they told me. Some with experience, some had taught there before. Of course being handicapped and being a local boy helped, I suppose. Being handicapped has its advantages.

Bonnie McCutcheon   **71**

But a funny thing happened. There was a Jewish girl named Sylvia Miller, who was hired to teach the year before Esma—because she didn't have any brothers and sisters teaching and Esma did. Well Tipper—I guess some of the people didn't like him. Anyway, there was a funny thing down in Warner's garage. Sylvia Miller's dad was there, and there was some guy repairing a car laying underneath, so he didn't know who was around. Some fellow was standing around, and he was talking about a Jewish girl getting a job that McCutcheon should've got. And he didn't know Sylvia's dad was there and overheard the conversation, see. And in fact I didn't get the job. But, anyway, she told me about it. Sylvia and I became very friendly. I used to date her and she used to come around and pick me up in her car. And she had money. She was already arranged to marry Ben—I forget his last name. He was a show salesman in Pittsburgh. It was kind of a lark for her. We dated some. The family was worried about it.

That was the year before . . . Esma was a neighbor kid, but I didn't get to see much of her. Esma didn't get to teach until the following year. And that was when I got to see her. The year I became principal, my second year, Esma taught her first year. But Sylvia was there the year before. I never felt resentment towards Sylvia, because I wasn't qualified to teach, even though some of the neighbors decided I should've gotten the job. I never felt they should give me the job. I guess maybe Will—he was active in politics and the Democratic Party—I guess he had something to do with it. Will would've used the politics because he wanted me to have the job. You see, sentiment. Because I was handicapped, they'd give it to a local guy. I know how some people were dying for jobs. I know some people who'd been working for Ford and been laid off. The reason I got the job the following year was this girl Mary McKinney got married.

B: They automatically quit?

F: Right. They had to give it to somebody else.

The second year at the Junior High I was made eighth grade teacher. See, when I was teaching seventh and eighth grade I was qualified only part of the time. But geography was my main subject. The county superintendent said I would have to take a geography course that summer. Well I remember I took them, then I didn't need them anymore. I took a couple of courses I didn't do well in. Whether I wasn't interested or whether I got in with people who were a lot brighter, I don't know. But I only got C's. Then I had to overcome those, you know. But I don't know what the hell happened, I wasn't much interested. Because I knew I didn't want to stay up there. Then they let me teach what I wanted to teach; that was Social Studies. There was an English teacher, a Music teacher, and I got to teach what I wanted to.

Later on, when Roosevelt came along we got the WPA, Works Progress Association. They had food for the kids, you know, made jobs for the people. I was in college when Roosevelt became elected. Yes, I remember about the WPA. Roosevelt he was elected in '32 and took office in '33. I remember the Social Studies teacher got a book something like a comic book called *The ABC's of the New Deal*. And the byline on that was "here we go after the dough." And, of course, there were a lot of Republican critics criticizing Roosevelt, you know. Talking about giving away money and stuff—he said, "we'll borrow the money. There's got to be somebody with money. There's some people who didn't lose out in the Stock Market crash." They borrowed money and paid them interest on their money, and put people to work. That's right. By the time I got to teaching they had these food programs where for a nickel the kids got a meal. For a nickel or a dime they got a hot dog and hot chocolate, or whatever. Roosevelt gave us hope, you know. It was a good feeling; it felt like somebody cared. It was really desperate for some of those people not knowing where to go. With Roosevelt it felt like someone cared. They had the WPA; they put the people to work. The men went—they got shovels and picks, fix the road, dig the ditches. And sometimes they would haul them on trucks and take them home. Ralph worked there for a while when he couldn't get a job. He wasn't very happy about it— very proud of himself. But I think it was something. Roosevelt knew they needed to work. The New Deal got people going and made them feel better. They had to get enough courage to get the wealthy people to start businesses, to start companies.

The thing I didn't like about Roosevelt was the repeal of Prohibition. I often think about it, you know. We're suffering from the sins of the past. After it was repealed it was fashionable to drink and it was approved. Parents said, "well if we don't give it to them, they'll get it somewhere else. Well that isn't the point. The parents didn't set a good example. And now we're seeing recently, in yesterday's paper, where drinking is finally dropping off. Maybe it's preaching, you know. Will was an example. I was ashamed of him. I didn't realize until later that he could get silly drunk on just a couple of bottles of beer. Maggie used to say, "I'll probably get blamed for it." She was the naggingest damned woman. I guess I inherited it from her too. She said she didn't know he drank until she got married. It's something that I never went and did myself. You could see how easily you can, you know.

But see, Jack Kennedy's father, old Joe Kennedy—he had bought up—when Prohibition came in—he bought up a lot of whiskey, and stored it in a warehouse, figuring some day it'd be repealed. And when the repeal came and he sold his liquor, he became a millionaire. I don't know whether that's where they got most of the money, but they got a lot of it.

But I didn't like it a lot. I think we are still seeing a lot of it today. Maybe I'm old fashioned and preaching. Well, I've got the money that I didn't spend on hooch. I did do a little bit of smoking. I smoked when I was hanging around with the kids in the evenings. I would smoke and they knew it. But, of course, in those days we suspected smoking wasn't good. But we didn't know as much as we know today. But I enjoyed it; it was a lot of fun, hanging around at night and then playing with the kids. Then I had them in school the next day. None of them ever got disrespectful.

There were a couple of kids I'd gone to Pitt with—John T. who was a math teacher, Mary H. was the valedictorian. She was one of the brightest students in the class. They hired both of them to teach at the Junior High. I was a second year teacher. But for some reason or other they didn't like me. Maybe they were jealous of me. They tried to find all kinds of fault with me, so I was glad to get out of there. The superintendent didn't want to send me over there, and I told him I'd have to go because I wasn't qualified. He wanted me to stay there as principal. I didn't want to stay there as principal because I wanted to get to the senior high. I didn't want to take the principalship because I'd eventually have to go and take credit for it. So they had to let me go take the job.

I taught at the Monroeville school for four years, then the junior high for three years. During the end of that time I applied at Westinghouse Tech. and got a job. Signed up to teach English in night school. And I did that for twenty-five years.

B: So you taught the employees?

F: Yes, they all had to be high school graduates. It was comparable to first year college English, I'd say. I taught Monday, Wednesday, and Friday. Only one semester did I teach all three nights. But I preferred Monday nights so I could work at the sale barn on Wednesday nights. So every Monday night for twenty-five years I taught students—never was off sick. The only time I missed was when some of the guys in the church wanted me to join the Oddfellows or one of those clubs. They nagged me. So finally I had to hire a guy to substitute—Joe Shaffly—he was a good teacher, one of the smartest students I ever had. He later became supervising principal at Mon-

74 Subject Lessons

roeville schools. But, you know, I was fooling around with those guys. The Oddfellows, they wanted to start a chapter in our area. I deprived them—the kids at night school—of my being there. Just for that dumb damn thing. And they wanted to get enough guys so they could have a group. I was disgusted. One guy says to me, "you'll get one hundred dollars when you die." I said, "I won't get it."

B: So that's what made you disgusted with the church?

F: The church—I guess it was really your mother who wanted me to leave. She's done a lot of my thinking, I guess. I've often let her decide a lot of things for me to avoid argument. She got fed up with the church. Well, the thing about the church was—I was disgusted with the way they treated Dewey Smith. He was a real guy, a regular guy. He was the pastor there when I was there. They decided they wanted to get rid of him. Some of the elders were snobs. They decided they wanted somebody a little bit better. But he was a really nice man—Smitley was. When they decided they wanted to get rid of Smitley—well he could see the handwriting on the wall. The guy they hired—his name was Ray P. I was so mad. I didn't like the way they got rid of him. They wanted to be classy, you know. They weren't that much. Just Fifth Avenue, Pittsburgh, just ordinary people, you know. I didn't see anything wrong with him.

B: Tell me about what you did on Wednesday nights.

F: I worked at an auction barn, a sale barn. I was a clerk. John was the regular clerk, but he needed help. People would come in in the afternoon and check in their livestock to be sold. When an animal was sold, it had a number and you had to see that the guy got paid. And you'd make out his bill, and write him a check. I'd be there at night to help him. I'd go over in the day in the summer. Wednesday was sale night, that was the big night.

B: What year did you leave Westinghouse?

F: Right after my daughter was born. I retired in April. I was teaching that year at the high school. I finished out the school year there. Then I went to work as a librarian for Carnegie Library in Pittsburgh—the science and technology department. I stayed there for a year. We had moved out to Armonk out on Route 22 by that time. It was fifty miles from Pittsburgh and thirty-five miles to Monroeville.

B: Were you glad to be done with school?

F: Well, I decided the library work wasn't so bad. I had decided I was going to get into another field of work. I could do better on retirement than by continuing teaching. It didn't break my heart to give up two classes. Then I became interested in the library. And I got to thinking that I'd learn more and more. Then it turned out that the

Bonnie McCutcheon

senior high librarian was going to retire and there was nobody to replace him. And I got to reading—librarians are going to be needed because Pennsylvania decided they were going to be needed. Pennsylvania decided they were going to spend more money for libraries. At one time they used to take some unsuccessful politician from the state legislature who lost his job—they used to take somebody like that and make him state librarian. But he didn't know straight up about books. So then they decided to hire somebody that was really qualified, and then spend more money on books. Then it became important. Carnegie Library had had a library school, but it was only operating in the daytime. It was certified and all that. But people were wanting to go at night, see? So they gave it up. The University of Pittsburgh were expanding because the chancellor had said, "well, we'll just move this library school across the street, and then we'll start it." So that's what they did. They started in the fall of '63, and that's when I got this library job. So I started in January—second semester the school was there. And by the time I got my degree they had been approved by the American Library Association, so that my certificate would be approved. And when I came to Elmira I didn't have to take a test to be certified.

B: So, how long did you work at Carnegie Library?

F: Two years, and then I went out to Illinois. I couldn't get out there until October. But as soon as I got there—I realized as soon as they signed me up, they didn't care. As long as they had a certified person for one year, to get certified themselves. After the first year they were hoping I would leave.

B: What did you do when you found out they weren't going to keep you?

F: Oh, your mother said, "just take the catalog cards and shuffle them. I took them and I put them in my pocket. Every night I came home I had a pocket full of cards. I took all the cross reference cards. They worked the hell out of me. They'd give me a whole list of stuff to look up. Well I did all of it. They could find the books, but the cross references . . . If you were looking up by subject, like Elizabethan Period or something—they'd have to find it some other way. I figure I took the equivalent of one drawer. But I went there because they offered me the money, and I left Carnegie because I wasn't very happy. The women at Carnegie Library were very resentful of me. This was reverse discrimination, see. I was a man with a woman's job. I've always done women's work. They were jealous because I started with a little more money than they started with. And they tried to find every damned thing they could that I couldn't do. Well I found all their damned stuff. They were trying to find fault every way they could. So I told the supervisor, Fox, I was going to get another job. Fox had a daughter who had won a horse at the county fair: a riding horse. Then he and I got interested in horses. So then I saw to it that my daughter had a pony as soon as she was born. Anyway Fox hired me partly because he wanted a man to eat lunch with.

Study Questions

1. Does Bonnie's method of transcription here enhance the sense that the narrator is educated? How has her transcription method affected the way you read the life history?
2. Compare this life history with the previous one. How do the different voices affect the nature of the underlying narratives?
3. How would this life history have been different if the interviewer were not the narrator's daughter? At what points do you think the narrator is acting specifically as a father to the interviewer?

4

Michael Avrut

Michael Avrut, like Bonnie McCutcheon, was an intern for *New York Folklore*, so I had the opportunity to work with him more closely than with many other students and, therefore, got to know him better than most. Ever since we first took on the job as co-editors, my wife and I had had a plan to do a special issue of the journal that was devoted to lesbian and gay folklore in America. As it turns out, this special volume ended up being the last one that we produced as co-editors, and Michael was involved in much of the production. During this period, we developed a solid collegial relationship because we each had things to teach one another. Michael, as a gay man helped make us aware of important issues within American gay culture, and we taught him the technicalities of publishing. We also offered him the opportunity to publish segments of the life history that he had recently completed in my fieldwork class, in the section of the journal that we called "Voice of Tradition."

The goal of the "Voice of Tradition" section was to give readers the opportunity to "hear" the authentic voices of folk practitioners with as little mediation from academics as possible. Both my wife and I were sensitive to the fact that the "folk" too often get packaged by academics and entrepreneurs, and this packaging may entail more disempowerment of them than empowerment. Sometimes—not always—scholars bring with them an assumption that the "folk" are not articulate enough to reach a broader audience without the mediation of a scholar. This may well be true in a practical sense: this current book, for example, requires a scholar's access to publishing. But it does not have to be true in an intellectual sense. We can let the people speak in their own words with only the most minimal mediation. My wife once mounted an exhibit by a local sculptor, and the only texts accompanying the pieces at the exhibit and in the catalog (Blincoe 1988) were transcriptions of oral descriptions of the pieces by the artist himself.

Michael's interview with Peter was meant to be the same kind of exposition of authentic voice in a very specific context: the socialization of a young gay man into certain aspects of gay sexuality. It has been noted many times that socialization of children is one of the key roles of the family in all cultures, but for gay boys and men there is a critical problem to be overcome. Socialization of gay boys into gay sexual practices and mores cannot come from their parents, because their parents are not gay (except under very rare circumstances). Because gay boys' parents are not members of gay culture themselves, they can offer only the most general of help in sensitive areas, should they even be sympathetic in the first place; but, more often than not, a gay boy is likely to conceal his sexual identity from his parents until the age of socialization is well past.

Thus the gay boy must find "parental" figures in the gay world who can act as surrogates—introducing the boy to the values, as well as the practices of gay love and sex. Michael's interview with Peter is a direct window into this socialization process. Yet, there are also specific historical dimensions to this interview. A great deal of the culture that Peter describes, such as the bathhouses, flourished in New York City prior to the spread and awareness of AIDS and now no longer exists, or exists in much modified form. So Peter is also introducing Michael to a historical aspect of urban gay culture that Michael cannot himself experience, but which he can nonetheless be intellectually rooted in through this process of socialization. Michael is finding his own place in gay history as well as his own place in contemporary gay culture through this interview process.

Once Michael had established his identity, he was able on graduation to put his knowledge into practice in his chosen profession of social work. He spoke to me some time after that about the complexities of being a case worker for AIDS patients and how his own sexual identity can be both a help and a hindrance in the counseling process. He also addressed the very delicate question of personal empathy versus professional distance in case management. Exactly the same issues arise here as in the interviewing process in ethnographic fieldwork. Michael feels that he can do better work as a case manager when he abandons his professional objectivity and becomes involved in the real life issues of his clients. He gains the clients' confidence and can be more effective in his advocacy. But there is an attendant emotional strain on him. Interviewing people in a fieldwork setting creates similar problems.

Michael modified my basic transcription method with a few tweaks of his own, although the basic concept is the same. His goal was to refine the process of accurately recording the rhythms and tempo of his interviewee's speech patterns. The authentic voice of gay men is a subject of some interest to linguists and queer theorists, and transcription is a critical problem (see Gaudio 1994; Livia and Hall 1997). He is also very concerned to show that this transcription is not a continuous narrative but, rather, short units edited together from a much longer set of interviews.

You will likely find it difficult to read this interview as it is written because it strays so far from conventional prose in its attempt to preserve authentic voice. One solution is to familiarize yourself with Michael's transcription conventions and then read the piece out loud. Start with just a few lines to get the general idea, and then proceed with the whole thing. Or . . . get a friend to read the piece out loud while you follow along with your own text. If you know an aspiring actor, this will be easy to accomplish. The whole point of the primary transcription method, with em dashes marking breath pauses, is to preserve the natural rhythms of the speaker's narrative voice. A great deal of a person's intended meaning in speech is conveyed through cadence, intonation, pacing, emphases, and a variety of nonsemantic components.

Life History

[]	a pause in speech of one or two seconds unless otherwise notated within the brackets by number of seconds
—	a break in speech, most often an interruption of the self and by the self
. . .	a small portion of material omitted
*****	a significant break between excerpted portions

Michael: You said you came out in '79?

Peter: '78.

Michael: '78. You first had an experience in a bookstore or something?

Peter: Seventy—no—it had to be [] oh, God—'78? Wait—yeah—it had to be '78 I guess. I came out in the beginning of '78. I had a girlfriend—and I went to—I told someone that I thought I might be sexually confused. She took me to a gay bar and I was very happy—and——you know—I met this guy—he gave me his card—that was his second night in the bar—and——I had never been to a bookstore.

I had a boyfriend for a few months before I think I had ever heard of a bookstore. I was trying to think about it today . . . This guy—we didn't get together on Friday nights because this guy went to the tubs. This guy was into very young looking guys. At the time I was nineteen, I looked about twelve—and—he used to go to the club baths every Friday night and I was just—I mean—to me—it was just [] beyond me—why would you want to go be with someone else when you could be with someone you care about? It wasn't a question that he didn't care about me. I knew he did. It just seemed odd—you know—I just thought this was weird but it was like this ritual he had. He was like twenty-seven at the time and—uh—he just went every week.

And then the first time I went to a bookstore which was my first—sort of—anonymous sex type of experience——[] I was in the City and I was meeting a friend there to go to an AA meeting and I met this guy. And we went. And I just kind of wandered around the Village. It was my first day in the Village alone. I had seen the bookstore with my first boyfriend when we went into the Christopher Street Bookstore and they had all sorts of magazines at the time and it was like a real bookstore and they happened to have a backroom and I said, "What's back there?" to my friend—and he said—"Oh, the same thing that's out here, only darker." I said—"Oh." I didn't really know much about it.

And then——this was the first time I was in the Village alone and I wandered around all day—just kind of feeling good about being there and—uh—getting hit on—you know—and that never happens when you're—you know—certainly not in New Jersey. And I——[] I wandered into the bookstore and——gave my—whatever money it cost and went in the back and I'm walking around and this hand came out of this cubicle and—like—pulled me in and at first I was going along with it I was like—wait a minute—stop—stop—stop— you know—so then I went to—to the area that was more well-lit and I started cruising—you know—this guy—just started— . . . Finally we went into one of the stalls and I guess we had sex and I guess we did everything that one can do in a stall and——then we went and had some coffee and then we made plans to meet next week and— uh—that was also the first time I ever got stood up—[laughter]—so I was really—oh, God—I couldn't believe he stood me up. I waited there for three hours where I was supposed to meet the guy.

Michael: Did you really like him?

Peter: Well—like him? No. I—I was just excited. I mean—I mean—I had had—[] you know—maybe I hadn't had . . . This is like the second guy I ever went out with or had sex with . . .

Michael: How old are you at this time?

Peter: Oh, God—like—nineteen . . . The first tubs I went to were the——[3] God—I saw an ad for it a while ago—I was looking through some old magazine and I saw an ad for it—and—Man— Man's Country—Man's Country—and they had a big truck—

Michael: Wait a minute—where is this? New York?

Peter: New York. Called Man's Country and they had a huge truck— an empty truck—a hollow truck on the—on the eighth floor of the club—

Michael: Oh—you were telling me about this place.

Peter: Was I?

Michael: You must have been, because I don't know anyone else who would have—[laughter] unless they have this in Chicago.

Peter: No—oh, they may. Every city's got a bathhouse with a truck, I'm sure [laughter].

Michael: Right. 'Cause I think there's a Man's Country bathhouse that's open in Chicago.

Peter: This hasn't—this hasn't been open for a while. I don't know. I don't think so. I haven't been to the tubs in years [clears throat]. And that was——that was just kind of regular again—you know—nothing—nothing too intense.

It was kind of regular stuff—you know—cruising—I always got a locker back then—you know—I'd—I'd climb the stairs—

Michael: What's climbing the stairs?

Peter: Climbing the stairs physically up and down the stairs from one floor to another. And you got a room and didn't have to climb. You kind of just sat there and waited.—

Michael: Now that's interesting. You know—I remember reading about this when I was fourteen. He was saying in the book that in the baths you could have a room and you could leave the door ajar to the room—how big was the room?

Peter: Oh, God—it fits this bed and four feet space next to this bed. That's about it.

Michael: OK—and depending on how you were sitting meant different things?

Peter: Yeah—like—if you laid down in your room on the bed—if you laid down there—uh—you were most likely into getting fucked if you laid down on your stomach——I think that chances were good that if you sat up at the foot—not at the foot—at the head of your bed—if you sat up—very kind of—like— looking kind of like—very stern—you know—you were more probably into getting your dick sucked—you know—that sort of thing—but then—you know—but at that time they were all so—you know—the bandanas were a really big trip. Everyone was sporting a bandana of one color or another.

Michael: On their hair or on their neck?

Peter: On their neck sometimes—well in the tubs sometimes it was it was on their neck, sometimes they put it right over the light bulb to kind of put the light bulb down a little bit plus you also knew what they were into—or maybe it was just draped on the side of the bed— like one guy used to have—at the Everards—used to have a brown and yellow handkerchief sitting right on his bed, so—I mean—there was no—no question what that guy was into.

Michael: OK.

*****

Peter: The Mine Shaft was—on Washington—in the Meat District just above Fourteenth Street—or possibly right below it—one or the other—[clears throat] I—I went the first time when it was very—— very quiet——one of my coworkers took me there and I was very—sort of intrigued by it—I used to call him my Mine Shaft— mate—and—I had a crush on this guy—so I was very—again, I was nineteen——the shit hit the fan everywhere, so he took me to the Mine Shaft—it was a slow night . . . and very serious crowd—you know—we were down—you know—they had a couple of levels—— one—like—on the first level in the back—you know—there was a sling and some guy was getting—you know—fist fucked or just fucked. They have stalls with guys getting sucked off——they had these long things where guys would lean over and just get their asses beaten—you know—with a belt or a hand——downstairs they had more of that plus they also had—like—kind of——two or three bath- tubs with lying in the bathtubs and getting pissed on—you know— the other side there was a whole sort of—like—water sports . . .

Steve and I were down there watching—and he—he looked very nasty and a very strong mustache, very strong features. He was— he came from a—mixed marriage so his—you know—he had very dark, strong features, but—you know——he was just very, very handsome and big and you know—he had a very deep voice . . . And at the same time we would be in the Mine Shaft and [] he would start singing like Diana Ross. He had this falsetto—I think it sounded just like Diana Ross and this was not a crowd that thought that was funny [laughter]. You know—this was serious. When you're into cruising, you shut the fuck up—you know—like I've been in—I've been in bathhouses where I've been yelled at for giggling—you know—it's very, very, very serious. You know what I mean?

Michael: What do you think the giggling does? It just—like—throws people off?

Peter: It throws people off. They want—they're like—in this mindset—[] you know—and every—every club—every disco—every [] after hours place—the Anvil————[] the Saint—you know—uh—[] they all had their different feeling about them but somehow, the same rules applied—you know—

Michael: It's like this sexual language and it does exist.

Peter: This sexual language and it does exist, exactly. It was like————I do think that people have become a lot more cynical and—and hardened as compared to—you know—the late '70s, early '80s—in the sense that—years ago—I mean—if you were gonna play the game—you know—you were in it to play and that was fine. You were serious, but it wasn't—it wasn't—it didn't seem so desperate—you know—there's such an intensity out there—like in San Francisco, I really felt this intensity with how people were responding—you know—never mind this whole idea of people don't smile at you unless—unless they [] intend to suck your dick or let you suck theirs. But this sort of—like—they're playing for keeps and I think a lot of it has to do with AIDS but—it really is a lot more intense than it used to be, but this sexual language—

Michael: You think now, they're playing for keeps?

Peter: I think now they're playing for keeps in the sense that they're a lot more serious—they're less willing to have a sense of humor about what it is they're doing. Years ago—I mean—people had a sense of humor, but it was also—I mean—the sexual language was one of—I mean—it was accepted if you're in a place like the Mine Shaft, some guy may come on to you that you're not really interested in, but that was kind of cool because [] that happens—you know—and now—you know—that shit doesn't happen. You just don't do it—you know what I mean. You gotta make sure that the guy you're interested in, cruising, is the guy that you want—you know what I mean? It's very, very calculated. Whereas before, it seemed a bit more————[] freewheel. You know—just—whatever. You know—but we understood—

Michael: Are you talking about the difference between teasing and not teasing? Like—you could come and go as you please while you're cruising, in the past, but now it's more like [] cruise me if you mean business, but don't waste my time?

Peter: Cruise me if you mean business; don't cruise me if I'm not interested . . . get lost——I'm serious about what I'm doing here—I know what I want and I can get it because I have a great body—you know what I mean—that sort of—whereas before—you know—ten years ago—there were a lot of nice bodies out there—real—a whole lot of pretty bodies out there, but not to the same extent that there are now—you know—homos just found out that they knew how to lift weights—you know—very recently—you know—and all of a sudden—they—their shit didn't stink——and I mean we all played the game in—in var—in varying degrees.

I can be sitting in a bar and have—you know—some guy that I think is an old troll come up to me, and I'm like—really disgusted—you know—I'm not—I'm—what I'm saying is I'm not putting myself above the mentality of the weightlifters simply because I don't have a weightlifter's body. [] I mean, that mentality, I think, goes down to everyone has got it to some extent, whereas before it seemed that people were more along the mindset of [3] we're kind of in this together, this is fun, we're having fun, it's sex, you know—we're having a great time, we're dancing, we're having sex, we're taking drugs, we're having—whatever—you know what I mean—but it just seemed a little bit less—[] um—[3] frenzied in terms of—or it didn't seem to really dictate the kind of person—you know—by by how many guys you had and now it seems that you—you are identified by the kind of guy who's going to talk to you. It's—I don't know—it's a whole other story . . .

I don't do well in bars. I don't—you know—and that's why I opted for the other places because I don't—[3] obviously I'm not—I'm not for lack of opinions and I'm—I usually don't have hard time talking to people but put me in a bar—I feel like an old troll and I don't have a thing to say—you know—and yes, there have always been exceptions to that on some nights—whatever—something happens—you know—but as a rule, I don't feel comfortable and I—you know—people—you know—and it—it has nothing to do with how I actually look—I know that, you know—and people can say, "Blah, and, blah—You're nice looking, and Peter, you're not ugly"—you know—but that has nothing to do with it because if you walk into a bar feeling a certain way, it doesn't matter what you know, it's how you feel about yourself and that's—and that is what's dictated to the rest of the crowd . . .

I feel real inadequate in bars—you know—in the sense of—I don't know what to say. I mean that's not always true—I mean I have gone to bars and gone up to guys and just had a nice time and met guys

and gone home with them in bars, you know—that sort of thing—
but I mean—what I—what I—I think what I've found so appealing
about the tubs or the sex places was that, excuse me—was that it
relieved me of any—[] any responsibility in terms of——I didn't have
to pretend that I wasn't there for sex, obviously, I think it was more
obvious to everyone including myself. I knew why I was there.

Michael: Well, it's like walking into a supermarket and pretending you're
not there for groceries.

Peter: Right, right. But a lot of guys do—you know—do that—especially in bars—the guys will walk into Stutz—I mean, uh—I don't
frequent Stutz, I go there once a year, if that—if that often, but you
go there, and I—I swear to God, if you say, "OK, how many of you
guys want to suck dick?" no one would raise their hand—"I don't
want to do that"—you know what I mean—I mean—no one's into—
no one's going to admit it in a bar. Now that's not true in the City,
they're a little bit more open.

* * * * *

Peter: Well, I believe that you can have intimate moments on a very—
[] on a very basic level with a stranger—no that's not true—that's
a lie.—[] I believe that you can have passionate moments with a
stranger. Intimacy, I think that—I mean—I—I believe I've achieved
intimacy with a great many of my friends——a couple who—you
know—interacted with sexually——[] but that was only—[3] it was
more a byproduct of circumstance instead of an initial motivating
factor with the intimacy in the first place——and I also believe that
a large part of going to these places in the first place was because I
struggled with the idea of intimacy—[] you know—and that this is
actually before—[clears throat] see now, I—now I think more than
anything, I'm in the habit of it and sort of comfortable—it's a very
comfortable place for me to be.

Even today—it's a very comfortable place for me to be—the sex
club. I don't mind it. I know what to do. I know what's gonna happen. I know how I'm gonna feel when I leave. So it's all—it's all very
safe for me in that regard, [] but before that——I think that—I think
that I honestly believed that one would separate the two in terms of
the sexual—the sexual aspirations and—and how you related to intimacy and never the two shall meet—you know—intimacy is more
a thing of—you know—it's not something that you had with a lover.
It's a very—it was very weird . . . You know——I mean, I view it a
lot differently today.

*****

Peter: I'm not really sure what my ideas of intimacy were at the time—you know—exactly what it was I was looking for—you know—I don't know whether I have a clear idea anymore—I mean I can sort of speculate now—. . . I guess it was a level of [yawning] looking for some sort of love—you know——[] very often it was just looking for fun—you know. It would depend—you know—no matter where I went, whether it was the tubs or the bookstore or whatever——a lot would depend on my mood. If I was in the mood, not really out looking for any—much of anything other than to have a good time, that's usually what happened. I had a good time . . . And there were no sort of expectations. [] I knew exactly what I wanted and that's what I got.

There were other times that I'm sure that I was looking for something . . . and didn't have—[] I don't know whether I didn't have foresight—you know—to know that's what I was looking for and to avoid places like that 'cause you're not gonna find it. You're just gonna go home frustrated. I knew that . . . I knew that something was—wrong if I—[3] if I went to the tubs. I fooled around with a number of guys and didn't—didn't have an orgasm every time, but fooled around with a number of guys—we're not talking one or two, we're talking—you know—a few, quite a few, here and there, whether starting something and not finishing or—uh—just going on to the next or whatever, but having, let's say an orgasm, maybe three times in the night—you know—and taking the train home. But, coming home and then masturbating—you know—after all that, still being horny. You know—I knew that—I knew that obviously I was looking for something else—you know—'cause nothing really satisfied me. If I was out looking for a good time, like I said, feeling good about myself . . . I would go out and do it and come home and be fine.

So, I think also, the kind of person I was at the time and probably still am to some extent was, I placed a lot of value on you can't get away—you can't get away from the physical aspect of cruising—I mean—it's all you have to offer when you're out there looking for sex and you have to have a place or any type of place, really, you know—because you decide that here's one of them, and you can get sexual with someone. Really, all you have to offer, at least initially, is what you look like. They don't know who you are, where you've been, what you're—you know—what you're all about. They just see what they see. And you know—you look at them and that's all you see. Maybe you're interested in who they are, maybe you are. Until you get to know them, you're not gonna know because it's a very, very one dimensional sort of approach—you know. What you see is what you get.

And—uh—I think that there is a lot—[] a lot of importance placed on—you know—this idea of this one's out of your league—you know—'cause he's too good looking—uh—this one's OK. This one's really good looking . . . You know—to turn around and see you looking at him . . . and then, of course—you know—there's this whole idea of—you know—this one can be out of your league just as much as the next one maybe . . . so it's—it's all really—it's a very mean—it's not—it's not a very nice——[3] it's not a very nice way to spend an evening with—with your—you know—your pushing 'em away or running after the next and—I mean—I just know that—I know for a fact that I have plenty of friends who I think are nice looking——and really none of what I think about them matters as much as how they think about themselves.

*****

Peter: I don't think that having an issue of intimacy or having problems with intimacy—I don't think that's—I—I don't think that's unique. I think we all have them to some extent. For someone to say—you know—"I think I have a problem—oh—actually being intimate with someone for a long period of time"—I think that a lot of people do. I think that one of the problems in the gay community, for gay men especially, who are so overtly sexual—I'm not saying that Lesbians are not sexual—I just think that men are overtly sexual. I think that—[5] I don't think that it's very unusual for—uh—[3] people to just feel like——[] I think it's easier for gay men to separate—[] you know—intimacy from sexuality. It's real easy for them.

I think one of the disadvantages, or advantages—I haven't—I don't think the vote's really in yet, we don't have this—you know—this whole concept of marriage to—kind of—force us into maturity—you know what I mean—that sort of thing. This idea that we will settle down. We can do whatever we want—you know— . . . I mean—we're already fucked, so we might as well enjoy ourselves. You know—that sort of attitude. . . . I think one of the things that works with a male/female relationship, certainly with marriage, is that you have those dynamics. You know—you—the balance and I don't think that you have that with—I think men as a rule, sexually, are very immature, in regards to their——in regards to their whole approach to sexuality. I think they're very selfish. I think they're very self-serving as far as their sexuality goes. You put two men together—you know—and you got—you got the two of them going at it and I'm sure there's a lot of people that would disagree with me. I think there's a real—[] I think that there's something very immature about gay men, about homosexuality——this is—this is not a value judgment—you know—I just think that we are. I mean—in some respects we are, it's much easier to be homosexual and in other respects, of course, it's—it's much more difficult. I mean—you don't get support from the community at large—unless you're in the gay community. You know—you've got to work for something extra. There's a lot of things that you miss out on. For better or worse, you miss out on them.

But I also think that—that we——[4] when I say "immature," I don't mean immature in the sense that that's bad. I just don't think that we—[] if you want—if you—I mean—there's no getting around the standard—[] the standard which we—base all our thinking on. And I don't think you can get away from the fact that we base a lot of our thinking on the heterosexual ideal. Again, I'm not saying that that's really a great place to—to—or anything to aspire to, but that's the way we're raised and we can't get away from that.

I like to think we can move beyond that—ourselves, in order to redefine our own relationships—you know—lover relationships and sexual relationships, friendships—you know—whatever—however you want to classify it, I can bet Gay men and women have to redefine their relationships apart from what they were raised with, but, really—again—you can't get away from it. It's just—it's impossible. It's the way we were raised. So, when I say "immature," I mean immature based on the heterosexual idea of what——a relationship is.

[10] There's a whole lot of—there's a whole lot of variables that—that—come into—why—why——the sex places flourished. Why—why—uh—they obviously came about. Because they were allowed [] after all those years of not being allowed—in part, because of the sexual revolution in general—and [] you know—I just think it's something that men want. That's why it works.

*****

Peter: We place a lot of importance, again, on the physical aspects of the person and the older you get—you know—you start to—you know—your body starts to sink and cave in and all that stuff and you become not—not nearly as appealing as when you were younger—

Michael: To who? Because old people find old people attractive.

Peter: Right, but the fear is that you're not—you know—when you're thirty years old I—you don't look at an eighty-year-old man and say that man is really attractive as a rule and you don't believe that that time will come. I think that's why—like—you know—like—I also think that's why gay men aren't so afraid of growing old. They know what they're going to look like—you know—when you go down to the sauna, here, you know—right here and you see these— you know—seventy-year-old men who've been swimming—you know—they've taken them a couple of hours to do two laps and now they're in the sauna. They're doing—you know—they're doing whatever they feel like doing and they're lying there on the bench naked and their bodies are not all that attractive—you know—not as far as I can [] see—you know—I don't personally find them attractive— or sexual, or anything like that and I know what I'm gonna look like when I'm that age—you know.

I think that for—uh—an older heterosexual, male and female, they don't really—like—see that. They don't see that as themselves when they get older—you know what I mean? They don't look at an older woman and say, "That's gonna be me." You know—but if you're a Gay man and—you know—what you're attracted to is other—other men, you see an older man and you say—that's what I'm gonna look like. Let's face it. We don't treat older people with a whole lot of kindness in our society. So that fear is that, that's what I'm going to be and I don't ever want to be that . . .

*****

Peter: There was this guy Jeff, that I was seeing a couple of years ago and—uh—I always found him really attractive—I mean—a great body, all that stuff. I liked him and we had really nice sex. It was very, very straight sex—you know—nothing out of the ordinary . . . what one considers ordinary—but I never stopped thinking about the things that I would rather be doing. Not while we were having sex, but—you know . . . So, when I was home and I masturbated or I—you know—going out and fucking around, I was looking for [] the kinky—you know what I mean?—and I never really liked—it never occurred to me that I would get involved in that sort of—in any of that sort of scene with Jeff.

You know—like—I just automatically separated the two—I mean—it was no big deal—I mean—I wasn't—I wasn't—it wasn't— it was like I said—it was kinky. Either thinking about being tied up or tying somebody else up or—or—getting into some water sports or——or—you know—dirty talk—you know—all that stuff. Nothing real extreme. Nothing really serious. More of a—of a head trip than anything else——and I just always naturally dissociated the two—you know. I'm with Jeff—we're having a nice time, I'm not complaining, but we'll never get involved with this sort of thing. I think—and I—I—I think that's probably more common than anything else—you know?

* * * * *

Peter: I knew—I mean—again, I knew—I had —I—I had some amount—some amount of guilt about doing the sex things——oh, I tortured myself for years about the water sports fantasies—tortured myself. I mean I just thought I was the most [] sleazy person—you know—for even thinking about it and it happened a couple of times, way back when, and I thought about them, but, [] and then I—I started going to therapy in, oh, God, it must have been '85—you know—it might have been '86—[] and uh—the first week we did my history—you know—where I grew up—you know—brothers and sisters. And the next week I sat down, took a deep breath, and said to him—"All right, I gotta tell you this one thing." And I said—I literally drove myself crazy thinking about this. The worst possible thing to have these thoughts.

And you know—and again—but I—I didn't really—I—I never felt guilty about being gay—you know—once I came out. Certainly, I felt guilty for years before that—you know—I felt bad. But once I came out and started doing it, I didn't feel guilty ever again . . . I mean—I—I had some reservations about the sex places in that there was something that told me this was not right——but more—more along the lines of—you're not connected. You're having sex and there's nothing wrong with it on—on a moral level—but it's—something's amiss—you know—so I had some reservations about it . . .

* * * * *

Michael: Can you define sleazy for me?
Peter: Heaven—[laughter]. Sleazy——[] in what way: The Sleaze Line? It's a San Francisco—you know—telephone number. You know—the Sleaze Line. There's a movie "Sleaze," too. Actually, it was the first movie I ever saw that had water sports in it. And—I mean—if you buy—if you buy the porno tape these days it's been edited out . . .

Michael: Is sleazy a value judgment?

Peter: Not for me. Not for me—you know—I mean if I'm in a room and someone—you know—someone—you know—you're going around the room and everyone's gotta say a word and someone says "sleazy," I'm—I'm over there. You know—I mean—I like it—I—I don't think it's anything—I don't use it in a negative sense—you know—like— "He's really sleazy" . . . So—I mean—sleazy? I guess, all pertaining to—[5] you know—what it is I want to do with that person.

Michael: Something that deviates? From the ordinary sex you had with—

Peter: Jeff.

Michael: Jeff.

Peter: Or Dave.

Michael: Tom, Dick, or Harry?

Peter: Any—any Tom, Dick, or Mary you can think of . . .

* * * * *

Peter: Larry Kramer . . . could be a little more explicit in his book. Talked about—you know—basically, the whole sexual nature of— of—gay life as it was back then and I think he was pretty clear that this was not—you know—all gay men but his whole—his whole premise was that we—we will kill ourselves—you know—this is before AIDS—but we will kill ourselves, at least spiritually, by continuing to conduct ourselves in this fashion—that we're not—you know—that we're more than sexual beings and that all we seem to want to do is to find ourselves as sexual beings.

But he exposed a lot of what was going on as did the movie "Cruising," and I think that's what upset a lot of people. They didn't want to be exposed. They liked the fact that they were working on Wall Street during the day [] in their—you know—three-piece suits and then going to the Mine Shaft at night in their leather outfits and—you know—and lying in a tub and getting pissed on and you know—they didn't want to be exposed. And I really believe that.

You know—and—and—my feeling was that—you know— with—unfortunately with books like [] "Faggots" and movies like "Cruising"—you know—let's—you know—"Faggots" was mass marketed—you know—so you could pick it up in the Grand Union in Larchmont. You know—and it was a best seller and it was a novel and—[] people were in suburbia and reading it and saying—"Wow! This is what it's about." Which was in part true. But people didn't know this is part of what this is about. And then you have people like my mother watching a movie "Cruising" or—uh—years ago——

ABC did a— documentary called "San Francisco: Gay Power; Gay Politics." Which again concentrated on the—on the leather crowd. And people like my mother would watch it and call me up and saying—you know—"This is—this makes me really nervous. This is really scary. Is this what you're into?" But, all of a sudden, people were—were being fed this information, which was true, but being fed the information in the sense that this was everything, which of course it's not. There—it's only a percentage of Gay men who participate in this sort of activity. So, it's—it becomes misinformation.

Michael: I think it also becomes misinformation if people don't understand that the s/m community is not a dangerous community.

Peter: No. No—I mean—ag—yeah—I think you're absolutely right. You know—I mean—it's—it can be threatening in that it looks dangerous. The——many of the people who are into it are extreme. There are many, many, many people who are into it, who you wouldn't know unless they identified themselves as such—you know—I mean—and that's—uh—[] you know—that's right down to the tattoos and earrings in the nose or—or the nipples or you know—or on the penis—you know—all that stuff, which is—when it comes right down to it, it's all just [] expression. I mean—you do what you do. That's all that's important . . . If anything, it's just interesting—you know—and that's what you do—"Wow! That's interesting. No. I'm not turned off by this."

Study Questions

1. How do you think Michael's training in life history method helps him as a social worker beyond his own statements to this effect?
2. Does Michael's particular transcription method capture the essence of the authentic voice of a gay man? In what ways? What are the limitations of this method?
3. Do you think Michael's interviewee is acting in a parental way toward him? Compare this interview with the previous two in this regard.
4. What do you see as Peter's goals in giving this interview?

5

Isadora Sahl

It had been my original intention when I first planned this book to have each of the interviewers write an introductory essay to put their interviewees and the interview process into some kind of context. I abandoned this idea for several reasons. One concern of mine was that this process could become an exercise of power on my part, although its intention was to expand what each of the interviewers had to say. I wanted to make sure that the interviewers included as much information as possible about the contexts of their interviews, what they had learned, and what they had subsequently done with what they had learned, but I was concerned (based on past experience) that some might skim or skip over important information. Therefore, I chose to interview each of them instead and, thus, accumulate information on what I deemed to be useful context. I included these interviews in earlier drafts of this work but eventually cut them out because, in my estimation, they added little of value.

The key disadvantage to presenting edited interviews with the interviewers is that I end up with more power over the process than I would like. The self-presentation of the fieldworkers becomes filtered through my needs in structuring this book, and interests that they may have apart from my concerns could be artificially excluded. To compensate for this problem, I originally tried to interview them in an open-ended fashion and to include as much material as possible (and also to let them see the finished product in case they want something added or omitted).

I also believe that the advantages outweigh the disadvantages (but only if you have unlimited space, and your readers have unlimited patience). For one thing, my students all got to understand what it was like to be on the other end of a microphone, being interviewed. Many of them who had never been interviewed before commented on how odd it made them feel. They were all quite comfortable talking to me face-to-face, but several felt that the introduction of a tape recorder[1] interfered with smooth communication and radically changed the nature of our relationship. This is a good thing. It deepened their own understanding of the interview process and helped them reflect on their own technique. Furthermore, when they were able to see the products of what I had done with their interviews, they had a clearer sense of the power dynamic involved in interviewing, transcribing, editing, and publishing.

Of more importance, though, is that the presentation of live interview materials gives me the chance to present their authentic voices alongside those of the people they documented. Thus, it is easy to compare the two and to see the many congruences of voice (and thought) that exist between fieldworker and narrator.

I am mindful that in the process of serving my own needs as a scholar I may be giving some aspects of my students' self-presentation short shrift. To compensate (partially), I am going to use this chapter to give one fieldworker two kinds of voice in self-presentation. Isadora Sahl first presents her introduction to her recorded life history in narrative prose that she wrote (the original version of this piece was not even written for me or this work, so that bias is absent). Then I present the contents of our interview together. I hope that, at the very least, this demonstration shows that there is considerable overlap in the substance of the two modes (written and recorded). I also hope that this exercise expands our vision of multiplicities of voice and the affective differences in the varieties.

Isadora's own life history (along with the example she presents here) raises a number of complex issues concerning poverty. For example, she identifies herself as having been raised in urban poverty, but this designation is not as simple as it seems at first blush. True, she was raised by a single parent in a poor neighborhood, and they needed food stamps and income supplements to survive. True, also therefore, that the social environment into which she was socialized was urban poverty, and she became a tough street kid as a form of self-defense. But her father is a college-trained composer with a modest international reputation, who has chosen not to take a "regular" (i.e., traditional middle-class) job so that he can devote his life to his music. For this reason, her background of poverty was the result of conscious choices made by her father and not from more conventional cultural or historical circumstances.

Isadora's background could be seen as confusing for her because issues of class and economics were not clear-cut. Economically she was poor, but she was raised in a solidly middle-class household. In an age of downward social mobility for the middle class, her situation is no longer unusual, but it does challenge old values and conventional wisdom. In many critical respects, her struggles look like the struggles of any child raised in poverty, even though she had advantages that do not accrue normally to the urban poor.

Thus, she went to college to get away from her old neighborhood in both a physical sense and an economic sense. Once at Purchase College she got a staff position and stayed over for holidays rather than going back home. In this way she cut off all ties to her former friends and their environment. She also saw a college degree as a tool in the process of avoiding poverty for herself. Both are common ideals of the urban poor.

As a consequence of shutting herself off from her old neighborhood, she lost touch with her own past and all the friends that mattered to her as a girl. The fact that one of them had died as a consequence of poor medical care troubled her, but she could not find a way to go back to her old home and find closure on this issue without opening all the wounds she was trying to heal. The life history project provided the perfect vehicle as a way out of her dilemma. She could go back and interview her friend's mother about the circumstances of his death. Instead of returning as a traitor, or turncoat, eager to leave the place behind her, she was returning as a social activist with their welfare at heart. Her key theme here is that poverty is not just an uncomfortable state of living: poverty can be deadly.

Her angst about appearing to be a traitor to her upbringing and old neighborhood is reflected in her own life story since leaving Purchase (as presented in the taped interview). She tried to pursue a "regular" middle-class life with a secure job that entailed a fat paycheck and multiple benefits, and a nice apartment in a safe neighborhood, but it did not work for her. The path of social action that her life history put her on called to her insistently, so that she has abandoned her "regular" job and returned to what appears to be her true vocation.

There is also a profound irony in this particular project. Her childhood friend Salim died because of inadequate medical care as a result of being a poor patient without the necessary medical insurance to guarantee the speedy service his acute asthma attack needed. Isadora had lived all her life without medical insurance and had assumed until Salim's death that to have no insurance was bad, or inconvenient, or worrisome, but that if you were young and appeared fit it was no big deal. But then she began a job that had a good medical insurance package that she immediately took advantage of only to discover she had a rare and virulent form of lung cancer that was asymptomatic.

A good job with good benefits saved her life. If she had remained poor, she would not be alive today to tell her story and that of her friend Salim. There is no more dramatic unity of fieldworker and interlocutor, and no clearer evidence that poverty is a matter of life and death.

Written Introduction by Isadora Sahl

For you, the reader, to fully comprehend the many levels of meaning in this life history, I think it is necessary to begin by explaining my own personal background and relationship with May Lin For.[2]

When I was born, on March 28, 1971, I lived in a tenement on the lower East Side of Manhattan. I was raised by my parents who were married when I was 1½ years old. Both of my parents already had children of their own. My mother had a daughter 5 years older than I, and my father a son 8 years my senior.

We have lived on or below the poverty line since before my birth. My father is a composer of music and my mother was a dancer until her early forties. Both of my parents are college educated and my father went to graduate school at Princeton.

My mother was raised by her mother, a divorcee, with her younger brother in suburban Maryland. She became pregnant and got married while still in college at Bennington University. After her separation from her first husband she moved to NYC and she and my father became involved shortly afterwards.

My father, an only child, was born in Boston but was raised predominantly in NYC in the Washington Heights area by both of his parents. He had also been married previous to marrying my mother. So I was born into a house with two educated parents, a half-sister and a half-brother who visited on the weekends.

My parents separated when I was 5 years old and I lived exclusively with my mother, seeing my father only on weekends or holidays until I was 8 years old. During that time, my sister lived with our grandmother (my mother's mother) while my mother and I moved around the country. She worked as a professor in residence teaching dance at one college after the other for semesters at a time. When I was 8 years old, we returned to the tri-state area and from the ages of 8 to 10 years my parents had joint custody of me. I should say that they had always legally had joint custody, but this was one of the few times that it was a reality. I would spend half the week with one parent and the remaining half with the other. While I was shuffling back and forth, I attended New Lincoln, a private school on the upper East Side. My father had gone to school there himself as a child, as well as taught music there for a number of years. My brother also went there for high school. I was accepted on a full scholarship as had both my father and brother, and was skipped from the 5th to the 6th grade.

When I was 10 years old my mother remarried and shortly afterwards moved to the west coast. I went with her only to return to live with my father after about 15 months.

It was when I returned to New York for the second time that I went to the private high school that I ended up graduating from. All school years not mentioned were spent in public school with the exception of kindergarten which I spent at Brooklyn Friends in Brooklyn New York. I had repeatedly failed the 10th grade in both New Lincoln and The High School For The Humanities, a public school in Manhattan and was enrolled in Elizabeth Seeger, a progressive private school especially designed to deal with students that couldn't, wouldn't or just plain didn't, excel in standard or traditional school settings. Seeger was set up so that it had enough grants, scholarships and other forms of financial aid to have about 5 students enrolled on full scholarships. I was lucky enough to be one of the few.

My brother is the person who found the school and without his help we could not have persuaded my father to give me yet another chance and check out the school. It turned out to be the best learning environment I have ever experienced, keeping in mind that I have gone to over fifteen different schools both public and private. The thing that in my opinion made Elizabeth Seeger so great is the same thing that made all the great teachers in my life different, and that is being taught by someone who is excited to teach you. To have a mentor who makes education interesting if not always fun is a person who is strongly dedicated to their work and to their pupils. That more than any level of education is what memorable teachers are made of.

Although within the school the socio-economic class walls appeared not to exist, it was very important both socially and emotionally that we had other peers from similar class backgrounds. Once school was over and most of the kids went to the subway on the west side leading them to their lavish, duplex apartments, we walked or took the East Side train to our homes in the tenements and projects. Obviously this is a gross generalization, for anyone who knows New York is aware that there are just as many beautiful, expensive homes on the East Side as there are on the West, but my point is that there was a segregation, subtle as it may have been, between the scholarship kids and everyone else.

There is a feeling that a non-wealthy child experiences when placed into a situation that simultaneously benefits them and degrades them on a daily basis. The parents of the child beam with pride at the above-average education their child is receiving, but the kids in the neighborhood want to know who you think you are that you can't go to school with everyone else. Beyond those difficulties you are reminded daily of just how the rich spend their money and live their lives; free of cares and worries about medical bills and the price of a gallon of milk. Those thoughts are not a part of their world, and you alone have to answer them when they honestly don't understand why you can't go to a concert, buy those designer jeans or how your parents could let you leave the house without a new winter coat. Situations like these bring the "minority" group together like no other. Partially due to this, I believe it was the private schools I attended that first brought me to the realization that I was living in two opposing planes.

It was at Seeger that I began dating James, also a student at Seeger on scholarship, and through him met his best friend and younger sister's boyfriend Salim and Salim's mother May. Over the next 2 years we formed a false family structure whereby Salim filled the role of the little brother I had never had and I the role of the big sister. May and I spent quite a bit of time together and although I wouldn't say she was a mother figure exactly she definitely was a person that I looked up to, as well as my confidant.

Having the extremely rocky childhood that I had, there was many a time that I needed someone to turn to for advice. Having the unusually close relationship that I had with both my father and my brother, I had a good network of people to turn to, but on reflection I believe it was because she was not related to me that I could really listen to the advice May gave me and discuss issues with her in a way that I at the time could not with anyone in my family. I can still hear her telling me that education was the key. If I really wanted to get out, go to college and raise my children in a "better" place, I needed to stop relying on men, especially ones who didn't have the same goals as I did, and get my shit together.

Once I entered college, we (May, Salim, and I) saw less and less of each other. James and I had long since ceased talking to each other and he frequently used Salim as a ploy to get back into my life: calling me up and saying Salim was in big trouble and needed my help etc. When James called me in 1992, it had been almost 2 years since I had seen any of them, and he again told me to call Salim. I told him that if Salim really needed me he could get off his ass and call me himself. Less than 2 weeks later Salim was dead and I was crying hysterically in James' arms in a funeral home.

When Salim died, it was one of the greatest shocks in my life. I had already outlived some people in my life but none of them quite so shockingly. My grandfather had diabetes, my grandmother had cancer and heart disease and some of my younger friends have been the victims of AIDS, suicide, or drunk driving. Even drunk driving has a place to put the blame, although it may be hard to do so when the blame rests on the deceased, but still the ultimate cause of death is easily found if not easily understood.

Salim's death was an extremely pivotal point in my own life because it forced me to go back home in a way I had not done since my first day of college. When I showed up at his wake I entered as an educated white woman, no longer held to my second family by the same bonds. When I left the lower East Side in 1989, I ran screaming and never looked back, until that day. I was greeted by James's younger sister Chantese, and instead of a hug I received shrieks of "Fuck You!" and "Who do you think you are? You left us and you don't care! Now you just like all the whiteys so what are you doing here?" and on and on.

It has been an extremely difficult process for me to incorporate the many different worlds I come from into one, stable plane on which I can peacefully exist. After the death of Salim, I couldn't repress this problem any longer. It became impossible for me to justify my moral beliefs or anything for that matter because I just don't pull from one identifiable source. I exist in two separate worlds and when Salim passed away my worlds collided. Westchester county and The Hill shook hands, each one shocked to see the other.

One day about a year later when I was coming to the realization that the topic I had picked for my senior thesis[3] was boring me to death and not going anywhere, I woke up in the middle of the night. I guess I had been dreaming, and I couldn't stop thinking about Salim. It is my opinion that Salim would not have died if he had been properly treated. I feel that his is a life that has been stolen, and it is also my belief that had he lived on, he would have had the fullest of lives. Therefore I write this paper for many reasons, the most obvious of which is to receive a diploma from SUNY Purchase. The other reasons are all twisted together, entwining each other; I write this to show that May's experience is a reflection of many people's experiences across this country; to explain that hard working "honest" people must struggle every day to keep one foot in the doorway of the white middle class world. I write this for myself, to learn and this time accept one of the worlds that I come from and have rejected. Lastly, I write this for Salim. So that people will understand the wrong that has been done to him, but most of all so that I can let him go and so that people can have the chance to learn about and share some of Salim even though he is no longer here to share himself. This is dedicated from my soul to the memory of Salim Dionysus Vega.

Interview with Isadora Sahl, Purchase, New York

(J = John Forrest; I = Isadora Sahl)

J: Tell me a little bit about how you got started on this project.

I: I floundered a lot to figure out what I wanted to do. For me the act of doing the life history was therapy. I was coming from a situation where the woman who I did, May Lin, her son who was very close to me had died a few years before while I was already away in college. And I had never had the opportunity or chosen to deal with that. I don't know what brought it to my immediate notice while I was trying to figure out what to do for my project. But it sort of all came together one day and I remember calling her and saying "would you let me, you know, tape record you and talk about you and write about you." And as soon as she said yes I came—and she said "good, do it, finally. You've finally decided to do something that matters."

J: Did you come through the EOP[4] program?

I: I didn't, but I come from urban poverty. . . . I was predominantly raised on the Lower East Side of Manhattan, mostly by my father who is a composer and a musician. My mother was at the time still a dancer, so I came from an educated white background who had no money. So it was like I was educationally wealthy, but a food stamps kind of situation. I always played in the streets and played with the gang kids, and this and that, but was sent to private school or something like that. So I lived a sort of dual reality. And then when I came to Purchase, when I decided, OK, I'm going to go to college—I had already cleaned up my act. I'd been a very . . . I'd had an "interesting" teenagehood let's say. I got into a lot of trouble. So once I cleaned up my act and went to college, I became like the perfect white woman. Not, maybe, to normal people, but certainly to the world that I had left. And, I really left. I didn't come home—I worked here [Purchase] over Christmas, over winter—I lived here all the time. It wasn't until I started to do this project that I even went back to the projects, and went back to those neighborhoods where I had played. So, it was a combination of a lot of experiences for me—I'd said "well now I'm going to be an educated white girl and I'm going to make a living, and pretend to be normal." And I had had a very negative response, particularly from the kids in this family that I ended up dealing with and from that whole posse or group of "fuck you, you're abandoning us because you can—you get scholarships, you get good SATs. How dare you." So my reaction was, "OK, well I will abandon you."

J: So you didn't go to school with these kids.

I: I went to school with some of them who also had scholarships. Once I'd gotten kicked out of all kinds of high schools and sent back to public school and dropped out of public school I went to a really small progressive high school called Elizabeth Seeger, which doesn't exist anymore. It was started by a woman who worked at a private school for years, and saved her money—and she and her partner started this school. My brother actually found it. And they gave me another chance as a junior, and gave me a full scholarship. My graduating class had twelve kids, and five of us were on full scholarship. So it's no surprise the school didn't make it economically. The son of the woman who this project is about—we got him into the school that I went to. We talked them into accepting him and "saving" him—blah blah blah. That was how some of my friends got in—we would bring them in.

J: So from high school you came here. What then?

I: I graduated school. I tried to go get a job as a teacher. Found out I couldn't get paid. Started working for Columbia—got sick of it and was about to get married and decided that wasn't a really good idea. So instead of getting married I moved to California—ran away. When I came back from California I got a full-time, fancier job with Columbia University and finally had full benefits, and this and that. So that was when I had the first probably full check-up I'd had for a long time. And they found this mysterious thing in my lung. So there was months of figuring out what it was. But I had surgery in December '95, and was diagnosed after that [with lung cancer]. Knock wood, I'm now completely cancer free, and didn't have radiation or chemo because I had a brand new form of cancer that they'd never seen before. I just had one huge tumor as opposed to it being in my lymph nodes or anything like that. They just took out that lung.

J: So you don't smoke anymore?

I: Hell no [laughs], and that's probably the only thing that would have made me quit smoking. It was just so funny. Well I mean it's not really funny, but I was such an adamant addicted smoker. They told me they would refuse to operate. I worked at the hospital, at the same time. So they said, "we know you and we're not going to operate on you unless you quit smoking at least a week before surgery."

J: So, getting benefits, having a regular job—that's what facilitated this. In other words if you hadn't had this job you would have died.

I: That's what they say.

J: So how does that make you feel about having a regular job?

I: Well, a job, quote unquote, is such a big thing for me. I come from parents who chose to make the sacrifices necessary in order to not have a normal job and in order to be creative, and to feel that they were doing what they were supposed to do or what they were meant to do. So once I had gotten to Purchase and graduated in four years, I was feeling so normal and I was dating this very normal man and I felt it would be sort of the right thing to do to try to have this normal job. So I really dove into it, and was really successful at it and was trying to make it work for a number of years, and kept telling myself that if I got high enough in academic administration at Columbia I could then transfer that over into policy writing, or something— back to the elementary education or kids in need sort of idea. But it's just bullshit really. Academia is better than corporate America in that I can wear my Birkenstocks and I don't have to wear panty-hose. But I was completely unfulfilled. I was making more and more money, I was having more and more responsibility—I supervised more and more people. It all seemed like the perfect right thing. But I just felt horrible. It's just like having to write a senior thesis, forcing me to deal with Salim's death and to deal with the fact that I'd left the 'hood. Forcing me to quit smoking and have surgery and lay there and think that I might die and that I had "the big C" and everything, forced me to say "what the fuck am I doing with my life? I'm so young and I'm already completely unfulfilled." You know, it seemed a little bit ridiculous. And that led me back *cautiously*—because then I became all of a sudden scared of not having benefits. But I came all the way back to saying, "well I'm going to try again to teach and to forget about making money" I have a big, big, huge, mammothly large issue with it. Because I'm not in a situation where there's anyone who can assist me.

J: Issue with money?

I: Money. I have a money issue. But already I'm working at Bank Street College. I took about ten levels downward—I'm somebody's administrative assistant—and already I am interested, happier. The people that I am conversing with are interesting to me; I'm learning something from all of them. And that is a lot more powerful and a lot more worthwhile. When I say I have an anthropology degree from Purchase people say "Oh I have an anthropology degree" or "Oh well I have anthropology and social work and teaching and that's why I'm here." I'm in a situation where I feel more akin to the people I am working with.

J: Well then, can you talk a little about how doing this life history project and being an anthropology major has impacted your life? What I'm wondering is if there is any way in which in your role as an academic administrator you were impacted by your anthro training.

I: Well I've been thinking about this, obviously, since I knew I was going to be talking about it to you. What I always am wherever I work is a supervisor and there's something about that—trying to look at a whole person and not just jamming someone into a fixed description. That's really the whole anthropological thing, it's not just the life history thing—which makes me better able to deal with diversity and better able to "conflict manage." It sounds kind of abstract, but I think it has a direct bearing, and I think it has a direct bearing on me being able to analyze what I was doing versus what I wanted to do, and the fact of how people react when they do what they don't want to do—and the long-term effects of something like that. . . .

J: Another issue I am working on in this book is the idea of reciprocal empowerment. In this situation right now, I hold the power—I'm directing things, asking the questions and so on—but I can give you a voice and empower you. In return you are empowering me because I need your story to make a book. So we can empower each other. I'm wondering if that power dynamic cannot also be effective in the workplace. That is, you can dictate to people what to do as their supervisor, and effectively disempower them, or you can share power with them and create a better work environment—and in the process help yourself. You empower them, and they empower you. . . .

I: As a matter of fact—not to cut you off—it was all men I supervised in one of my jobs at Columbia—my own issue. Those guys all call me, all email me. I haven't worked in that job for almost two years. We formed a bond there. I was their boss, but there was also mutual respect. This might be a little different, but I was thinking when you were talking about the give and take of power and I have two responses. One is, I'm still in touch with May and her kids, and I think that we're in touch more because I went back and I did that process with her. So that's one thing. Another thing is, as far as her empowerment, she has multiple copies of my thesis. She gives it to people. Since then she has married, she has her master's, she bought a house. She has done all these things, and she said to me just the other day, she said "you know, I think part of the reason I made sure to buy a house was because it was down there [in the thesis]. It was written. People knew I said I was going to buy a house. And if I didn't buy a house . . . you know what I mean?" She felt she had made a commitment by telling me and it helped her carry it through.

Life History

(Isadora has placed her questions/comments in square brackets)

Okay let me tell you something; um, I got a lawyer. I got a lawyer from the CORE, the coalition for racial equality. A girlfriend of mine, she knows somebody who works for them, and they recommended a lawyer who knows how to deal with these cases and with minorities, um, he's at 250, um, Broadway; he's in the Woolworths building, and he's supposed to be a reputable lawyer that in fact he's the lawyer that, this particular law firm is the ones that like started malpractice at—the guy who's the partner and then he passed away, lawyers would come to watch him. so that's the way he is, ya know. and so, I forgot their names, can you believe it? That's because I just have them like in the back of my mind. And I went there and I met a doctor and he asked me all these questions about you know; what had happened and what I had seen. You know he took down the medical stuff; you know, and as a doctor, he knew. And then they wrote me and told me that I had a case, against HIP; and the hospital. Because they knew we had a case against HIP but we weren't sure about the hospital. The HIP clinic neglected him, the HIP doctor. Then when he went to the hospital, the hospital neglected him . . . It was like inevitable. He was just gonna go that day. because, you know, if I was right there to you know, to make sure I followed up because he was in the ER with Shirley, and she called me. They were at the HIP clinic, right. And then, the ambulance took 'em to the hospital, so I figured he was okay. when I got there my son was gasping, he was gasping for air. And then I, then I, and he was in the emergency room I was in the waiting room cause they said; we're gonna have to stabilize him and then they said they intubated him so then I said, okay maybe, you know. They said don't worry—that does happens to asthmatics—because we got him before he didn't get any air—which was a lie cause when they did the autopsy . . . he, he said that that's not true, cause he had a lot of fluid in his lungs. So they didn't get any; he didn't get any oxygen . . . Anyway, at least, they're suing them. They're suing the doctors, the HIP center, and the ambulance.

[Who helps pay for the lawyers?]

No what it is, is when you go to a lawyer whatever they settle for they get uh, a third. So, if I settle for a million dollars they get a third of that million, and then the rest is mine.

[Is the HIP clinic still open?]

Yeah. But they changed their policies because of Salim. Yeah. One is cause somebody just told me that, that his mother belongs to HIP and

Isadora Sahl

she's asthmatic, and now with asthmatic patients they take them right away. So, at least Salim didn't die in vain.

[What happened with the clinic?]

I reported the doctor . . . So he was reported to the office of professional, . . . whatever . . . professional conduct. I reported them, they came here, they just, we had to explain the whole story, Me and Shirley had to go through the whole thing all over again, . . . and they said, you know, the guy who was here who's the inspector, he said, there's probably nothing gonna be done to him, but this will go on his record, and if something else happens they'll have this on his record. And then we'll see what happens. But, you know, but he's being sued anyway, the doctor's being sued so, that particular doctor and the HIP, center. They're being sued. Because that's negligence; on their part and negligence on the doctor's part. Cause even if the HIP center didn't do what they were supposed to do the doctor should have did what he was supposed to do. And he didn't even bother to call the ambulance. So I don't know I don't really know who my lawyers are suing. They left him in the waiting room for like 3 hours, he was there from like 2:30 til about 5:30, she called me at 5:30, and she said, they just saw him. I'm like what? And I said go back there and find out what's happening. Cause then, I knew that, when you have an asthmatic it takes a long time for them to, you know you could be sitting there, but they take you right away, but they're medicating you, and they just checking you, that's my experience with asthma. With him they didn't even do that, none of them checked to see how far his breathing was they didn't check, you know a doctor, shoulda put a stethoscope to see how, badly he was breathing and wheezing, and how clogged he was and he didn't even bother. So, he was negligent, I mean. They gave him 2 shots and it didn't work. Obviously he was really out of control then, so, he said take him to the hospital, um go in an ambulance or get a cab, and that's still no way to treat an asthmatic, because in a matter of a few seconds, he could've went from this degree to that degree, and he still, and he refused to come to the phone or talk to me; I couldn't get him because the clinic was closed and there was nobody in there but the doctor alone with all those patients. There was no attendant, no nurse, nobody. How can you leave somebody alone like that? How you gonna have patients sitting there, everybody leaves at 5 o'clock—see ya! They gotta have a staff that in case patients carry over, there should be a staff on emergency you get overtime, but that's . . . So, we got to the hospital, I ca- the ambulance, I called the HIP center too, the HIP emergency and said what kind of policy is this the doctor doesn't call the ambulance the patient does? I never even heard of this. They didn't wanna say anything, of course, because they're protecting their own I said, well is this the policy? They said, Well I don't know and, let me contact the doctor, so they musta beeped him, and then I at the same time, called the ambulance, I called the ambulance, the ambulance got there, I told Salim hang on the ambulance is here, it's coming, so hang on. And, they got him in the ambulance. So I figured okay, he must be okay, cause they gave him oxygen, they gi- rush him to the hospital. They'll take him. Whatever they gotta do, they gonna check. Not knowing, taking my time going there! I took about 45 minutes. I even took the bus! because I said well, he's in the hospital, who would ever think? You know? I just never in my, in my, in my imagination, wildest imagination never! Because I've always been with Salim. When he was in the, hospitals, and, we've been lucky though, we've never had to wait, he's got asthma, they've taken him and I've been there. I figured him being grown, I don't know I just, maybe, maybe that: Salim always used to tell me, you are too naive Mom. You think the world is, is a good place, and it's not. And I would, be: But it has to be, there's good people. And he would always tell me: you are so naive, you don't know what's happening in this world. And I guess he was right, because I was naive. I really trusted, these people, you know, like, Oh! I would never do it so why would they? You know? Taught, uh, learned some, unfortunately, my son had to die from it, but, when I got there and then the doctor, you know, he said okay well, you know you gotta leave, cause you supposed to leave. There's supposed to be care taken, I knew he was really in pain then, because he couldn't breathe and he was probably you know like bugging-out. And um, then he was intubated and I stayed around for about an hour and they said, you know, there's really nothing I can do. I just checked on him but I knew he didn't look right. His color didn't look right, and I figured they're intubating you on oxygen you look like your asleep, but he looked like he was, distressed, his body, his facial expression didn't look like he was just resting and he was sedated. And, then, he had, then the next morning, they cal-, I, I called. Shirley's mother called and she said you better call the hospital, Salim's had a cardiac arrest. So, about 6 o'clock in the morning he had a cardiac arrest. If it wasn't that Shirley called, his mother called at 6:30, we probably wouldn't have known, as soon as he, but, I'm gonna give them the benefit of the doubt and say they were trying to stabilize him, so they didn't even have time to call his mother. But they should have, that should have been one of the calls they made, because in case he woulda died, I should've been, I should've been on my way there. And he was a kid! See, that's another thing that they didn't, somebody must not have been looking at his chart! He was only 18, 19! So, still, he's not a grown person. He didn't come there on his own. He had a mother, they knew I was there with him, he lives with me! Now all that information was there. It wasn't you know, but they took it upon themselves that, you know, they didn't call. And then, they said that he had a cardiac arrest and they were stabilizing him, but I knew, they were hiding something. They didn't wanna say, they made it sound like oh, we got him stable. Then, but, but, it wasn't true, they never got him stable. They, they were trying to. And when I got there, they were still trying to stabilize him, they knew something went wrong, they don't know what. So that's when they took a CAT scan, because they figured, they said Oh! you know when you have cardiac arrest, you move them, you know the, the oxygen isn't flowing so they gonna check to see if it damaged his brain, and they claim, then everything happened so fast, they said he had a, a, they said he had blood on his brain and very little brain activity. So, then I said well, what's the chances of him ever getting in, I said look please tell me the truth, and she said; even if, he came out it wouldn't matter. So, I said so what you're saying is my son is, gone? And then, they came back and said there was no brain activity. That he was . . . But they knew, you know they try to be soft, you know somehow they try to cushion over it. It just happened so quick. There were a lot of questions I wish I would've asked, but I didn't. I think it would have made a difference, in my mind as soon as they said no brain activity, I already knew, me working with children, that are retarded, that, he's a vegetable. You know, then, after that I learned all the other procedures. The, worst part I think was, was during that time after they told me that he had no brain activity they said, oh did he have, he must have had an aneurism. From all, and the, the severity of the asthma attack, made the aneurism explode, that's why he had brain, blood in his brain, so. That's what they were claiming. Okay? That he died of an aneurism. Then right after, here comes these people asking me for his organs. So right away I'm like no, no, forget it, you know I can't. You know, and uh, I said: no, I can't deal with it right now. And then, that's when everybody came to the hospital, and the next day, then I decided to give his organs. He saved 3 people's lives. It just sounded so gross when they came. What they were afraid of, I think there were 2 objectives there. One objective was, that he was young, and that if they didn't take the organs before the rest of his body started to deteriorate they wouldn't be able to use it. So that was one objective. The second was, I felt like they were trying to hide something, else, from me. So, I wasn't really sure, and that was confusing and I had to make this decision so quickly, under all that pressure, but, you know, when I got home, the next day, I made my mind, I said okay that's fine, and the next day I signed his organs away and everything else, you know. I knew there was something else happening, you know, but I knew it wasn't just the right time to find out what, actually was going on. I knew then, cause I said my son, I knew this just wasn't acceptable for a kid to come in with asthma, a healthy kid, to just all of a sudden die? Please! And if it wasn't for my sister it would of never got on the news, and I probably would of never, dealt with all of this, because I wasn't really thinking about it.

He really didn't. . . . He never got. . . . You know he used to be out, he has the little asthma stuff like that, the inhaler. That stuff was terrible. I wish he never started that shit, because Salim has asthma, since he was about two. And I, used, herbs, I never used the medicine they gave me, and I controlled it. When Salim got about 14, he started, he only got an asthma attack, really bad like maybe once, or twice a year that I had to take him to the hospital. And as he was getting older it was becoming less, then all of a sudden when he got about 14, it was getting bad, and that's usually not the case. The case is, that when you get older, but I told him, I felt, I said Salim it's the way you're eating, Because I've always kept you on a certain diet, I watch what you eat, you can't eat late at night because your digestive system, it builds up too much mucus and you tend to store it in your lungs, because you, you have asthma. So, you need to eat less, you need to eat more vegetables, you need to drink more water, you know, watch your bowel movements, all that stuff, and he was neglecting all that, eating late and, and not eating for long periods, stuff like that, and I felt that, that had a lot to do with . . . Plus, asthma's emotional too. And, even though Salim fought, it, it was because I was there telling him, No, you got, don't give in to it! And he was strong and he knew how to breathe and to relax, but, I don't know, I find his death still, you know, very strange, and like it was, he was the sacrifice for, in a sense like my happiness, because, I mean we struggled all our lives, I have, and because he's dead, and I have this court case, there are a lot things that, my grandchildren and Aisha's children and Kai's children will benefit from. Cause, it ain't gonna be a tiny bit of money that they're gonna get. So I try to look at it like that. Well, he's dead, but, his nieces and nephews are gonna remember, uh, if it wasn't for your nephew, uh, your uncle, you wouldn't have what you have, or you wouldn't be able to finish school because he, I, I'm gonna make sure that the money's set up that, that you know, that it continues, so, you know. Sometimes it happens that. . .

[I never saw him have a serious attack, I just don't understand.]

He, he didn't, it wasn't a serious attack. But because of neglect, you know, sometimes your asthma gets so bad that you may need an epi, okay? Some, you need it! Because the pump isn't enough, so you need an epi and you need to get an IV because that's what they should have did, they should have put an IV, at HIP they should have and if they couldn't, they should have got, as soon as he got to the hospital an IV should have been inserted. And then, the uh, cause the, the nebulizers, because the epi is one way, then there's that nebulizer where you, you, take in the stuff, the medicine, it's in the bottom and there's a vapor coming out. There's a lot of different things. He's done the epi and then he's fine. And if they see two epi's ain't working, they say okay, we gotta put you on a IV. They, somebody is sitting there, making sure that he's drinking water, cause he's never been alone, see if I was there, this would've never, cause, I would've been breaking. Scuse me! Hello! You know, but he was in there alone, and, and I, he was like me, he trusted they weren't gonna leave him there. So. It's like weird. Anyway, so. We'll see what happens. You know it could take a couple of years, and whatever. I probably would've never done this, I mean the guy I spoke to at court he had said listen, your loss is something that can't be replaced, but, the only way that these people are gonna feel their loss, the loss that you feel, is through their pockets. Cause th-, see they, they haven't lost a son, you have. He says you gotta think of it as a business now, and it's like hard to think like, but, but my son is not a business! But, Salim would have wanted me to fight, you know and to go on, and to get the money and whatever it is that I have to get, so, you know. I signed everything I had to sign, you know the lawyers are really good, they've been calling and they been writing and I've signed a few things. And now it's just waiting. Now, now it's them negotiating. That could take 2, 3 years, 5 years, depends. You know, some people say you never know. Sometimes it could take 3 years, sometimes it could take 5 years, sometimes it could take 60 years, you don't know. But whatever, whenever it comes, even if I'm not here, Aisha and Kai will have it. You know, it'll be in my family, somebody in my family will have to get it. I mean, it's not gonna just go, down the drain . . . That's it in a nutshell. You know, anything else?

[How did you deal with it?]

It was hard to uh, um like, I always talked about it and people would ask me, and they said: you don't—I said, I don't mind talking about it. But it helped me, it was like a, a therapy for me to go through the whole process of remembering detail by detail, you know, what happened, what he looked like, because, seeing him laying down like that was, that's like my last memory of him and it's like, oh my god! You know I don't wanna remember my son laying in a bed, with a tube down his throat, IV's and all those machines all around him. But I talked about it, and I kinda like, pushed myself through it, you know and now, the memory is there, but it's not as, it doesn't feel as, intense so, talking about it helps, a lot, it still does. You know. It still, I still talk about Salim's funeral, like I don't wanna, you know, you you, you have to talk about it, and otherwise, if I don't, imagine if I kept all that inside me?!

[What about Kai and Aisha?]

I force them to. I bring it up, always, I bring up their brother all the time. Salim woulda liked, you know, certain things. A movie. Oh! If that movie would've been out, Oh Salim woulda loved that. Or, Salim woulda did this, or we would've liked this. And I'll mention it to them, in the beginning, Aisha was like . . . yeah. Kai won't, it's hard to say with Kai, because he doesn't really . . . he hasn't really said anything. I even have a book about death. That I had since Salim was like, three. I don't know why, I just picked it up and said I don't know, maybe one day I might use it. And I read it to Kai, and we read it together, and I was waiting for a reaction, I asked him, and you know, I explained it to him, you know what it was about, you know a grandfather dying and how people die, and blah-blah-blah, and he didn't say anything. And then, you know, I, I try to ask him you know, how do you feel about your brother not being there and do you miss him, and what do you miss about him the most? And I'll say, well I miss this, and what do you miss? Little by little I think, I don't know, I think because he's small he, it, hasn't really hit him. With Aisha, I think she looks at me. If I fell apart, she would. But as long as I'm, hanging in there, she just follows my lead. It's just like when, when the, when all of it was over and now we have to go back to reality, that was like the hardest, thing to do! It's like, okay kids! We can't stay in this house together and cling on to each other! We have to go back, to school and to work and to be, be, uh . . . So, my therapy was, I was out of work for like two weeks and, it's a Friday, and then we were going on, like a break, the spring break, that just passed. So I said, let me go in, Friday. . . . And stay, you know, like let people, cause people around my job are gonna come to me, they, eh are you okay? Are you, you know. I said I need to get that out of the way. So that when I come back, again, it'll won't, people won't have to come to me and say, May I'm sorry, or uh, How you doing? And, so I did that and that made me feel better, and then that week I just kinda like rested. But every-, uh, the kids! I guess because, they saw me go and I just continued to, cause I had to go to school too! And they didn't think I was going back to school. They like thought, she's not coming back. And everybody looked at me, and I'm here! I missed two weeks but I caught up! And uh, it was surprising, my kids, they did fine?! You know, Kai Hsing and, Aisha did okay but, I think it was because I did okay.

[Were James and the other kids there all the time?]

Yeah they came, they came around for a little while, but then, after about a month, things started to go back to normal, and they, you know, they didn't come as often. And then, when they started to stay away, James, it never, bothered him, but I think, uh. Isha, and Amalik, it was very hard for them to come by, James didn't care! And James is the one that reminds me the most of Salim! Because I look at him, and he just makes one move and it's like, Oooh-ish, isn't it?

[Can you talk more about that?]

Well, there was a lot of um . . . You know and I, I know James was deeply affected by it. More than, anyone.

[I think it's the reason he's in army.]

Yeah it is, I think it is. That he said: Lemme, I gotta definitely do something! Yeah he does. He wrote me a little, in fact in back of that picture he, I didn't read it when I got it, and then I read it and I was like oh my gosh! He said, I'm in it he keeps saying I'm gonna be the son. You know, to show you, so, that made me feel good. But um, I thought, when, Salim passed away, and all his friends that he had, I thought maybe that would, like change their life, and it did because, but it didn't change it for the better. A lot of them got worse like, Amilik really,..he went off the deep end. He really,.. and then, then, when Jerald left- died, that even made Amilik.

[Can you talk about Jerald's death and Jerald?]

I don't know if his mother knew as much as I did, because, no, she didn't, but I knew, because Salim would tell me. And I knew that he was into smoking, and dealing, whatever, and guns and whatever. I knew he was in there, doing it, and when he went to North Carolina, and after Salim passed away, Jerald, in fact couldn't, didn't even go to the funeral. He couldn't, he couldn't deal with it. At all! And he never showed up. He came to the house, but he didn't come to the funeral. And um, he would call all the time, to check and see if we were okay, and uh, two days before he died he was here. And I was at school, and he saw, Kai Hsing, and Aisha and Anthony, and he it was a Wednesday, and he left Thursday, and he died Friday, they shot him. And I had asked him: Jerald, you okay? and: Yeah Ma, I'm gonna come home now, and I'm not, and I'm gonna, you know . . .

[How did you raise Salim to not do drugs?]

You know, it's, I don't know why. And neither is Aisha interested in it, and she has friends that, smoke. But um, I smoked and they were little. When they were little and my Mom, and I was always very open with it. They were 5 and 6, uh like a Bambu right here. And it was just that way, and we'd smoke at the kitchen table. And my mother used to say: Ah, you shouldn't do that! and, I said, but if they gonna learn about drugs, they gonna learn here. If I hide it they gonna learn it anyway! So this way it's right here for them, the roaches, the Bambu around and my mother would have a fit, because of it. But when Salim got about

10 years old, he told me he didn't want me to smoke anymore. Cause he had these friends, these oriental friends that he hung out with, and he had started to, he wanted to bring them over. And he says: And I'm not gonna bring them and have you here smoking. So, now, it was a reality check for me because, I never told him he couldn't do it, I never said anything about it I just did it. But here he was in school and he was learning that drugs were bad, in all forms. I couldn't really argue with him and say, no they're not! And, because the reality was they did do these kind of damages, and yet I smoked it, and he was intelligent enough to argue with me and say: How you gonna tell me? So I said, I'm not even gonna bother, so I just had to stop. So I did. Because I felt, if my child is pulling my coat, hey, it's time for me to give him some respect. All my friends, and my family, my sister and my brother, they said: you're fucking bugging-out. Who is he? He's just a kid. I said, but he's my kid. And if, I have to give him that respect, this is his house, this is not your house. You can't come here and smoke anymore, you're gonna have to find another way. You can't hang out and smoke cause Salim doesn't agree with it. It kept going on, we, so I stopped smoking. And then, they, people would still come here and try to sneak, and go in my room, so Salim would tell me: What do you think I'm stupid? Auntie Mei Yuk goes in there. I said, but that's Auntie Mei Yuk, I'm not smoking. "But, how do I know that?" I said, but Salim, I wouldn't lie to you. I'm not! If I was smoking I would just tell you, this is what I wanna do if you don't like it..? Yeah! But I don't, and he said: "Well they're, you know, they think I'm stupid. And I went to them, I said, you think he's stupid. Now he was like 11 and 12 now. He's getting a little older. He says: "I'm not stupid, I know what the deal is." And, and, they said: Well he's just a kid. He's no-, you the one that supposed-. I said, but, you think by going in the room that he doesn't know what you going in the room for but he does. Because, I never closed my door on my children. I've always kept my doors open. You know, where they could come in and go as they please. You know and a lot of people'll say, Oh but you need time. I said if I want time then I shouldn't've had children. That's the bottom line! Your world is kinda re-arranged around their world. When they sleep, you got time, when they're up, doors are open, and that's the way it is. Whatever, one day we were here, not in this house, in the other apartment. We were, I think we were gonna do, blow to tell you the truth. And, they so, Salim and Aisha knew we were gonna do something. Uh, they put out their books on drugs and showed it to us. Me, my brother, my sister and our nother two friends. They said: "Do you know what drugs do to your brain?" . . . said, that's it! You guys ain't doing no shit at my house no more. I felt so guilty. The guilt alone just

killed me, you know to live with that guilt, and I, I said, I can't do that. I can't because I'm living a lie here! I'm telling 'em not to do one thing, and they're, catching me! And you guys, are getting even more problems for me because these are my children! So, that was it. I just said, then I just turned around and said that, I don't want any smoke, any blow, don't even come up here and even, you know, try to . . . and then I just don't, I haven't, it's been a long time, 10 years maybe. The other day, Kai's father told me: Do me a favor, go down- upstairs to the store, and go buy me some E-Z wider. I said, What? I'm gonna do something like that and, first of all I don't have nothing to do with it, and then second of all if I go upstairs and I'm buying it and somebody, is in there, watching me buy it, how do I know 2, 3 years from now, my principal or some-body, I'm in a meeting or a big event that this lady remembers that she saw me buying E-Z wider? And she may be the lady that tells the other man not to hire me, for a teaching job or a higher position! You never know who you may meet! And I'm not, I, if I did it it's different, but I don't and I'm not gonna take a chance, so he, couldn't argue with that. He said okay fine. I said, no way, I'm not gonna jeopardize my career for some bullshit like this! Buy a pack of Bambu for you?! And I can't say I never, inhaled it! But it, it just that, it's really funny how, You know, I think that the one thing I was telling one of my friends, that I think I re-gret ever doing was, was doing any drugs. I really do, because it, it was a phase, and it was stupid because you really didn't get anything out of it. And, I remember my mother telling me, May, if you start one drug you'll lead to the other. And she's right, it does. There's no way for you to say, I'm just gonna smoke reefer and that's it. Th- no-, you could! That could happen! But, the chances of it, let's say that you just gonna smoke weed, you decided and you're not gonna do anything else, it's not, because if you're around, those, those kind of people, it brings, those other kind of people. Once you started, those, that world opens up to you. And that's their, you know, I, I'm lucky, that, I've never been into drugs because, I have my kids, and I couldn't really like, do it the way, other people could do it because I had, the kids. So I couldn't sit here and, smoke that much because, as much as I would smoke, they still, I still had to tend to them, so I had to like, no, I have to first take care of my kids and then I would smoke. So, you know it wasn't, I would smoke at work, but, not as much with my kids. I would smoke more, outside of the house than inside. My friends, they would all hang out here because they knew it was okay for them to do it in my house, this was like the house to get high in. But now, it's not the house to do anything. But I, I'm glad, that Salim and Aisha never, and I hope Kai Hsing doesn't either. That they don't. Because I don't think that, that's a, it's just something that, I don't think you can, it doesn't have to be, a necessary part of your life. You know. It was a time for us because that was the time, but now . . . I don't know. The way the things and the drugs . . .

[It's all so interrelated.]

And it just brings you into that world. It's easier. Because it, it just, leads from one thing to the other. In this neighborhood it does. And I'm glad Salim never was . . . you know, he was a dud. Aisha's a dud too.

[How did he involve himself with the rest of us and not participate?]

You can be part of the world but you don't have to be, completely a part of it. Right. You have to, stay-hold, hold your, values. And he, but, that's because I think that, my kids definitely, I have very, they're very clear what their values and what their priorities are. Because I've stressed them over and over and over again. I mean when I look at my kids, I, I know a lot of parents are having a lot, a lot of problems with their children. And uh.., some have been in private schools some of them have not, and I try to look at them, and say, what is it that I've been giving my kids that they aren't giving them? Their kids, and a lot of them are, these are wealthy, people. What, what's lacking there? And, what's lacking is, is communication, to really make really clear what is it that you want from your children? What is it that you want from them because they don't know what they want. And you gotta, and if you don't know what you want, how can you make clear to them what, what, they should have? So, I think I really stressed those values to uh, my kids, you know, to be honest, to be truthfu- you know to be honest. That education was the key. You know, that they were minority children and that, the world was not set up to make, to make it easy for you, to, as a minority child. And you have to realize that and, you gotta work hard. The only one who's gonna try to make it as easy for you as possible is me! So you gotta work with me! We are working together here. That's what I always told them. We're a unit. If you don't do what you're supposed to do it's gonna effect all of us. So, if we just kinda like work together, in the end we're all gonna have. It don't look like we gonna have now, but it will in the end. And Salim, and Aisha know that. And they see what comes to that. And I think that's important, I think that parents try to um, be the dominant factor in their, family, you know. Especially single mothers, cause they have to, play those two roles, so they really have to, either they learn to be real, real strong, or they're real, real soft. It's hard to be in between and you gotta be. You gotta be that loving mother and nurturing person, but at the same time, you gotta be strong, and you also have to know how to pull the resources. Because you can't be everything so you, you gotta know how to grab certain things and people, to pull into your world, to make up for the losses that you don't have. Because there's no, how else can you do it? You can't do it by yourself, and you gotta have, surround yourself with that support group. It, it can't always be your mother, and your family and your sister so you gotta have friends, go on vacations, you gotta seek that kind of support. That's, what I really think, that, that is the point. Seeking those resources, you know to be resourceful, and to, make your children become that way. Because that's the reality of life, you know. There's no way you're gonna sit there and think things are gonna come to you, you gotta, reach out, and don't be afraid to take, and to give.

[Anthony lives here, for how long?]

For about 3 years.

[He's Kai's father?]

He's nobody's father. He's really just, my um, companion. He has no influence on my children whatsoever. Yeah they tolerate him because of me. You know it's always, Mom, you're okay? As long as I'm not miserable they're, they'll be okay. Salim, never liked him. Because Salim, you know, he had a big mouth, and they would argue and you know, he just had a way of talking, you know, talking a lot of shit! That of course I, I, me knowing him, because even my mother wanted to kick his ass. You know, he has a really nasty, I would tell him, listen, the way you talk to me, why don't you go out there and talk to them people out there. You know you take it out on me! And that's what he did. And uh, a few times that he was like, yeah, you know, he'd start cursing and going off and Anthony would be like, I'm tired of talk like that. I said, pay him no attention. This is not your place Anthony. You know, he's disrespectful, you're looking as the man and I'm your woman, but that's my son! So don't get involved. Anthony had a bad habit of making, saying stuff, to me. Salim don't play that. You got something to say, you know, state it correctly. Because, Salim was brought up to tell you how he felt! And he didn't hold his tongue! And that's where him and Salim, and, you know Salim tolerated him, you know and after a while Anthony learned not to say anything. And like, if I would scream and complain, that would like, get Anthony excited, I said listen, my right as a mother is to complain and scream and bitch, because that's my right! I gotta go in the house, goddamn you kids you, and, that is what I'm supposed to do. You have to just be there for me, you ain't, just listen and aa, okay, you know and that's it. But he just never knew how to do that. And, Salim knew that, and I mean, I mean, Salim told me: "I know you not marrying that man Ma. Cause he is not the husband that you need." I said, no son I'm not don't worry. And, it's the truth, I'm not. I have no intention of . . .

[Is he the first man in the picture for a long time?]

No. No, Kai's father was with me for a long time. But, um, they had, no influence on my kids. Maybe with Aisha, cause when I broke up with him, Aisha was upset. And Kai was small, a little bit, but Aisha was really upset. Because she was spoiled by Kai's father, you know she was like little Daddy's girl and stuff. And uh, she was little. She was about ten. And it really bothered her, cause I was with him since she was two. So we were together a long time. But, I just, um, and that's why I really stayed with him that long, because of, not Salim, cause Salim couldn't give a damn! He didn't care about nobody but his mother! But Aisha and Kai I was afraid how they'd take, how would they take it, but I realized I wasn't happy. And I wasn't giving my children what I needed to give. So I broke up with him. And then I met Anthony, like a, like a, well I broke up with Kai's father a couple of times, like two times, and this, the last time was it. But we were a little more stable. Cause we were here. And I was in school so I was a little more focused. I felt a little, a little better, and they, then, by then they got used to it. And when I met Anthony he was just somebody that they knew made me happy. Him moving in here was a mistake. Ha-ha! But um, never let him hear that even though I would tell him that anyway. It was, it was a mistake because, he has benefited from living here, but I haven't, and neither have my children. He's just there. And, he's just there he serves no purpose, whatsoever! It's sad but he doesn't. And that's because, you know what, you look at yourself as a, as a, single woman, always thinking in my mind, that men, I need a man to help me with my children. And I never needed a man! It was a facade! It was an illusion that I created in my mind, that I needed a man to help me with my children, because I never did! Salim became a man because of me! Through all those bumps and ups and downs, not knowing his father, and me talking to him but not meeting him and all kinds of stuff he had to go through. I don't know how he did it, but I, I was the one that made, kept him going through it. Through school, and all the other stuff, he wasn't sure, getting to Seeger. Even through grammar school he had problems! But I was there. It wasn't his father, it wasn't no man, and Kai's father wasn't there, he was there, just giving the little amount of money that he gave, and I'm still thinking I, know, but I always knew how to reach out. Because I've never been afraid to tell people my business. Because there's no secret, my life is an open book! So what if I'm telling you about Anthony or anybody else, my whole job, my, people in my room know. Cause, when I feel that way I have to say something because, I'm not gonna come to work and be like: Hi, how are you, good morning, everything's fine. And I'm working with you everyday, I'm gonna say, No! I got some serious problems! You know? And that, somehow it's made me work it through, it made me, keep a clear mind, and focus, and so, you know, that's the reality. I mean, somehow, Salim made it. Aisha has, with all her ups and downs. Her father was no damn good. He died, God rest his soul. In November, he just passed away. Yeah, we've been funeral hopping. It's been a, I think I need to open up a funeral home, and tell people how to have funerals now. Cause, I mean . . .

[How did it affect Aisha?]

I went with Aisha, and you know, I said I don't wanna go because you know, I didn't like him when he was alive, so I don't wanna go when he's dead, it don't make a difference to me but you are his daughter and you need to be there. And you know, it's sad for us because it just re- you know, it reminded us of what we just had to go through. And it was hard because, I lost my brother first in May and then I lost Salim in February. And then Jerald was close to me and then my ex-husband, so these are really people that have . . . Jerald I wouldn't say, but my brother, my son and my ex-husband, those are people that are very close in my life. This is my daughter's father, I mean I can't, he's my first husband, my only first husband I ever had! Ha-ha. I probably ever will! But those are, close, people, you know? It's taught me, I've learned a lot, from it. I learned that through death . . . people don't change, some people. That, you think that, that the way it's affecting you it's affecting everybody else but, it isn't. It's affected me a lot. But, there's people, that just go on, like nothing happened. Which I guess is healthy but at the same time, I don't know. I think that, I think it should make you more in touch, with reality. That life here is very short. And love the people that you love, now. Don't be a hypocrite when they die and tell 'em that you love 'em while they're in the coffin. I think you need to make sure that, they know I love you, you know, not when they're sick in the hospital. You know cause I think that would really make me feel guilty if I never said to my child, I love you. Or that they never were sure that I loved them and then they died. You know. That's the first thing that came in my mind. Like when my brother died, I kept thinking, I said, I, I know I was a good sister. I was there for him, I cleaned his butt when he was sick, went to the hospital, went out of my way when I was tired, you know to get out your bed, you just took your clothes off, you laying down and somebody calls you? That's love! And I told Salim and Aisha that. I remember, I said, this is when you know you love somebody. When you tired, and you don't wanna get up, and you get up anyway! That's love. And I said, you remember that, because it's easy to do it when you, oh! no problem, but when it's a problem and you go like, okay. Cause you deal with the pain, and my brother was a pain because he wanted um, he was, he and my mother didn't get along, and I was like the only that he really wished to talk to. And I would go, and I would talk to him and try to calm my mother down. And, he died of AIDS. And thank God he didn't really suffer, because he didn't really, go through that whole . . .

he went into a coma, and they thought, the doctor said: He's never . . . this is it, and we just waiting for him to die now. They brought him to the room to wait to die . . . he woke up. Then the doctor said he's never gonna leave this hospital. He walked out the week, week after. Okay? He died in his bed where he wanted to be, in the house. Cause he knew, see my brother was really bright, and he knew what AIDS was and he knew as long as he was in the hospital they were gonna poke and experiment and do everything. And there was nothing else he could do, let him die in peace. And he was right, and, that's the way he died. At his home, which was good.

[That was the cause of death?]

No, see, the, when they came, we knew he had AIDS. So, he just, went to sleep. And, the day before he died, I went to the house, and he was like: May I'm goi- I'm just tired, and he didn't want to eat. And I made him drink some soup. And he was just kinda weak, and he said: I'm just tired. Could you just sit here with me. My feet are cold. And I was rubbing his feet. Just rub my feet 'til I go to sleep. And I just had that feeling, I don't know. I said, do you wanna go to the hospital? He said: No-no, just leave me, I'm just tired. And he went to sleep, and he didn't get up. I think that's a nice way to die. Just sleep yourself into . . . you know just, go to sleep. But to be under those, you know, foreign people all poking on you and everything else. You know so, it was okay like that, you know. We survived.

[What do you want to say about it?]

Being a single parent is a big, big issue for me, big issue. Big, big issue I think, and and especially, in a environment like this. But, I think there are a lot of resources here, and uh, if you need help, you can get it.

When Salim was growing up, I put, tried to get him in the Boy's Club, because when Salim was in the 4th grade, he was having all these problems in school. Okay? Always. He would have teachers that just didn't understand him, cause he would do weird things. He would talk to himself in class. He would take out the textbook and read it. While the teacher's teaching, he was up there reading out of the textbook in his lap. They didn't understand, they said something's wrong with him. So when he gets to St. Joseph they want him tested, no problem, we'll get him tested. He wasn't doing well, academically. So, they tested him and the psychologist found out that the part of your brain where your math develops, was very immature, but the part that develops reading, was, extremely mature. He had a 8th grade reading level in 4th grade. So the doctor said, there's nothing wrong with this kid! Except, there's nothing wrong with him, he has a, single parent, something gotta be wrong with him. He's gotta have emotional problems, this is a mother who's single, black child, he's gotta have problems. The psychologist told them: Leave him alone! Cause he's intelligent! The only thing the psychologist said was: He's too attached to you, and you need to break that. It, it wasn't easy, but I was doing, he was close to me, because I spent everything, all my kids were always with me, so that's when I started letting him go to, you know he always went to daycare and stuff, but then I went, I put him, I made him go to sleep-away camp. And I convinced him, that it was a good thing for him to go. And he went there every time. And you know, just so he could get away from me but, you know the tie he had with me, I don't think it was ever gonna break. You, if you had tested him again if he was alive, they woulda said: you're too attached to your mother! Because he was, I mean he would, he would stay home and it would be fine for him. He couldn't care and, to punish him, I was like okay Salim no TV, he couldn't care because, he would pick up a book and stay in his room all day and read it. Now, you couldn't say no reading Salim as a punishment. You couldn't do that to Salim. He say, I don't care, I'll stay here, he could always find plenty of stuff to read. It didn't bother him. He was just that kind of a kid but . . . being that he was, a different kind of a kid, I always wanted to put him in like a gifted program, or an excelled program. He's gifted but, the programs that, in this neighborhood they don't have it. The ones that they, that were, far, how was I gonna get him there? Cause I would have liked to have put him in Hunter, and typical—I didn't have the money to do it, and I think that it's too bad that I think a lot of children that, minority children that are in like my situation, that they, there's not even resources to pull these children out, because there are a lot of gifted children here. And, parents, a lot of parents don't, they know there's something special about they child but they, what do we do? You know? You know, how do you, where do you go? You know is there a program that just takes these children? You know is there somebody, a head hunter, looking for, gifted children in a ghetto?

[What about the Boy's Club program to place kids in boarding schools?]

What they're looking for is, see cause Salim dropped the Boy's Club cause he's not very sociable, and that's too sociable for him. With Kai Hsing, he's in the Boy's Club, and what the Boy's Club does is if you're a good member, like Kai Hsing doesn't get into trouble. Cause you'd be surprised, those kids are wild in there. And what it's showing you in the Boy's Club it's giving them discipline, and values and priorities, which Kai Hsing already has, so he's like a step ahead. When he's down there playing he knows how to work with the team, you know he doesn't fight. So the, people in there like him. So what they do is they'll recommend certain kids to be tested. And, and they also recommend them to go away for summer camp, and the summer camp is like a summer school, summer camp, so he has, school in the morning and he, in the afternoon, he has recreation but, structured sort of you know. So they always chose, choose Kai Hsing and Kai Hsing takes like this aptitude test. And, he'll take the test, and then they look at his grades, and the people that recommended him at the Boy's Club and his teacher, and there's a lot of boarding schools that are, that take a few hundred or whatever amount, I don't know what the number is, of kids, and takes them, and enrolls them in boarding school, and they stay there, through elementary, through high school, and if they do well they'll even pay for them to go to college. So Kai Hsing has, he took the test three times already, and um, passing on- if he doesn't, if they don't get him this year, like they didn't take him last year or the year before, but he gets, but he goes to the camp. So he's getting that, reinforcement no matter what. And he likes it and they like him. Now this year, he'll go, I don't know which way he'll go. Either the boarding school or the camp. He's willing to go, which is fine. You know it's kinda, you know the only thing with Kai, like the summer school, he did very well because they had a, a cooperative learning. Do you know about that? Okay, they do a cooperative learning, while in Catholic school it's all traditional rote learning, which is boring! And Kai Hsing unfortunately, is—the only one who's a good rote learner is Aisha. Even me, I'm a half and half, I can learn rote, but after a while I gotta be doing that cooperative thing here. Because I just don't keep the concepts well that way. So, and Salim was definitely a uh, a cooperative learner, he was not a traditional rote learner. And Kai Hsing, and, is the same way. So he's not picking up the things he needs to pick up, in, school. He's learned the fundamentals. His reading isn't well, and it's not, at first I thought, he couldn't read well, cause they said he wasn't reading well. He was like under, like a 6 month under his uh, grade level. So I said let me check it out; so, you know, I let him read to me, and I'll find out his mistakes, is it, is it actually, you know, phonics, is it linguistic, you know, what, what is his problem? So, it's, wasn't none of that. The problem was, is Kai Hsing like to, jump quick, he reads like, you know he'll try to skim quick, and like he doesn't, and I tell him you can't do that, because you're not that good of a reader to start skimming. You got to become an avid reader for you to start to get the gist of what they're trying to say. Because his comprehension skills were, were low, and that's because he didn't read word for word, he was trying to go on- because he doesn't enjoy reading. So, he hasn't been doing that well. He keeps taking those tests at school and he scores below, his reading. So he always goes to summer school for reading. But when goes to the summer school; they are like: "This kid is unbelievable!" and he's, he's the leader, in the room, he's so, he, I mean he was like, high in everything. Language arts, reading, spelling, math everything. But it's a different environment, he doesn't feel as pressured, he does his work, he's not with me now, I'm not there nagging him! So, you know, it's showed another side of Kai, because, a lot of times, you, we think that the teachers know what they're doing, but they don't. They don't. And, and I mean Salim got shafted a few times, with that, with them trying to uh, put him down and I didn't, I fought, but not as hard as I'm gonna fight for Kai. Because there was a teacher of, of Salim's that said um, one teacher, cause he used to read, he used to bring books to school. And she caught him, and she didn't, their first meeting of, each other, they didn't, she couldn't stand him because Salim was in 7th grade, he was, she didn't like him. But she caught him reading these thick books, you know like the *Swords of Shenaro*, college level books, and she realized this kid, this kid reads. So she started to bring him books, about you know, like that gothic stuff and uh, you know those weird uh, what did he like? You know he liked all those uh, mystical things okay, so she started to bring him stuff like that, and then, she never bothered him after that. And once he, Salim, knows that you accept him for who he is, he'll do whatever you want. You try to make him something he's not, he's gonna fight you all the way. So that was one problem with her, he did very well in her class, and next year, this teacher said: He had to read, uh, *The Lion The Witch and The Wardrobe*, by C. S. Lewis, and he never got, he never bought the book. And he was upset, "Oh, he didn't bring the book in!" I said well Salim read that book in 4th grade. "Oh, well he couldn't have." I said don't tell me cause I worked in the library, and I brought him all those books! I never realized that the book was, a, a, a 8th grade book! I just knew that Salim liked to read, so I used to bring him stuff and he used to read it! And he read the whole series of C. S. Lewis. He read it when he was in 4th grade. "No. He doesn't know it." I said Salim this teacher got it out for you, you gotta prove to him that you are not what he thinks you are. He thinks you're an asshole and you're a dummy and you're not. So, I said Salim you gotta fight this, he already has in his mind that you, come from a single parent. you, you're, you don't know, you got emotional problems. He took the test. He had to do a whole test on C. S. Lewis and he passed it with 100 percent. The teacher never bothered him after that.

You know, it's just too, you know, I, I fought them, now with Kai Hsing I'm having the same problem. I know Kai Hsing has potential, he has to be mo—he's not motivated in school, with his teacher. He doesn't like writing, he's failing a lot in social studies and science, and he doesn't bring the books home to study, and I could study with him and he's not doing it. But I've done everything I can, I'm, I'm a good example, I study, diligently. I, I talk to Kai, Kai you gotta bring the book I'll work with you, I'll make the time, as long you do it. But, what is his teachers doing? How are they motivating him? So now, I'm gonna go in there and I'm gonna question them. You see a student that's not motivated, it's obviously not lack of motivation from his parents cause you know me, and it's not that I don't motivate my child. Now how dare them even, and they better not insinuate it, because they, the, there's no way! So now I want to know what are you doing to motivate him in school? To hav- keep him with the desire, the eagerness to learn? Cause you're gonna lose him? Nothing! So I'm gonna throw it back at them! How dare you? You're putting it all on him and me, what about you? No! Oh, wait 'til, I can't wait to go on Thursday. You know I've let it go and let it go, and I went to the teachers the last time, I said, I think Kai Hsing is failing your course. I'm in school, I've been in, I have a very hectic schedule, and maybe I'm not making enough time, to really get on him but, Kai Hsing is 12 and he knows his responsibilities. But, he may need more structure, he may need so, I put him in the after school center-thing for a little while, but I couldn't afford to pay, for it anymore, so I had to take him out and he kept asking me: "Mommy please, I'll do my homework." And he still, messed up. So now I'm like oh, I should've kept him in there what am I gonna do? Then, I finally had a long talk with Kai. I really had one of those, guilty mother talks, have you had one of those? That your father or mother made you feel so guilty? That how could you do this to me, you've hurt me so much, I feel so bad, oh, your brother would have flipped if he woulda been here, and, and he cried. And that made me feel like, okay, maybe he just needed that little talk. I don't know what good it does. And he started, like I'm working hard and can't you, so that's what I felt as a mother I have to appeal to that kind of a, like, this beating, yelling, punishing isn't doing it. I have to, to just say, c'mon, you're hurting me, and you're hurting yourself and it hurts me to see it. So he's been trying, but, he may get left back. Cause he's failing, he's failing social studies like by 2 points, like 67; science 68, uh, religion, and sometimes, they didn't say he was failing, the, the teacher hasn't said he's gonna get left back. I don't know why he hasn't said it. Okay, I, I'm afraid that they might tell me this time, well he hasn't made any improvements, and now it's one more quarter left. But Kai Hsing said he's really gonna try hard to bring it up, because he's not failing by that much, so his, he could. If he was failing like 40's and 50's, but he's not. He's got 67, 68, I'm like Kai, this is stupid now, so, I don't know, but I'm gonna throw it back at the teachers. Because now that I'm a teacher, now I understand really, and I know what it is, even though I don't think they believe I'm a teacher for some reason. I really really have that feeling. Because I, last year, when I had told his, other teacher that I was teacher and that I taught handicapped children and I was going for my master's in special ed, and she calls my job, during the day, got me out of my classroom like several times to complain: Oh, Kai Hsing's giving her a hard time. Which is bullshit. So, one day she called and, they, they, they had to go and get me, and they must've said: "I have to get her out her room, her classroom." and she said: "Oh, I'm so sorry, I didn't mean to get you out your class, I didn't realize, that they had to take you out." And then I said, she don't believe that I'm a teacher. Because, just as a professional courtesy, I, you're a teacher, you're my friend and I know you're in your classroom why am I gonna do that, I'm a teacher I already know that you're busy. I'm not gonna take you out, stop you from a, a lesson, or whatever you're doing. But she, didn't realize that, and I have that, I just, I don't know I think that they look at me as they just don't believe. And they make assumptions on Kai Hsing, like one of his teachers last year, the one who had Salim, who gave him the books, said he's nothing like, compared him to Salim. Like Salim and Aisha I don't remember with them, but Kai Hsing is very, you know, he's different, everybody's, every child is different. And he said: "Well is he spoiled?" And then I said, well Kai Hsing, all my children are spoiled, because they're my children, I said but there is a part of Kai that you don't know. Kai Hsing is a very good helper, better than Salim and Aisha, he's always been the kind of kid that, you don't have to explain things to him, Salim was always selfish in that way. But Kai Hsing, if he sees the table dirty, he will clean it. And, Salim wouldn't do that, so I said, you just have to give him that, he has to feel comfortable enough that he can do those things for you. So she started to give him some errands and more responsibility and, I don't know if that, well, he passed. But on this assignment, I don't know, what's happening, but I'll have to find out, what, what actually is he, what is this teacher doing to motivate my son? Because he's not, doing anything.

[What do you do?]

Well, I think that if, I keep on his, if I tell Mr. Simon that I know what the deal is, and what are you doing and reverse it, you're the teacher, now you gotta motivate my son because I'm motivating him! What are you, what are your suggestions? In your classroom. What are you gonna do during class time? To motivate him into, studying right? Are you gonna take him on the side maybe, maybe you need to talk to him alone, to show him that you care. Maybe he feels you don't, that you're just looking at the kids that are doing okay, and he's a little different, so you're not taking the time out. Yeah, that's what I'm gonna tell him. As a teacher, the kids that we, we're supposed to spend the most time with are the children that are going on the wayside, not the ones that are okay. You know? That doesn't even make sense! Why do I teach?! You, you're a little different, you're not following the, crowd, so I don't want nothing to do with you. And then they'll just get up and try to embarrass you, and you do not embarrass a 12-year-old. Especially a 12-year-old boy. You're better off saying, Kai, could you stay after school? I'd like to talk to you. You say, Kai, what's up? You know what's happening here? So, I'm gonna give him a few lessons in teaching. Yeah! Cause I'm sick of this. You know they're making me feel like I'm not doing what I'm supposed to do, I said wait a minute May Lin. You know, and not to say anything about white people, but throughout my life, it's like, I've had a good rela . . . you know, good relationships with white people I've never had to feel, um, that being black, that they've stopped me from doing what I've had to do. I have had a couple of incidents where I felt, like, if I wasn't black they wouldn't speak to me this way. I've had like two incidents. And, you know, and this school is one incident that has made me feel that way, has made me feel that I'm a single parent, and my son and my children are in a category, and they're already categorized. And, um, I feel that him being a white teacher he's not really, looking past all those prejudices and looking at, these children as children. There's not that many of them that do, you know?

[Do you feel trapped by the underprivileged world?]

It's hard, like at least you understand and that's because you, you've like, um, lived on both sides, but that's okay it's good to do that. It's too bad that everybody doesn't do that. There's not enough black people that haven't lived on, on a, on the side of white people or have assimilated, we, we've had to assimilate their culture, but, between minorities, like Caribbeans and, and you know Puerto Ricans, all the other Caribbean islands, African Americans won't, assimilate into their culture, and they won't do the same into ours, and we're all the same. If you would just take a bit and piece of everybody, you know we would understand, each other better. Yeah! Because everybody has their own culture and their own values, and culture has a lot to do with you know, where you get your values from, and there may be things that you may be doing, that I could say I really don't agree with, but it's culturally okay for you! Just like it's culturally okay for me. I, I have a white teacher, friend of mine, who was saying, oh, um, people, they should have it from like the government where there are certain ways you should raise your children. So I said, let me tell you something, I dare anybody to tell me how to raise my kids! I made them, and I take care of them! And what you may think

Isadora Sahl

is right for your kids may not be right for mine! I said, and you being white, your way of raising kids, you don't believe in hitting children, see but I do, I didn't at one time, I was into that Piaget and all of that stuff and I thought that was it and then I said wait, that psychology shit is out the door, it's time for me to kick some ass! This is not, I can't talk to my kids and say, honey, you really need to, it's not like that, I had to really show them; if you mess with me, I'm a hurt you! As much as it was against my whole, my whole thing of doing it, it was just against me, even though I was raised to be, hit like that, but I didn't want to do it to Salim and Aisha, and I, I didn't really have to until they turned out to be teenagers! We had to go, fist to fist with that, it wasn't like: I'm gonna beat you, like my mother did, but I had to use some violence, which in a white world would be, I was abusing my kids! But that what's they'd think. And I had to tell her no way! You have no right, and no one has any right to tell somebody how to raise your children. And sometimes, you may think it's wrong and the kid comes out fine, and he'll thank his mother for doing whatever it was! So, you can't you know, but that's how people think, it's terrible.

. . .

Before I lived here I lived on Columbia St. with my mother. I used to live on Ludlow St. when, I was born on Ludlow St. on the lower East Side, and I lived with my Mom and my Father, my Mom and my Dad. Then when I was about three we moved to the projects.

Whatever, then we moved to the projects. I was about four or five, then we lived on Baruch drive, with my father for about a year, a year or two. Um, then I lived with my Mommy until I was about 19, on Columbia St., and, then I got married to Aisha's Father and we, we, we lived in two places. I lived on 2nd street for a couple of months. Still on the lower East Side, then after 2nd street. I moved to 4th street. I lived on 4th street for about three months, and then I moved to 595 FDR Drive, that's still in Baruch. I lived there, I lived there, 'til . . . I'm a tell you, just wait . . . Salim was about, I been living here about 9 years, 10 years. Salim was about 13 when we moved here? I lived there for about 12/13 years and then I moved here. So I been living here, Salim was 13, Aisha Was 10, I think he was 12, Salim was 12 when I moved here, And Kai must have been, 8 from 12 is what? I'm bad, Kai was about 4. Kai's 12 now, so I been here about 8 years, it'll be 9 yrs. in July. I been living here 9 yrs. The reason why I got the projects was because Aisha's father was a—was a Veteran, and so when we applied and because he was a Vietnam Veteran we got top priority. So we applied to the projects and we got in here in like 8, 9 months. Because he was a Veteran. So that's how I got this apartment, really. Cause once you get into the projects then you're here, you're in.

Now, this is gonna be a good story. In FDR Drive was a two bedroom apartment, okay? and I lived there with me, Aisha, Salim and then Kai Hsing came! It's very crowded now because Aisha and Salim shared a room and then I shared a, and then I had, so now here I had all three of them in a room, but Kai was just small then so it wasn't too bad. What happened is, for some reason the lady downstairs, she started to complain, and she went to housing she put me through a lot of charges. She complained to housing, and she got the cops to come to my door, and knock. 8 o'clock in the evening the cops would come to the door and they would say: "We got a complaint of noise but, there's nothing happening here!" So I says no we're sitting watching, me and my children are sitting here watching television. So she kept on complaining, the cops kept coming and I says "What's going on?" Housing called me in and I was working I didn't have time to take days off, finally I took a day off, and they told me that, I met the assistant manager, she said well she's complaining that you make excessive noise. She brought me down, she sent me a summons. What she did was she got, she did this for a couple of months, she went down to criminal court and got, brought, brought up charges on me, that I made excessive noise. Criminal court now! I had a subpoena! To appear in court, I had to take a day off! I had to go to court. I went in front of the judge, the judge looked at the summons he says: "first of all, you know, he said okay what's the complaint?" I said, well your honor she is complaining that I make a lot of noise, and I really don't know what she's talking about. And, the judge says: "first of all, we don't do this here, this is not charges that we take up in this courtroom." He said "you'll have to go speak to a mediation court, where they settle this kind of problem." There's a word they call this, something like residential problems whatever. So, that lady started screaming: "No! You don't know what she does, she makes so much noise I can't sleep, late at night." And he said: "Miss, you need to calm down, we don't take care of this here." She made a big scene, I was very calm. So then we go into court, we go into this mediation center. And I tell you, Izzy, she put me through a lot of changes, she was constantly harassing me, knocking, you know, sending the cops up. And I was just, I was going through a lot of changes as it was, you know with Kai's father and all of this is happening, I think had just started school too. Just started school. I said "oh no they coming after me. I'm trying to do something positive, and here come this thing on top of me." Everything is, and I left Kai's father, I'm on my own now, I'm going to school take care of my kids when I got to do every, now, here we go. Housing is you know, like, believing this lady? Until I finally go in and say, you know, listen, why is she doing this to me? I don't, I've never had any problems. So the lady who was in housing, she got to like me, you know and she said "well, you know," and I said "you were siding with her," she said, "we didn't know who you were" and this and that. I said "she's making complaints and I'm not even there. I work and I go to school, I'm not home, my kids aren't home until the evening and they got to get up and leave the house at 7 o'clock in the morning, how late could we be possibly up?!" So then I made a deal with her at the office, she said: "We can't move her from that building, but, you got to be kidding, we can move you to a three bedroom." Housing doesn't do that. Once you're in, and got one bedroom and you have twenty kids you gonna have to live in that one bedroom, they don't give transfers, in here, they used to a long time ago, but it happened that, there's no people, there's no a, they're not making a, middle income or low income buildings anymore. So people are desperate to get in here, because unless you make a good amount of money it's hard to find a place to live! So, I said okay, they said "well where do you wanna live?" I said "well I would prefer," they said well do I have a preference. Where would like? So I said "I'd like to live up on Columbia, because my Mom and my Aunt live here." And the schools and the stores are closer cause I was all the way back there. Leaving that building. That building is locked! It's quiet, it was clean. I could leave my door open. My neighbors knew my kids. I was very comfortable in there. I could send Salim and Aisha down in front of the building they would watch them. That's how the building really was. So, it was hard, it was hard for the kids, leaving their home. "Come on guys," I said "we're gonna move," but they didn't like it. I said we're gonna, we didn't, we didn't know when we were gonna move but they said in the contract they asked me if I wanted to live on FDR Drive, I said no, I don't. If I have to wait it out, I'll wait it out until, until the building I want comes through.

I go to court, the lady she's there, she's bitching and complaining, she said that I can't live with the policy, she said: "I can hear bobby pins drop on the floor." They already knew she was whack see, yeah they knew that something ya know, and housing knew! They moved her to my building cause my building was the quietest building, and she had been complaining in the other building she lived in she had problems with it. So they said, "well, we'll put her in a building that's quiet and people are good, how much problems could she have?" But she managed to harass me! And she just moved into the building, everybody else in the building knew me cause I'd been there since I was pregnant with Aisha! So, so we were all very comfortable, we all knew each other, and here comes this lady from nowhere harassing me! They were like "oh my god are you in trouble?" Yeah, so she said that I dropped bobby pins and I made noise 'til 2, 3 o'clock in the morning, I never seen her! I didn't intervene, you know, cause I you know, cause I wanted to get us out of there. I was like then it be my turn and I can testify. I left my number so they could contact me at work, and I go to school. How I'm up 'til she said 2, 3 o'clock in the morning. There ain't no way I could hang out up til 2 o'clock in the morning, and get up to go to work. My kids, and I said my children leave at 7:15 in the morning. They get up about 6:30 I got to get them breakfast and they're out by 7:15, cause they gotta get on a bus to get to school. So, she had no idea you know, that she's busted. So they dropped it and they said okay, you know just make sure you know, that then she said she had heard the big wheel, the big wheel you know Salim had a big wheel. They said okay well, try not to have the big wheel in the house if you know the kids ride it, they made up some bullshit that would end it, but, in essence it helped me cause I got to move out. And I got a 3 bedroom.

The reason why I have this apartment is, this apartment was, a good friend of mine, he lived here with his mother and father, and he told me: "My mom and dad are leaving this apartment." And this apartment was in good condition because his father had made like you know little improvements and it wasn't falling apart. And my aunt lived in this building so he said May, go to housing, and tell them you know that this family is leaving! And you tell them that you want this apartment. So I went up to housing, I told them about this apartment and they knew about the problem and that there ain't no problem, they knew that, they wanted to get this problem witnessed, this lady kept comin-in, still complaining even after we went to court! She still was going into housing complaining about me! So they wanted to get her off my back. So they said, okay we gonna let you have it. So start getting ready, it's gonna take about a month painting and do stuff, okay. Pack, I pack my stuff. I'm all ready. I had, there's a guy you go to in housing that, you let him, he puts you down for the apartment that you're supposed to get. And I noticed when he put my name down he put it in pencil, I didn't think nothing of it. So now weeks are goin by and I know that, now, he don't know that I know the people that lived here. See, I know the people left and I'm waiting like what's up with the key? I'm packed, boxes and everything. I go in there the guy tells me "ooh my goodness!" "Oh I gave that apartment to somebody else. Oh I, I don't know how that happened." I be like wait a minute, but I came in here, I specifically and told you that I wanted that apartment. I told you my aunt lives in the building, I have small children, I need to be near. This way I have some help with my kids. Um . . . but that was a way for me to get in here. And the guy says "Wow I gave the apartment up, can you take another one?" I says "no, but, you said you were gonna give me this one!" "Oh well uh, we'll have to think of something else." Now everybody, for some reason, everybody in the housing office they knew me, because I was in there a lot and they knew me. So, my assistant, you know everybody like has an assistant that helps you with your housing problems? She said, "come here!" And she called me over so she could see. She went to the manager she said "listen this is the lady that's been having problems with that tenant and you know we're trying to get her out, and she was promised this apartment in 140, now the guy who does the transfers says that they don't have it anymore, she's gotta take another one, she's been prepared to go, blah-blah-blah." He said, "well, hold on." He called him, he said "you got the apartment." He said, "here are the keys." What happened is, that guy, he, found out later on that this man was taking money from underneath the table, and somebody wanted this apartment, and he had already got money and told them, he can have it. But, somebody overrid him, you know the manager, usually the top people never know what's going on, but because this lady liked me, she pushed, and I got it.

So then we moved in here and this is not the nicest building because they used to sell drugs all in the front of the building. They'd be lined up at 12 or 1 o'clock. Cause then I started working at daycare so, I would come home at lunch time, thick with people! Because they were trying to—see what they were doing at that time was there was drugs being sold on the avenue right here. They pushed them out from there and they came to this building. So, this building was like oh man, and that door, no, it was never locked. It was always broken, okay, so my kids had to live here. My kids hated it. Oh, they hated it, Salim just hated it hated it hated it, because they weren't used to being you know, you know we live in the neighborhood we were fortunate to live in a build-ing that was you know, you walk in, it's clean, no graffiti. You could walk in the hall with your shoes off, that's how clean the building was, and it was a project! It was part of this projects but it was clean. And the people lived there were there for a long, a lot of years so, they were good people and housing didn't just move anybody in there, they were particular about who they moved in the building because they knew the building was a good building and they wanted to keep it that way. Now I heard it's coming down, it's not as good, but still, compared to this one. We lived through a lot in here. Then, for some reason, the building changed, I don't know why. It changed. No more drugs, no crime, they did a whole new, in the last couple of you know, in the last couple of years it's been pretty good, Like 5, 6 years. They got rid of all the drugs. Now we got a lot of kids, cause they hang-out in the building. That's where the graffiti comes. Cause there's a lot of kids in the building and there's no control. And there should be cops here, especially on this corner, because this is an active, corner. So there should be cops always around getting the kids out. But at lunchtime the kids come in the building, eat in the building; they smoke, they do whatever. So, that's how I'm here. And I hate it with a passion.

The only thing nice about this apartment is I have a beautiful view of the river, I have a nice view of uh, um uh, the city, that's it.

[Is the rent the same as the old apartment?]

Same rent, it goes by my income. I'm at the high, right now I've reached the, I pay 600, I pay, okay, I have air conditioning, I have to pay for the air conditioning outlet, I have to pay for it. I pay, like 7 dollars a month and I have two, I really have four, but I just pay for two. I have to pay to, as far as the maintenance, because I use an air conditioner I pay 14 dollars a month. Plus our parking is like 11 dollars and 40 cents, a month. With all of that and my rent at 619, I pay 645, a month. Now, 619 I'm like, see right now, what they used to do with housing is it goes by income. When I get a raise, they get a raise. But right now there's a thing called a ceiling. The ceiling for a 3 bedroom apartment, in housing is 619. I've reached the maximum. This ceiling, if I don't question them, they try to rip me off, but I already know my rights, they have to keep my rent at 619 for the next 5 years. That's how I'm a get out of here! With my income going up, they can't charge me anymore rent, cause that's a lot of money for a shit place like this. For 300 dollars more I could live in a nice place. Like for 900 dollars even 850 I can, live in a nice place. But, I figure, my plan is, I'll stay here, and I know my rent's not gonna go up, and when I leave here it's not gonna be to an apartment I'm, I'm, we really wanna move into a house. Cause that's, that's what I wanna do! How I'm gonna do it, I have a few things. I have, I have a few things I been working on for the last couple a years, you know like these new projects that you can, you know you put a little stake in it and one of it is, like, living in housing I been getting a lot of things um, people that live in housing they try to get them houses on a lower, uh, cheaper, uh, like they build up certain areas, like in Staten Island and Queens and the Bronx. So I've applied to those places. Now even though . . . really I don't make enough money. Cause my salary is about 28,000 dollars, right now. Now, when I graduate, it's gonna be more. I'm waiting for a raise right now, plus we're gonna get raises, there's a lot of things, plus I work overtime. When I work in the summer, that's 6,000 dollars overtime that I make. Plus I work after school. That's another 6,000 dollars.

So I make 12,000 dollars a year just on overtime. So that's how I make my, and overtime is a lot, because the 6 weeks I work in the summer is, working every day from 8:30 to 2:30, that's how teachers get over. Then I tutor in the afternoon 2 days a week, I make 30 dollars an hour for 5 hours a week. So, you know . . . for 5 hours. It's in a group home with juvenile delinquents. These girls are rough! These are group homes where girls, girls have, are put in there because, they, got no place to live. And they, most of them aren't in school, and I have to tutor them. They're very hardcore girls, they been in jail, they do drugs, they been pregnant, they been stoop sisters. They've been fucked-up. . . . So I do that, I like it, it's interesting. It's sad . . .

I'm in a program, in the board of ed, it's called citywide program. Which is special ed, it, it's special ed, but this program is funded more than the regular special ed. So I gotta go, these kids in citywide programs you got, emotionally disturbed children, you got the multiple handicapped, these are severe, these are special children. Learning disability is one of the 40 other problems that they have. That's, they put these kids in the citywide program. We have a 12 month program for them. Now, you as a teacher don't have to do it. It's up to you, I like to work in the summer, I have a job. What happens is, I get paid, they give me 5 checks that I regularly get. But then, I get paid every 2 weeks during the summer. So I have my regular paycheck, that I would get anyway, and then I get the extra money for working in the summer. And I get 3 weeks off! Now I could have the whole 2 months of summer off, and I'd still get paid, I'd have my paycheck, but this is extra 3,000 dollars cash, after taxes I get. . . .

That's not including, now that I, I'm gonna have like, 3, 4? I had applied for a promotional differential, cause now I have a bachelor's, and I have 30 above my bachelor's and 36 in a specialty. So that's how the board of ed pays you. The more credits you got, the more money you make. That's how the board of ed works. You got more credits, it could be in uh, polar ice or, ice skating, you got the credits, they gonna give it to you. What happens is, let's say you came in with a, a bachelor's in, what's your major?

[Anthropology.]

You could be a teacher, but, you have to take 24 credits in education, and then you can education as your minor. But they gonna make you take some education classes, if you wanna stay there as a teacher. With me, I wanna be a teacher, so my master's is in special ed because that's where I wanna be.

See I have another plan, because my master's, most master's are about 30, 36 credits. Mine is 28, my school offers me, I'll give you another graduate, I'll give you an MEd which is a master's above a master's, for 12 more credits. I'm gonna have a MEd, which is a master's in education with a specialty in special ed. Now, if you came from another school, and you wanted that MEd, you gonna have to take 30 credits there. But, I already have, all the preliminary stuff they needed. I, I'm at the school, so they offered that to me, all I need is 4 classes and I have a MEd. So, oh, ho ho ho, so now what'll happen is, instead of me taking my differential in the board of ed, and saying that I have a master's, and then I have to get 30 above to get money, they also have something where you get, 60 above your bachelor's and then you get a raise, so I'm just gonna apply for the 60 above, cause instead of waiting to get, I, for me to get another 30 credits is stupid, because I don't need it. So I wouldn't need it, cause I, I had thought, I knew had to get my 30 above, because that's the only way to make a decent salary at the board. That's, cause, you can get it in anything, you could take anything, basket weaving, they don't care! And they offer a lot of classes for free. A lot of teachers will do that. But I don't wanna do it like that. I wanna degree. I want, something else. It's non-metric, so I'd rather just do this, so this summer, I'm gonna go for my MEd. 12 more credits, big deal! And they pay for it!

[What is the starting salary for a teacher?]

$20–26,000.

[Is that just special ed?]

No. No, regular ed and special ed make the same amount of money. $26? Yeah, and look how much I've gone up. And I've been there 4 years. We haven't had a contract, in almost 2 years. So were on a very low salary, and the board of ed has- I should really be a little higher than that. But they screwed me somehow. You know, they, they, we go a step every year, and I'm on another step, no, I'm about the right step but, we've gotten, the, the last contract we had made this deal where you all go one step together. It's like $500 increase, you know, a year. That's what we've been getting as an increase, $500. But now, I put in my differential, and I'm waiting. It's gonna be almost a year in June. I'm waiting. But they owe me from that time, they pay me for all that time, so I'm just waiting. It'll be a couple thousand dollars more on my salary. I'll make about $31,000. It still isn't a lot for a master's. It's stupid! Then I'll wait another year, when I finally complete my MEd, and then I'll apply for 60 above! That's gonna take them another year. That'll hike it to about, see, depending on, it's maybe $34,000,.. yeah, cause I'll be up to, it'll be about $34,000, $35,000. That's still not a lot of money.

But I really don't plan to stay with the board, I really don't. My plans are to, get, get what I can out of them, all of the experience. Cause the board of ed will teach you, you know, they can throw you in situations that, are impossible and, if you can do that, I think that you have a good background, I feel I've been lucky, I've had a good background, you know I have a lot to offer kids, and there are people that work in, that make these decisions, that don't even have, never have been in the classroom and taught, and they're the ones that tell, make curriculums up. How do they get in!? They only get in the position because they, they have a job experience, but not in the field of education. In supervising, making proposals, you know, stuff like that, but they couldn't tell you a child from a frog, you know they just don't know enough. And they don't, they make the decisions and hopefully, you know I'll eventually get into that kind of thing, were I can go in there and, and really help the children. So that's it.

Except, someday you'll come to my beautiful house. I wish I could design my own house. Oh man! I could tell you some, I'd like a house where you know, like, upstairs it would be my bedroom and then I could look over, like have it like a deck sort of. Like a loft, where I could look down into my living room, with a nice fireplace right there in my living room. Oh my god! My kitchen would have to be, huge! Big counter in the middle, cabinets all over the place! Spiral staircase right in the middle of the living room you know? Oh man, to go upstairs, ah, yeah! That's it! . . . You never know!

I, I'm hopeful. We'll try to get a house someplace. It doesn't make sense to go, to another apartment . . .Well, you know, they have some houses in the Bronx, that they're um, building. I've seen it! And they're building houses there and what they're offering is, you have to make about $40,000; about, $40,000. It's a 3-family house, so, now I could have somebody move downstairs. I gotta have, I need about, maybe $4,000, to put down. And I don't even have that. So, that's what we're, I'm working on. I'm trying to save money this year. Try to put every penny I have in the bank. Maybe something'll come through or, you never know, I, I have a lot of people, that I'd be surprised, that would lend me the money. You know that's, you know, I've been lucky like that, you know and people believe me, they know I'm not the kind, you know, the kind of person would rip them off or something like that. You know and then I know that Salim's case is still, on. So, I know, you know, that that's gonna come through, eventually! It could take 3 years, it could take 5 years. Meanwhile I could buy this house, and let's say I borrowed money from somebody, hey I'll tell 'em: I guarantee you you're gonna get your money back because, even if I go my daughter will give it to you! Because the money is coming! It's just that I don't have it now, I don't, most of the people that I am close to know that, so, if I can save half of it and, just borrow the rest, then hey! I'm gonna do my best. That's what I'm really working on, but we're gonna go see what the house looks like first.

Study Questions

1. Do you think Isadora comes across differently in her written introduction versus her self-introduction in her taped interview with me? How different is her voice in the two? How different is the content?
2. In how many different ways does this life history show that "poverty is a matter of life and death"?
3. How does Isadora challenge your ideas of what it means to be poor?
4. To what extent does Isadora's interviewee conform to stereotypes of poor urban single mothers? In what ways does she differ?

Notes

1. All my interviews were conducted before digital recorders were available.
2. This section was originally the first chapter of her senior BA thesis
3. Required of all Purchase College seniors.
4. Educational Opportunity Program for poor and educationally disadvantaged students.

6

Onalie Mesa Oakstar

One of things that turned Onalie Oakstar on to anthropology was the discipline's long and abiding interest in kinship and the family. She was delighted to learn that there are numerous family types beside the nuclear family in cultures throughout the world, all perfectly functional, and all adapted to the social and economic circumstances that produced them. Commonplace information in anthropology thus stands in marked contrast to the popular Euro-American conception—occasionally finding voice in political circles in the United States under the rubric "family values"—that the nuclear family is both universally ideal and normative.

Onalie's interest in the anthropology of family and kinship stems from the fact that she was raised in a single-parent household, and she found the experience overwhelmingly positive. Although she recognizes that some children might be disadvantaged or negatively affected by being raised by a single parent, she is not convinced that this must of necessity be true, and is interested in presenting an alternate opinion.

She does not believe that single parenting is preferable to the nuclear family, but she does think that each case must be viewed independently of cultural customs and norms. In addition, she believes that there are deeper values that can override issues of surface structure. For example, she believes it is preferable to live in a single-parent family filled with love than in a conventional nuclear family devoid of love. She also recognizes that the nuclear family meets certain needs of a child that a single-parent family cannot, so that even in a single-parent household, those needs must be met somehow. If, for example, a child in a nuclear family becomes alienated from one parent, there is still another parent to turn to, so that the child is not left isolated and alone. In a single-parent household the danger of alienation is potentially greater, and the child may therefore fear alienating the only parent it has if there is no one else to turn to. But, aunts or neighbors can serve as parent surrogates to turn to when estranged from one's only parent. Thus, the deficiencies of single-parent households need not be fatal weaknesses.

Onalie was pleased to discover that one of her fellow students at Purchase College also had an unusual family structure that he, too, was very comfortable with. For the early part of his life, Ben was raised by his biological mother as a single parent, but when he was a teenager she entered a stable lesbian relationship, and Ben ended up with two mothers. Overtly, he too is overwhelmingly positive about his family experience, although he acknowledges the rough spots in the transition from one to two mothers.

Onalie's interview with Ben, thus, functions as a self-affirmation for her own feelings. She can be reassured that she is not abnormal just because she was not only raised in but actually liked a family structure that the mainstream commonly sees as abnormal (even though single-parent households are now statistically more common than classic nuclear families in the United States[1]). This interview was thus mutually supportive. As such, it was an extension of their basic friendship, which also had this supportive quality to it. What was interesting to me, and was frustrating for Onalie, was that Ben became nervous and easily distracted when she tried to capture the essence of their friendship on tape using my prescribed informal interview format.

The problem was solved when Onalie switched from audiotape to videotape. Ben was at that time in the acting program of the Division of Theater Arts and Film at Purchase College: a budding actor. Once a camera was turned on him, he was filled with poise and self-confidence, and he became willing to talk at great length about himself. What is presented here, therefore, is a transcription of the audio portion of the videotape.

Although Onalie's solution was ingenious, one might be led to wonder to what degree such a method created a self-conscious performance out of the life history process. My answer to this is twofold. First, I would argue that for whatever method is used, there is an element of self-conscious acting out a part in all life history interviews, so that what is produced here differs only in degree and not in type from the other interviews presented in this volume. I might also add that it is hard to conceive of an actor not performing when put in a formal interview situation (whether it be in front of a video camera or not). Second, when reading the interview, while there may be passages of self-reflection that appear to be in a somewhat rosily romantic vein, there are many others that are plainly self-critical or reveal obvious weaknesses.

Another important feature of video use was that it gave me greater insight into certain aspects of the interview process than usual. This is because Onalie set up the video camera on a tripod so that it could take in the whole of the sofa where Ben was sitting; because Onalie sat beside him on the sofa to conduct the interview, both were on camera all the time. I was able to see her gestures and behaviors as much as his, even when she was doing nothing but listening. In general it was much easier for me to give a general critique of her interview technique than if I had access to an audiotape only. Because of this, the tape is even now occasionally useful as a teaching tool in my fieldwork class.

Onalie presents the interview here somewhat like a long actor's soliloquy. This is reasonably faithful to Ben's way of talking. Onalie actually asked very few questions and did not interrupt or fill pauses when they occurred; she simply let him talk and tell his own story in his own time.

Life History

I went to private school—to a Quaker school—from Kindergarten to second grade. In that school I made one really close friend who's still one of my best friends. His name is Glen. Then I went to school in Jenkintown from third grade on. It's where I grew up. Jenkintown is a small town; it was and is a major part of my life. It really shaped my life, because Jenkintown isn't normal as far as towns go. It's very very small. My class—I graduated with twenty-eight people. So it was like I went to school with these people forever. So I knew everything about everybody. The school was small. We didn't have to have cars because we walked to everybody's houses. But then some of us had cars. I drank a lot when I was around sixteen—well, like tenth grade. I drank a lot and then stopped drinking when I started smoking pot. Smoked pot a lot. Jenkintown was just really fun. But as far as an artist is concerned. It didn't nurture me as an artist. I was an artist as much as I could be in Jenkintown. But I was caught up in the logistics of being in high school: the girlfriends and all that shit.

When I was a kid my mom worked all the time. She works at the university school of social work. She's a field placement person. She places people after school. When I was younger I would go to an after-school program, I don't know how long. And then for a period of time I had a babysitter after school named Jane who was also kind of a housekeeper. Jane was really cute even though I wasn't old enough to understand why. But I really thought she was hot. She had a Camero—like a black Camero, or something, with silver seats. It was so fucking cool. I had a cat when I was a kid, named Foxy Moses Baumen. We got the cat—someone came to our door, with Foxy in a basket. And I wanted to name him Foxy, and my mom named him Moses because he came in a basket. He died while Jane was there and that was a trauma because I had never dealt with that before. It's really vivid. I then got a kitty cat who's still alive. She's like twelve, and I love her tremendously. I feel very connected to her. The thought of losing her is a really scary thing to me, and it's something I don't give much power to because I'm afraid of it. She's a major part of my life.

My mom and Margaret started dating—you know—seeing each other, but I didn't know that that's what was going on. I just thought that they were friends. We'd go over to Margaret's house for some time and hang out, and she'd come over. That was around when I was twelve. I remember that Margaret wasn't at my bar mitzvah because they had gotten into some kind of fight around then before she moved in. I hadn't a clue about what was going on. Then Margaret moved in. Maybe I was thirteen and a half, or something. So she started to become a part of my life. I'm jumping from subject to subject. Let's see—I had always been able to relate to women—to girls—like in high school. And I was always able to do that really easily, I think because I was raised by just my mom. There's a huge feminine side that I am able to be connected with. I figure that's a very good thing.

I played football for junior high and then for the first year of my high school. I liked it. I liked the feeling of hitting people hardcore. I liked that but it really wasn't my thing. So I stopped doing that, and I managed the girls' lacrosse team from ninth grade to eleventh grade. And then twelfth grade I helped coach the junior high team. But tenth grade I decided I wanted to play girls' lacrosse because we didn't have a guys' lacrosse team. I played the goalie and I got a lot of shit for it. But I really felt good about it. And the other teams started forfeiting games and wouldn't play us because I was a man. Even though they said that it was dangerous for a man to be on the field. Even though I was in the goal and these girls were coming up to me—throwing these hard fucking rubber balls—four hundred miles an hour at me. And I'm the dangerous one! So I backed down and I stopped playing so the girls could have a chance to play. But I got in all the newspapers and stuff. And really I wasn't that good either, which is the ironic part.

I have always been an artist, but I never knew what it was to be an artist until I got to Purchase. I was, technically, a really gifted visual artist. So I would always produce these things that really looked cool and looked good, and people would be amazed. But I didn't know what I was doing it for. I didn't have a reason to do the art. I just did it. And for most of my youth, that didn't bother me at all. It got to be senior year in high school and I had to decide what I wanted to do for college. I just started becoming blocked as far as my artwork went, and I couldn't figure out why. I was so frustrated: I couldn't do anything that I liked, and I didn't know why. I came to Purchase for a portfolio review, and I got into all the colleges. I got into the best art schools in the country, but I just freaked out because I didn't know what I was doing. Then I came and I heard a lecture on the acting department here, and they made it sound as if acting was something that could happen, you know, that you could make a career out of—which is something I had never thought of even though I loved being on stage. I was on stage a lot in high school. There was a core of us who did these plays with a man named Tom Large who was the English teacher. He also directed these plays. There was, like, five of us, and we did everything. We built the sets. I made the posters, I designed the posters. We acted in it. I did the sound for some of them. And it was just like we did everything. It was like what real theater is about, even though I didn't know what real acting was. So I came to hear this lecture, and they convinced me that that's what I was meant to do. I came here. The first year was really tough. I had to deal with a lot of stuff I didn't understand. As far as emotional life went, it was the hardest that year—that year and the summer after it. It was the hardest year I ever had to go through because there was so much growing that needed to happen, and a lot of diving into the unknown. What I learned was that art and life go hand in hand. I needed to learn things about my life and my relationship with my parents and people before I learned what I needed to learn in acting. And it caused a lot of havoc in the house. Me and my moms, we never really fought. Everything was always hunky-dory, you know, in an OK way—because, I mean, it was OK to live that way as an adolescent. Then when I had to become an adult, it was hard for my mom to take because it had to do with communicating with each other on the same level: on an adult level. It was hard for her to take. Our relationship up to then had always been . . . Everything was . . . Anything that we wanted, that she wanted or I wanted—we'd get it through guilt. Instead of just asking for something it would be like "oh I wish I could go out to dinner tonight." Or, I don't know, she'd say "hey, you want to go out to dinner?" Oh, I don't know—and that kind of thing. Instead of my mom—let's say she wants me to go get her a Coke, she'll whine about it, or something, you know. She'll be like . . . oh it bugs me to think about it. So I started dealing with that. I started being totally honest with her, with everything. I knew that I had to just start saying what was on my mind, because that's how I needed to free myself emotionally. And I just started doing that. It freaked my mom out and we got into all these troubles. And I was having a hard time because I was going through that summer. I was having my heart broken at the same time.

I feel that a broken heart is the hardest thing I ever had to deal with. At the same time I'm a different person. I feel like I understand life more than anybody because of that. Now that that is over, in a sense—myself as an artist, an actor especially—there is so much that one has to act that's on a level that's hard to understand without experiencing it. There's nothing, there's no thing more painful than that. So I kind of feel like I've gone there—to the depths of myself—and seen what it's like in there, in the darkest place, and learned from it. Mom had a hard time understanding what that was all about. I think she could probably feel threatened in a way if I had another woman in my life. She supported me being an artist, although I'm not quite sure she understands what it is to be an artist, why it is I did things that I had convictions about, that I did in order to be different because I liked to set myself apart from people. I don't know if she understood that. I don't even know if I understood that. I really want to work in the theater. I have what it takes as far as looks goes, and talent, to do the Hollywood thing, to make a lot of money. The only reason I want to do that . . . Well there's two reasons. One reason is so I can make money and so the moms can stop working and that I can set them up. Because I really want her to stop working soon, because I want her to be able to live life—live on the coast of California. The other reason that I want to be famous is so that I can go on the Howard Stern Show. But other than that there's nothing really great about being famous. Because that's when basically life changes. That's the part that scares me. So I'm always in a dilemma about that, although I see myself going in that direction. It's just going to happen. But once I have the money, I can do whatever I want in the theater. Nobody in this country understands theater anymore. I want my mom to be able to stop working. I mean I want her to keep working, maybe I want her to sculpt again. She used to be a sculptor. I want to switch the roles, you know, because that's what should happen. I mean, this country is so fucked up. They put their parents in homes when they just don't want to deal with them anymore. I really feel that the role switches at one point. That the child should take care of the parents. I want to buy the moms matching Lexus, you know, I want them to be set up.

Margaret—in high school it was always "why the fuck is she there? Why is she there man? Why is she there? What right does she have to tell me to take out the trash? She doesn't live here." There was always that in high school, that was partly, I'm sure, feeling threatened by her since she was now obviously a major part of my mother's life. Here I am, the single child spoiled beyond belief, and this other person comes in and takes over. When she first moved in she didn't have her own phone line. She was always on the fucking phone, and I'm just like, "get out of here, I don't need this shit, you know, fuck." But there was never a problem with her being a woman, which is something I take pride in—being so open about people—coming from Jenkintown. Jenkintown was utterly shielded from the real world. We had one black kid; his name was Jim. And to the Jenkintonians he wasn't black because he was Jim, and we grew up with him. There was a lot of ignorance in Jenkintown. I was on the forefront of speaking out against the ignorance and I always got into arguments with people about that. And people would always blow it off. I think that even though they acted like they were blowing it off, I feel that I made a lot of people think, you know, I made a lot of people open their eyes and wonder what they felt and why they felt these things. By the end of high school people would always apologize if they said something that was ignorant in front of me. I could tell that my presence would make them speak a little differently. So I was always proud of that and . . . back to Margaret. It wasn't until the summer—that summer— the summer after my freshman year. It wasn't until after that summer that Margaret and I . . . I mean we had an OK relationship, but now it's like, I mean she's definitely my mother. She's definitely that part of my life now. And it's fantastic to have two mothers who spoil you. I mean, she gives me money each month the same as my mother does—well, not as much—but she gives me "mother money" every month. Anytime I want art supplies she's like my—what do you call it?—my patron. She's my artistic patron. She supports me; she's there for me. If I need her we can talk about anything. Definitely a parent—and I'm extremely grateful to have that, you know. So many people I know don't have one parent that loves them, I have two that believe that I am the greatest thing that was ever produced in the history of the universe. Support like that is essential. Support like that is a gift from the goddess. The gift from the goddess. As a kid we're talking about turning that stepparent relation-ship into something that's meaningful, and I know so many stepparents that just don't do that because they themselves aren't in a place where that's possible, you know. I feel that it's the stepparent that needs to make the first step because a child doesn't know. A child has a hard time understanding what's going on, you know. It's hard to see a parent fall in love with somebody else. Margaret was really good at that and it wasn't until I came into my own that I could return it to her. Yeah, I think it's a big relief to her that it became that way.

I can't remember when it was. I'm pretty sure that I figured it out—what the deal was—pretty early on, you know. But I didn't—I mean my mom—they never actually told me until I was leaving for college. But I knew what was going on because they slept in the same room. My mom brought me up—raised me so that something like that wouldn't even faze me, wouldn't bother me at all. Though she didn't trust that—I guess because she was scared to tell me for some reason. I always tried to, like, trick her into telling me, or something. Like "yo, why do you and Margaret sleep in the same room? Why doesn't she just take that room?" And this and that. And, "oh well because it's easier. We don't have to, you know, get a new bed. It's easier this way, you know." Stupid things like that. I don't know why she never told me. But there were times when, like—first year or so—maybe a little less, a little more, there was tension between Margaret and me because . . . I don't know, just because. There was, you know . . . Like, she'd really get on my nerves easily. I'd be like, "why is Margaret always on the phone?" She used to be on the phone a lot. She's a social worker too; they're both social workers.

I guess I was in seventh or eighth grade when it started. Come ninth grade I started dealing with it on my own because, you know, friends would come over and I would have to, you know, explain what's going on here. So I assumed that they were lesbians, and that's what I told everybody. And, Jenkintown is a small town. They're not really exposed to many things like that, you know. I'm, like, one of three Jews there, there's about four black people, and nobody ever knew what a gay person was. So what I did was make everybody accept that that was the case, and so it wasn't strange. And it worked. That was my way of dealing with it in school with my friends. A year later and everybody knew what the moms were, you know. If I said "the moms" everybody would know what it was, and it was accepted. I mean, we have a really good relationship. For the last, like, three years of high school we had a good relationship. If my mom was away and Margaret was there she'd be, like, the mom. I got arrested once for having beer in my car and she had to come pick me up at the police station. And I hang out with Margaret as much as I hang out with my mom. We spend days together the same way my mom and I spend days together. And I call her at home, you know, and when we go on vacation we all go on vacation together. Like I said, they both support me here at school, and Margaret paid for all my guitar lessons last year. She pays for most of my artistic things—magic markers and artistic supplies. And Margaret taught me how to drive a stick. I don't know many people who have a really good relationship with their parents the way I have with Margaret and my mom. I mean, surface-wise, it doesn't look like it's normal, but it's more normal than

Onalie Mesa Oakstar

most of the people I know. I can talk to either of them about anything. They're both social workers, so it's like having two shrinks in the house.

It was the day before I left for college, and my mom took me out to eat. And she told me . . . well, she asked me "what do you think about Margaret and me?" And so I realized that this was it—that she was finally telling me. And I was like—"well, I'm kinda"—well I told her that I was—that of course it, it, of course it, you know, doesn't bother—and that I—"that I'm a little disappointed in her for not trusting herself and the way that she raised me—that she couldn't have told me before—and that I've known all this time—that everybody in Jenkintown knows because that's the way I dealt with it." And so she was really happy and also she felt bad. I mean she was crying—everything was really happy. And then, you know we saw Margaret—Margaret was crying. They were both really happy that they could finally get it off their backs, you know.

My grandma used to live in Florida, so when I was a young kid we went to Florida every Christmas. We would hang out with her in Florida; Miami. I remember her house pretty well. I was a young kid. I don't remember when she moved. She moved to Atlanta eventually, which is where my Aunt Ruthie, my mom's sister, lives with my cousins Lisa and Todd. But, I remember we'd go down there and we'd go to the beach sometimes. And my mom and I would go—every year we'd go. We had a ritual where we'd go to Burger King and get burgers and we'd go to the airport and watch the airplanes land and take off which was, like, I loved. I've always been obsessed with flight and Superman. I was a Superman fan. So airplanes really amazed me. Later, in high school, we'd either go to Miami or Atlanta—whatever.

Later when Margaret was living with us she'd go with us, she'd go with us wherever we went. During the summer I went to camp and then at the end of the summer for a week we'd go—my mom and my best friend Roger who lived up the street would go . . . I mean, one year Margaret came up with us, I mean, that was later . . . One year my grandma came up there . . . One year a friend of my mom's came up . . . to the mountains near Ithaca college. It was a place called Montour Falls—really small. The postcard would always say "where in the hell is Montour Falls." Small place. And they had this mountain house—Nettie and Erwin. It was on the side of this mountain and the house was really beautiful. They built it; it was wood. And there was a lake, a small lake there—and it was all really private. It was theirs. And that view was really amazing. It was just such a fantastic place. And Rog and I would fish. All we'd do there is just sit at the lake—at the lake all day and fish—and swim in the lake. And we'd be kids and just play in nature. Later, I don't remember when, Erwin died and Nettie had to sell the place because things reminded her too much of him. I mean, Erwin was the first person in my life, who I knew that well, to die. He was a really great person. He told stories and stuff and I really like him. Recently, at the end of my freshman year, I went up . . . Roger went to Ithaca for a year and we went to get him—me and Josh from my company. During that we took a ride to Montour Falls—and drove up there and walked up to the mountain house just to see it. And nobody was living there because they hadn't sold it yet. And that was really emotional—to go up there and see that place. It was just so strange. So after the week in the mountains I would spend a week with the Brennars—Roger's family— and we'd go to the shore, the New Jersey shore, and spend a week there. That was after a whole summer of camp. And the shore is great. We'd just go there and be kids too. We'd play Uno a lot. I learned how to shuffle cards at the shore. One summer—one summer at the shore—this was the best thing that ever happened to us. We were at the shore. It was the summer right before my seventh grade—right before my first year in junior high school. In Jenkintown junior high and senior high were the same thing, I mean, they were in the same building. And we were at the shore, and it was, like, the last—it was the day before we had to go back and go to school. Uncle Buzzy—Roger's dad . . . We were sitting in the living room playing Uno and then he said "guys, I have some bad news. Jenkintown's on strike. You're going to have to stay here another week." We were, like, wooooo. And it was so awesome. Man, we just stayed another whole week. We did just, like, nothing. We just stayed there and had a great time. And it turned out that they were on strike for fucking three and a half weeks. And by the end of the strike we were like "Oh my God, let us please go back to school." It was funny.

My mother really brought me up well, I mean I was really . . . I knew a lot as far as where I was in my development. I still do, I mean, I was an older kid than most kids were, you know, so that I understood there was fear involved on her part, you know. And there was fear on my part too because I never really confronted her about it. So it never really—I mean, it didn't really bother me that much. I mean, it could have been a man. It wasn't really the coming out of it that got on my nerves, you know, but there were times when her presence—Margaret's presence— was the thing that bugged me out. You know, I lived my whole life with just my mom—like, I'm it for her. Then Margaret's all of a sudden this huge presence in the house. When she got there first, she was always on the phone, she was always on the phone. She finally got her own line. So there were lots of times when I was just like "man, why is this person—why is this person here?" She'd just taken up my space and all this stuff. But that had really nothing to do with the fact that they were lovers, or together like that.

Well, I didn't feel, like, that . . . I never felt as if they were lying to me. I felt as if they were too scared to tell me that they were . . . That it was a scary thing for them. But I didn't take it—I didn't take it as them lying. I didn't get mad at them for that because it really . . . I knew that it had its life and that it would eventually—that it would eventually come out. And the older I got, I mean, the more I talked to people about it. And my sister and my brother and like . . . And my sister said once that she walked in on them—which is like—I remember that conversation really well because that was, like—that was the absolute confirmation of what it—what I had thought. So that was really fantastic to hear because it was a confirmation. It was, like, definitely then, you know. Before I had just, like, guessed and I was pretty sure I was right. They slept in the same room. The more time we spent together, the more she came, I mean, the more that she became a part of my life, and the more she became a parent to me. My feelings for her were as a person not as a lesbian and as a stepparent too. I mean I think I had a relationship with her as a normal kid would have with a normal stepparent, you know, taking a healthy amount of time to accept that she's in my life. And, all the, like, the struggle or the growing that needs to happen in accepting something like that happened in a normal way. I feel—to me it was a great experience. I mean, I knew it at the time—just to know that I was able to accept that in such a quote unquote normal fashion. My friends accepted it because I accepted it and so now she's—she's—she's—my mom. She's my second mother and I talk to her. I talk to her as if . . . the same way I talk to my mother. And we talk about everything. She's like a second guide for me. Having two women in my life like that has definitely had an impact on my life. And now that I'm in a relationship—a serious relationship—with a woman, I realize that my knowledge of— of—of . . . I guess my accepting of the feminine side of me—which is a huge part of me—growing up with them . . . I have an understanding of what it is to be a woman in this society that we live in, and how hard it is. So now, that being in this relationship, and finding a woman who is very comfortable as a woman, and me comfortable as a man—I think that their being there, the moms, has informed me more than I can really convey: in every aspect of life—in theater—and understanding what it is to be a human being. And, a lot of men don't get that, you know. A lot of men are afraid of that side because of the society and how society portrays a woman, and how society portrays a man, and what that is meant to be. I am very grateful for having that experience.

I'm a very good communicator now as far as honestly communicating with them. Margaret's pretty good at that. My mom's not as good at communicating straight. But basically we all communicate pretty well. I mean it's my . . . I mean, it's my house as much as it's their house, you know. I have friends over when I want to. I mean, I'll ask if I can have friends over and I can entertain there. I mean, we all have . . . It's our house. It's Margaret's as much as it's mine, and it's my mom's as much as it's Margaret's. It works pretty well. There's not really a dictatorship in there. It's not like my mom is the dictator, although she is, like, the man of the house. She is, like, the head in, like, certain aspects. And, you know, it's definitely a different house when I'm not there. When I am there it just turns a little different. It just changes a bit because I leave my shit all over the place and they hate that.

The summer was a very big turning point in my relationship with them. I started seeing this therapist, Jackie, who was a gestalt therapist. And it was such a fantastic experience with her. I mean, I went in with a goal to achieve. I wanted to—I needed to open up my emotional life. I needed to be a good actor or else I was going to get kicked out of this program. I think a lot of actors' problems are that they focus . . . When there's a problem in the work they focus too much on the work and not on life. And it's in life that the problems have to be solved—that the problems have to be discovered and solved—before it can happen on stage. And so I found that out in that summer. We started working on my reacting to things—I mean, in the house with the moms. There'd be so much guilt involved—or guilt—and things that would cause things to happen inside and never come out as they actually happened—come out as a processed thought of what's going to happen if I do this. What's the best way of doing it? How will I change it so I can get what I want?— and all this bullshit. And so what happened was—with Jackie—I started working on that. I started reacting in life to what I honestly felt. And so all of a sudden in this house there's this one person who's reacting to things like that and being totally honest and it kind of came in conflict. There were big, big arguments that weren't—that didn't have to do . . . I mean it wasn't like they were aware of the reason that the conflicts happened was because I was being totally honest with them. They weren't really willing to accept that or willing to accept that the conflicts happened over stupid things. But the thing that I was clear about was that there wasn't really a way to say "look, we've got to start reacting" because they weren't—they weren't listening. "We have to be honest with each other." One thing that Jackie would always say to me was that it's me that feels guilty. They try to induce this guilt, but I'm the one that has control over feeling guilty or not. And so I stopped feeling guilty. When I stopped feeling guilty there was havoc because—because—because that's how we've always lived. So I guess I was clear on the fact that the way I'm going to get them to relate to me the way that I want to relate to them is just to keep going at this full speed. And eventually they started to accept the fact that that's the way I'm going to be and to communicate with me—if they have to communicate with me—the way that I want to be communicated with, or else there was going to be—or else there was nothing else to do. Around the same time—the end of my junior year—I fell in love for the first time (I'm now in love for the second time). And that experience, that year, was really amazing. And I'd felt nothing like it, and I really connected with this person. Her name is Season. After that, after we connected I went away to camp—to work the camp which was really . . . We were in the same place then and we could have gone from there and grown and grown and grown. But I left, and from then on we started growing apart. But I was still in love. I really realized that this is somebody that I really connected to—and you don't meet people like that very often, you know, it just happens that way. So this freshman year she started seeing somebody over at camp. She started seeing this other guy that she really liked. And so it was a big struggle my senior year. We were talking and not talking, and realizing that we were both in different relationships and all this stuff. And freshman year I was thinking a lot about her when I was at college, and always wondering "I need to go back and see if it's still there." Then we saw each other my freshman year—that summer—during that summer. We started seeing each other for about a week or so. What I realize now was that this was a really major point in her life where she had to make a decision about . . . I mean, she had been in this relationship for two years and what we had was still there in a sense. I mean, when we saw one another it was really amazing—the energy between us was still there. And she had to make a decision on whether she was going to pursue life with me or keep going with this guy. And I didn't realize I had to give here the space to do that, and I wasn't really giving her the space. And, she decided against staying with me which was really hard for me to accept. And I didn't accept it until this year. I mean, I guess I couldn't accept it. I didn't know what—I couldn't understand. I said, you know, "there can't be anyone else that I connect to like this. This is unbelievable—and she's just turning away. How could she turn her head?" And so how that transfers into my relationship with the moms was I was going through this—my mom was not listening to the fact that I really cared about this and she would not be sympathetic at all. She wouldn't listen to the fact that I was really depressed and, at the same time, working with Jackie. Then the biggest fight happened about Season. We were downstairs and I said something about her. God, I can't even remember now—it's in my journal. I could go back and look at it. She said something and then my mom made fun of me—and I freak. So this is while I was in the stage of reacting—and I reacted and I freaked out. I told her—I said—I yelled "don't fucking mock me." And I walked upstairs and sat down and started writing in my journal—and she started crying. And Margaret came up in a fury yelling all this man-woman bullshit. Like I was using my power as a man in this argument. And that pissed me off unbelievably because I thought I was relating to her as a human being—as a peer—not as a mother. I was relating to her as an adult and they can't deal with that. And so it turned into this man-woman bullshit. And, I left the house for, like, three days and I didn't come back. Then, one night when I wanted to sleep in my bed I climbed up the side of my house into my room so that I wouldn't have to walk by them. It's really amazing to have that experience because the hard part for my mom was her loving the fact that although the house is not a "normal family values" house we had a great relationship and everything worked well. So all of a sudden all of this conflict happened and she thinks that was hard for her to handle. I don't remember how that particular argument resolved but towards the end of that summer we were relating differently. They were accepting that I had grown from—I wasn't a child anymore, you know. And that was something that I had to accept, and I was accepting it. I went back to school and I wrote this monologue about Season. We had to perform a monologue for our acting teacher the day we got back. And, I wrote that monologue and it was so close to me. And I performed it, and people were just amazed to see me there—open and expressing myself. So, by the end of the summer I had accomplished what I set out to do. It felt really good that I took control of my life.

Study Questions

1. Does Ben's narrative come across to you as more staged and artificial than the others because he is an actor and the interview was captured on videotape?

2. What do you think of Onalie's transcription method, treating the life history as a single narrative without intrusive questions? Does she lose anything by erasing herself in this fashion? (One of the critiques of classic ethnography is that the ethnographer recording the material is usually absent from the account.)

3. Ben talks a great deal about being emotionally honest. Is this life history an example of emotional honesty? How can you tell?

4. Most of the interviewees in this book are much older than the student fieldworkers, but Ben and Onalie are the same age. Do you think this situation made a difference to the way Ben narrated his life? If so, in what ways?

Notes

1. US Census data are hard to interpret because of confusing definitions, but the consensus seems to be that single-parent households with children under eighteen account for around 23 percent, whereas classic nuclear families (a husband and wife living with their biological offspring) now stands at 18 percent.

7

Janette Yarwood

On occasion students ask me if they can conduct their life history interviews in a language other than English. I am generally reluctant to allow this because it creates more work for the student in that they have to transcribe the original *and* provide me with an adequate translation. Also, depending on the particular language, I might be hesitant, because if I cannot understand the language in question, I am not able to be attuned to the original authentic voice. I am reduced to appreciating only *what* was said and not *how* it was said. This defeats much of the purpose of the life history project for me. I can be persuaded, though. If the student is absolutely committed, and if the substantive promise of the life history is self-evident and weighty enough to compensate for the other problems mentioned, then I give the go-ahead.

When Janette Yarwood came to me and said she wanted to conduct an interview with an immigrant from Puerto Rico in Spanish, I asked a few questions about the content, and then acquiesced. Not only was the content of interest in its own right, but I read Spanish well enough that I did not require a translation. So the main issues of extra work and authentic voice being lost did not apply.

The life history that Janette produced was good, as I had expected, but it also raised some issues that I was not expecting. I was, for example, a little surprised at Janette's rather wild and creative spelling in Spanish. Frequently as I was reading the transcription I had to say the words out loud to understand them, and only then I realized that she was not aware of Spanish orthographic conventions but was using a sort of Anglo-Spanish phonetic spelling to write what she heard. When I asked her about this, she said that she grew up hearing Spanish and often speaking it because her grandmother and elder relatives spoke only Spanish. She explained that her grandparents were from Puerto Rico. Her parents' generation spoke English but maintained their fluency in Spanish. Her generation spoke enough Spanish to interact with their elders, but Janette noted she had very little experience with reading and writing Spanish because her schooling was all in English. Not only that, a vast gap also existed between her ability to comprehend Spanish spoken to her and her ability to express herself in grammatical Spanish.

Janette's experience relates somewhat to the experiences of a child of immigrant parents in that she sits in a halfway position between first-generation adult immigrants who are fluent in their native tongue but not so much in English and third- or fourth-generation descendants of immigrants who speak only English. Her day-to-day transactions in the world are in English, and that is where her primary fluency lies. But in order to have contact with her close family, she needs to maintain a level of understanding of Spanish also. To get by in Spanish, her primary need is to understand what others are telling her. She has virtually no need to read or write Spanish, and she has sufficient knowledge to make herself understood when necessary.

I understand Janette's experience because, for somewhat different reasons, I share some of her fluency problems. I was born, and learned to speak, in Buenos Aires where, although my parents spoke English, I was surrounded by Spanish speakers to whom my parents also spoke Spanish. This experience left me with a reasonably empathic understanding of Spanish but limited ability to write or speak it. When anyone spoke to me in Spanish back then, or I had to read a passage, I was on fair ground. But if I had to respond or write something, I got into trouble. This curious linguistic halfway house stands as an index of the cultural limbo that many child immigrants find themselves in.[1]

These linguistic problems got yet more complex as Janette pursued her life history project beyond my fieldwork class. She did the requisite interviews and transcriptions for me but then decided that the material was rich enough to be able to expand it into a senior thesis. She had to do more interviews and introduce some formal analysis, but this was a well-worn path for many of my students. The snag was that I was due for a sabbatical during Janette's senior year and therefore could not be her thesis adviser. Finding another adviser was easy enough, but the person she had to work with could not read Spanish. So Janette was forced to translate all the interviews into English.

The translation process was fraught with all the well-known problems, chief of which was the question of how to maintain the colloquial feeling of the original Spanish in English. The result was highly commendable, being both accurate and reflective of the original voice. To get a sense of the Spanish version (including all the idiosyncrasies of Janette's transcription) I have given a short excerpt from what she first presented to me, followed by the entire life history in English translation.

Janette was personally connected to this project in a number of different ways. The woman she chose to interview was her boyfriend's mother, and she had some very specific personal goals. She knew the woman was a substance abuser and had tested HIV positive, and she knew also that these facts had completely estranged her from her children (including, most especially, Janette's boyfriend). Her first goal was, therefore, a basic humanistic desire to understand the woman better, which she thought might help her to help her boyfriend deal with his home life better. She knew that the woman could not tell her story directly to her children, but there was some hope that if she told the story to Janette and Janette wrote it down, the children could read it and begin to understand their mother better. Direct communication between mother and children had long since broken down, but with Janette as the intermediary, this indirect method held some promise.

Janette's goal here raises an important issue for life histories in general. Not just because of estrangement but for all kinds of reasons; older family members may have difficulty talking directly to younger relatives. Sometimes it is as simple as people just not being able to find the time to sit and listen. Life histories documented by third parties can thus be an important vehicle for recording precious family information that would otherwise eventually be lost. The fieldworker (as outsider) becomes a conduit for communication *within* the family.

It is also important to note that of all the life histories I have supervised, this is the only one in which the fieldworker began with a distinctly negative attitude toward the interviewee. Janette started this project because she wanted to help her boyfriend in his relationship with his mother, as he was too close to the situation to help himself. Her first thoughts were, therefore, for him and not for her. She hated what his mother had done to him, in fact. But the life history process made Janette see her in a different light. Her own feelings went from hatred to empathy, and so it was as (or more) transformative for her as for her interviewee or her boyfriend. Indeed, it was this transformation in her that was the catalyst for her being able to act as an intermediary for other members of the family. There are a few celebrated cases in the anthropological literature of fieldworkers actively disliking the people they were working with, notably Colin Turnbull's experience with the Ik (Turnbull 1972), but they are extraordinarily rare for obvious reasons. That makes this project all the more precious. The fact that ethnographers habitually choose to work with people whom they like or are attracted to in some ways is a major flaw in the method, and in anthropology as a whole.

Because Janette came from a family of Caribbean immigrants herself, she was also interested in understanding the world of immigrants that she grew up in. Some of her old friends became addicted to drugs and alcohol, or tested HIV positive, or were murdered, or ended up in jail, and some, like herself, had ambitions that drew them out of that world into a safer one. But unless she were to theorize that the ability to leave the ghetto depended on luck or random acts (which did not seem intuitively correct nor especially hopeful), there had to be causes that could be identified. This life history represented a first effort at finding those answers.

Janette went into public health administration on graduation and had a long-term goal of qualifying as a doctor. She took pre-med courses to make up for holes in the science training she had missed at Purchase College in preparation for applying to medical schools. She saw her training in anthropology as important in making her a culturally sensitive physician, and pointed out the ways in which she had already been able to use her life history work to good effect at the Health Department.

She also presented me with a nagging problem (nagging for me, not for her). She thoroughly enjoyed anthropology. At the time, she wondered if she should throw over the medical stuff and enter a PhD program in anthropology. My concern, which she adequately expresses herself, was that by becoming an anthropologist her work would become part of the great academic paper chase, whereas as a culturally sensitive doctor she would almost certainly make a real difference in people's lives. The reason that her struggle at that time touched me so much is that I too once had aspirations to go to medical school, but I made a deliberate decision to change paths toward what eventually turned into a PhD in anthropology. I am not perpetually sorry that I made the choices I made, but I do have my regrets (and I did eventually train as an emergency paramedic).

Janette eventually decided to attend the CUNY Graduate Center for a PhD in anthropology instead of qualifying as a physician, and on graduation she spent much of her career as a public policy adviser in Washington, DC. She explained to me some time later that she made the choice to go into policy rather than become a professor because, once again, she felt that applied work could have more of an impact in people's day-to-day lives. After working in policy for years, she returned to academia so that she could reflect upon her experiences. She is now on the faculty at Yale University.

Life History (Excerpted from the Spanish Original)

J: yo quiero saber de tu vida entera no solamente de lo malo que te paso yo quiero saber lo que usted cre que es lo mas importante de tu familia del viaje de Puerto Rico donde naciste cuando naciste

S: me paso lo que me paso a los diez años entonces tuve que ir de mi casa yo segui andando hasta que tuve a la hija mia a los quince años entonces segui mi vida pa aqui pa alla hasta que mi dio con irme a club y esa cosa usted sabe después de alli tuve a mi otro hijo como a los 23 años en ponce donde yo cai presa después yo fui a buscar lo pero no me lo dieron nunca yo lo tuve presa después sali y me ajunte con el papa de Gabriel entonces como sufri mucho con el y eso decidi a venir a este pais sali en cinta con Francis me vino a este pais y el se vine detras hasta que tuve los otros hijos de el . . . .

J: usted vino a quedarse con alguien?

S: cuando yo vino vine en case de mi mam porque no tenia mas sitio entonces de alli coji un furnished room entonces di a lu a Francis y eso fue en Dekalb Avenue y tuve a Milagro y después a Gabriel y me quede aqui viviendo tu sabe la vida esa . . .

J: me puede decir mas de cuando usted era joven de donde naciste donde vivia que hacia

S: yo naci en Puerto Rico en Yauco en un sitio que se dicen los guandules entonces desde que yo naci mi vida era yiendo al rio labando ropa estaba en escuela de chiquita pero no llege ir mas de a septimo de alli no fui mas porque usted sabe mi mama nunca mi dijo vaya ni ve ni na después a los diez años me paso lo que le dije pero mi vida fue asi en mi casa usted sabe y tuve una vida asi no fue muy bien ni buena sufri bastante también . . .

J: me puede decir un poquito de tu mama

S: bueno cuando yo era chiquita ella no era tan buena conmigo cuando yo cresi me daba mucho me trataba mas mal que a los otros porque habia veces que yo tenia que lavar al rio a veces no todos los dias . . .

J: usted era la unica hembra?

S: no, en cassa somos tres pero hay una que es abnormal de la mente entiende hay otra y yo hay otras mas pero de padre y madre somos tres entonces las otras dos son de otros hombre usted sabe pero la que estaba en casa conmigo era mi hermana Maggie que era usted sabe la mas aquel esa era la santa y yo la la pues tenia que labar planchar siempre con mi trajecitos largo y si no lo hacia me daban hasta que yo misma hice mi vida tuve que hacer mi vida fui a escuela a esa edad y pues de esa edad me gradue y no fui mas . . .

J: OK despues que le paso eso a los dies años que hiciste te quedaste en casa

S: despues de eso yo me fui pa como me quede en casa pero cada ves me estaban con cosa y eso entonces conoci una muchacha de aya en Puerto Rico y me invito para un sitio que se dicen aca lina y ella me dijo que era una casa de trabajar pero no era eso era una casa de como una barra como una casa de sita estoy alli entonces sufri mucho porque imajinate yo no tenia mas que entonces me fui a Yauco otra ves y alli fue que sali en cinta de esta Anna Milagros a los quince años entonces volvi otra ves al mismo sitio hasta que empese a usar drogas y todo . . .

J: eso empeso alla en esa casa

S: no eso cuando mas joven . . .

J: cuando eso le paso a los dies años usted no se lo dijo a alguien como a su mama

S: yo le dije el dia que eso paso fue que yo iba para una fiesta patronalles usted sabe pues entonces iba un hombre que estaba enamoro de mi pero yo no sabia el tenia como como algunas quarenta

Life History (English translation of the full interview)

Janette's questions are marked by an asterisk (*)

You want to know about my life when something happened something bad that . . .

* I want to know about your entire life not only the bad things—I want to know about what you think is most important—about your family—about the trip from Puerto Rico—when you were born—where you were born.

What happened to me happened to me at ten years old. Then I had to leave my house. Then I kept on going until I had my daughter at 15 years old. Then I kept on with my life here and there until I started going to clubs and things like that—you know? Then I had my other child at 23 years old in Ponce, where I went to jail. Then I went to get him when I got out but they didn't give him to me never. I had him in jail. That's where I got together with Angel's father. Then since I suffered a lot with him and things I decided to come to this country. I was pregnant with Michelle. I came to this country and he came right behind me and then I had my other kids from him.

* You came to stay with someone?

When I came here I came to my mother's house because I didn't have nowhere else to go. Then from there I got a furnished room. Then I had Michelle that was at Dekalb Avenue and I had Jessica and then Angel, and I stayed living here, living you know that kind of life . . .

* Can you tell me a little more about when you were younger where were you born—where did you live—what kinds of things did you do?

I was born in Puerto Rico, in Yauco, in a place that's called Los Gandules, and from the time I was born my life was going to the river to wash clothes, and going to the hills to get coffee. Over there people had to go pick their coffee. I had to be getting different fruits and things like that. I was in school from little but I didn't get to go past the 7th grade. I didn't go after that because my mother never told me to go or I should go or nothing like that. My grandmother is the one who raised me. I was never like mother and daughter with my mother because she never really cared about me. My grandmother is the one who raised me; she took care of me. I went over there because my grandmother had a daughter that was a secretary, and I used to wash and iron for her, and she used to pay me. She used to say she wanted to take care of me. She used to say "you come live with me I'll raise you and you can be somebody in the future." I would stay for a while but my mother would come for me. But then she would send me back. She never really cared about me. So I would go back to my grandmother's house. I used to pack a dress in those milk boxes, that's what they used to use for suitcases, and I would take some panties and I would go. It wasn't far, maybe three, yeah three of our blocks, until ten years old when that man abused me. I didn't know he was watching me. But my life was just like that. It wasn't that good, not bad, but not too good. I suffered a lot too you know—

* Can you tell me a little bit about your mother?

Well when I was little she wasn't good or nice with me. When I got older, she hit me a lot. She treated me worse than she treated the others because I sometimes had to go wash at the river. Not sometimes—all the time—everyday . . .

* Were you the only girl?

No. In my house there was three, but one is not right, you know, like, retarded. In my house there was eighteen, one other girl and me.

Janette Yarwood

There's one more but from my mother and father. There's three girls and all the rest are boys. I'm the oldest of all of them, of the ones that lived with me. Maritza was the most . . . she was the saint and I was . . . well I had to always be ironing. I always had to be wearing long dresses and skirts—and if I didn't do it I got hit, until I had to make a life for myself. I had to make a life. I went to school until that age. I graduated and I didn't go no more.

* Did you have a father?

My father lived with us and he wasn't that bad he was nice with me it was my mother who didn't like me and I had brothers they even abused me you know they even did it to my children I can't really talk about that because Michelle doesn't really like me to talk about that they did it to my other daughter Anna too she told me one day she had to go to the hospital one day and while she was crying she said mami Maria—I'm like this because they all abused me—she was only eight years old you know my mother raised her and she said they all did it and she was scared to tell—it wasn't only to her it was to all of them but you know I can't really say anything I don't like to talk about it but God knows and they know that's serious abuse because they knew how I was and they abused me but they abused my children too and they never treated them right you see Angel goes over there and he doesn't say anything but he remembers everything they never treated him never well not any of my kids did they treat right I wasn't and Angel or so good but I went over there sometimes and they threw me out and I had to leave with my kids one time Angel had to stay over there when his father had beat me up and they used to hit him with sticks and he got really sick if you would have seen him my God he didn't even look the same he was so pale he didn't eat.

* OK after that thing happened to you what did you do did you stay at home?

after that I went to—no I stayed at home but they kept saying things to me bothering me and things like that—then I met a girl from over there in Puerto Rico and she invited me to a place that over here is called whorehouse (lina) but she told me it was a house for girls like for us to work I was there and I suffered a lot because imagine I was only—then I went back to Yauco that when I found out I was pregnant for Anna at 15 years old then I went back to that place—I couldn't stay at home—I started to use drugs and everything else.

* That started in that house?

No that when I was much younger.

* When that happened to you at ten years old did you tell anybody—like your mother?

I told her the day it happened. It's that I was going to a carnival, you know, well there was a man that liked me but I didn't know he was, was, like, forty. Well, I saw he kept walking behind me and following, but, like, I didn't imagine that he . . . I was with my little brothers and when I tried to cross the street he took me by the arm and he took me to a place called Ponce and it was there that he took advantage of me. Then when I bothered him and cried and begged him to take me home because I couldn't, I didn't dare, I didn't know how . . . and on top of that I was bleeding a lot. And he didn't want to look like he was scared. Imagine a ten-year-old girl and him. Well, then I told him "please take me I won't tell on you." Then I couldn't even walk. Then he took me. Then when I got home, I told mami that I got my menstruation, you know you bleed. But they didn't believe me and they beat me, and I ended up in the hospital that same night for two months, because he, you know . . . I was young and the beating on top of that. Imagine. Well, after that they didn't treat me the same. Well, I kept on with my life until today.

* How was your life with Angel's father—was he your first boyfriend?

No. I had a lot. I had like a mountain of boyfriends, if you could call them that. But he was the one you could say was like a husband, you know. When you live, and I didn't want to stay in that life, and I just got out of jail . . .

* Why were you in jail?

They accused me. It's that I hooked up with this girl, and they said I, you know . . . when you forge checks. Well after that I got out of jail, at about, at about 25 years old, I lived with him. No I got out maybe when I was younger, and I met him, you know, we were in the same place. And him . . . well if you look at Angel and you look at him, he was the same. I mean when he was younger they were the same. Angel is more humble, but he was the same. I mean quiet and he looked so serious, and I said "well maybe my happiness is here because I want to get out of this life." Then we started. But from the time we started, he was beating on me, hitting me. I didn't even eat because there was times he didn't bring me

Janette Yarwood

food and I couldn't go out. That's when I got pregnant with Michelle. That's when they said Michelle wasn't his, and when he found out I was pregnant, he told this girl to hit me in the stomach so I could lose it. Then after that we got back together. He took me to a lot of places. Then in San Juan I found a way to get a plane ticket to come to this country. I was already pregnant. Well I don't know how he found out where I was or my address. And I had Michelle, then I had Jessica . . .

*So you stayed with him?

No, I didn't stay with him because he beat me. He came and went when he wanted to, you know, and I would call the police. But the police didn't do nothing to him until finally one day he disappeared. I haven't heard from him. Look my hairs stand up now that I'm talking about him. I heard he got killed, I don't know what happened to him. I just know if I saw him I think I would pee on myself. It's been a lot of years since I seen him. One time, when Angel's father got out of jail, he saw that I had a baby [David] and he asked me whose it was and where was the man? Well, that night he took David and he said he was going to throw him out the window. Well, a friend of mine stood in the way, and they arrested him, and he got five years. That's when they were going to take the kids away again, but I sent them to my mother's house alone, and they suffered a lot there.

* Were you in jail a long time and how was it?

5 years. That was horrible. There were a lot of fights, people getting killed. I suffered a lot in there. That was in Yauco. The food was bad. They didn't treat people right. They put people in solitary confinement when you did the littlest thing. That jail was really bad.

* What about when you got here?

Well, when I came here I was a lot more calm and they gave me welfare and they gave me everything for my apartment. I kept my apartment fine until I started [drugs] again. I mean it's true I suffered a lot because he came to the apartment and broke things. But life was easier than over there. Well here it wasn't so hard when I first got here. It was hard because I went to my mother's house and it was still the same? She had to be hitting me and things like that . . .

* How was it after you had your children?

When I had them it was fine but since I had to be running here and there, well that's when they accused me, because I drank too. I wasn't taking drugs but I drank a lot. That's when someone accused me—that I had my children in the streets, that I didn't take care of them. Then one day when I lived in Brooklyn, I was outside with the children. Jessica was playing in the pump [fire hydrant] and a boy pushed her and she cut her foot. They didn't take them away that night but they took Jessica to the hospital and I took the other children to my mother's house. The next day I took David, he was the baby, and my mother called them and told them that I was drinking and taking drugs and I was sometimes . . . And the social worker came and they went to court and they took them. They took my children.

* Did you ever have help with your children

No, I raised them myself.

* How did you start using drugs—here in New York?

In Puerto Rico I already used them. It started in Puerto Rico. I was, who knows, maybe 12 years old. When I first got here I didn't do it, but after a while I started. I met some people and I went to some places and that's how. In Puerto Rico I started in a club, in a bar, you know. (long pause) Well, they took my children because I was drinking and I took them with me when that man beat on me. I ran away with them. Sometimes I went to my mother's house, but I couldn't be there either because there were problems there too. Then there were times when I would drink and take them with me, because I thought that if they were with me nothing would happen to them. I used to take them with me I didn't believe I wasn't taking care of them, couldn't take care of them at that moment, because if I'm in a bar or in the street I'm not taking care of my kids. But for me, I was taking care of them. There were times they went hungry because I would buy them things but not like if they were home. But when he beat me up, their father, I had to be running away. Sometimes I went to my mother's house. If not I stayed in the street. That's when they, well, you know, they took them away.

* How was it when they took your children away?

When they took my children, I know I wasn't doing right by them, because I had to be running or because I was drinking. But when they took them away, first they took away the older ones. But I suffered more when they took David because he was the youngest. Then I started to drink more and do more drugs because I thought being high or drunk would give me relief. But when I realized that nobody was going to help me, not my mother or my family, I asked them for help. But, they would tell me they're not going to give them to me. Then I said, "see no one's going to help me, look at me, I'm worst than the bums" because I used to sleep in the streets and in parks and I didn't eat for days and sometimes I didn't bathe for days.

* Did you have an apartment?

No, I lived in the streets like that until one day I said, "God help me" because my children are first in my life and I don't have nobody to help me. Then I went to see where my kids were, and my mother wouldn't tell me where they were, and they were telling my children, "that mother of yours is a drunk and a drug addict." It was true. I won't lie, but to tell me they didn't know where they were? After that day my mother stopped talking to me and I used to go to court. But sometimes I would go a little drunk. Then the judge told me, "you have to accept that you are an alcoholic, you know what it is to drink 5 bottles of liquor and wake up and drink again." But I didn't want to accept it. The judge wanted me to go to a program but I still didn't want to accept it that I was an alcoholic. I could only accept that I took care of my children, and the lawyer would ask me "how are you going to take care of your children if you're always drunk and live in the street?" But I still didn't care. I wanted to be with them. Then I thought, "it's true," and I had to accept the fact that nobody was going to help me, because I had to go to court by myself. Well, I went to the program and, thank God, in five months I didn't drink or take drugs. I gained weight, and, well, they gave me my son David, but Michelle, Angel, and Jessica didn't want to come back to me, because, you know, that lady treated them good, you know, better than I did.

* About how old were your children?

Michelle was about ten, Jessica about seven, and Angel was five. David was three. In that program they taught me how to take care of children, how to talk to them, and after about eight or nine months they gave me Jessica. I had to fight for the other two, but they didn't want, you know, they messed with their minds. I don't know. But she would tell them she cared about them a lot, but not Jessica. She said she always wanted to be with me. Then after some time they stayed with her about six years. Michelle was already a teenager and Angel was pretty big by then. They only came because one day the judge told them, you know, you have to go back to your mother, because your mother has changed her life around. But they still didn't want to come, and the judge told them, "that lady is not your mother and you have to give your mother another chance."

* And once they were back with you how was it?

The one who was always with me was David, and right away Jessica started to get some friends and she started to miss school until . . . I don't know if she like some boy, but she came home at three in the morning. I don't know what happened, but if something happened I know it was my fault because I was drinking and I told her go buy me a beer. I sent her with a man I didn't really know, and I was so busy thinking she was with that man. I beat her with a belt, and that's when she left me. After that she got, I don't know, she started going to clubs. And one day, not too long ago, she told me she suffered a lot, and she decided she wanted to go back to her foster mother again, and, well, she was older, I couldn't tell her anything. But Jessica came back because she couldn't be running the streets with her foster mother and I tried, but she wouldn't change. And she always threw in my face that she was in a foster home and that I treated her bad. She brought up all the things I did to her in the past, but the others didn't do that. Michelle stayed with me, but she fell in love with the man she's still with. She was about 14 and she got pregnant at 16 years old. She was nice with me. Her room was always clean. Angel was like that too. He never hit me. But one day, he was already older, I went to hit him and he held my hands. The only one that came out like that was Jessica. She always used to hit me. Sometimes David throws the things I did in the past in my face. Angel was never really with me. One day he sat down with me and he said, "mami if you keep on doing these things I'm leaving." Since he was so young, I didn't believe him. I was going to change, but I kept on doing the same thing, and, well, that's how he left me. He was younger than 16 years old. He would leave for a while and come back until he finally left for good. But he kept going to school, he never stopped going to school. But sometimes when I think about Jessica it bothers me. Her husband hits her, and she hits her little girls, and she doesn't think. She doesn't change. She's just like me but she doesn't take drugs or drink, and I try to talk to her. I tell her when I had little children I used to hit them, and I thought it wasn't abuse. But now I know yes it was abuse. But then she says, "what about when you hit me with hangers and sticks and everything else?" and she starts to talk about this disease that I have.

* What is that mark on your head [dot in the center of forehead]?

That was here in this country when I was . . . I had my children. But, I would go to this place. Well, they told me if I didn't mark my forehead I couldn't come in, and, well, since I was in love with this man, well, since I wanted to get in I did it. I was about 39 years old. That's why I say sometimes people do crazy things, because I did a lot of things to my children. If I had to stay in the streets I would do it with them. But not now. I did those things when I was high or drunk. For me that was nothing. God knows if I could have done something horrible like those women you see on the news do, like kill their kids, because you're not thinking. Who knows? Maybe they don't even remember. Sometimes I tell my daughter, Jessica, "I wasn't a saint but you have to learn." If you hit one of those little girls and they die even by mistake, you are going to go to jail and then you're going to say it wasn't you, or it wasn't your fault because you did it when you were mad. She says "I know how I hit them." But she hits them with her fist, and they hit the wall, and I tell her I see the abuse. And she says, "don't you remember when you hit Angel in the head or when you hit me with hangers." I tell her, "I know I did all that, but I didn't have any sense, I wasn't right. Right now I think about those things at night. It's true I started realizing it late but I know what I did. I ask God for forgiveness. I mean, look at what I did to my children. But then I say, "look how I was, and all my children turned out good, because, look, Angel is the son of a man who is so terrible because he hit me so much, and look at my son how he is. He goes from work to his home from home to his school. He doesn't hang out. He has a nice place. He has no bad habits, thank God." Michelle, either she has a husband and a house, and now he doesn't hit her. Jessica is the only one, but she's not bad because she has her house. She doesn't have much, but she has a roof, and she doesn't do drugs. I can say that about her. One time a man got her into it, but she left that alone. She doesn't at all, or David. He hates everything, and it's a miracle because he saw everything I did. I took him with me all the time. He could have said, "let me try it," but up to now he won't, thank God. I'm happy and proud that they educated themselves. Everyone is surprised and says how in the world a woman like you could have ended up with kids like yours?" They're jealous. You know my mother raised my other kids, I have four more kids, and one got killed by a gang at about 24, and one killed herself, and my son died of AIDS, and the other one is in the streets, and one lives in Puerto Rico. I think he is not doing so good. He does a lot of drugs, you know, and my mother raised them, and she doesn't drink or have any habits. And I was opposite, and look at how my kids ended up. People say, I don't know how you could have raised your kids." Well I raised them, and I didn't raise them. It's like they raised themselves, because look, Angel came to me crying, and he was young. Sometimes I say, "why did I do this?" He told me, "if you keep up this life I'm leaving." He left and he never came back, and he got an apartment. When he graduated from high school I didn't even know he was going to graduate. One day he just called me, and came to get me to go.

. . .

I remember one time I didn't have money to pay rent and the landlord took off the door and we had to live like that. Imagine me with four kids. I had to put a blanket to cover the door so no one would come in. I always had to change them from schools, because we were always moving. I think in one year I must have had 40 apartments. There were times that I would find things in the street, and I would feed them right from the street. I could give them food, but I wanted the money. I wish that I could change all the horrible things that I did, because I did awful things. I would not have done drugs or drink. That makes you a different person. I say this now that I'm old, but I guess maybe it's not too late.

* Tell me about when they told you that you have HIV.

Well I felt as if they told me I had a cold. Every once in a while I cry. I think more about David. I know I have the virus not the disease and so I know I can live for a long time if I take care of myself. I don't really think about that a lot. Right now I don't take drugs but every now and then I drink. Not like before. Maybe once a month, because I can't take it. I wake up sick. But some days I wake up wanting to. It's true. I can't drink one, because if I drink one and someone gave me the whole store I could drink it all. I'm not one of those people who can drink one I have to keep on going.

* When you think about your children how do you feel?

I feel proud because of the way I was, how I was they came out good. Not even Jessica is that bad because she doesn't drink or smoke. I feel really good about Angel because he's in college and he works so hard. And Michelle, well, she moved from my house at 16 years old and she went to a college and she's still with the same man and she has a house. And David, he's the youngest, and I really worry about him, especially since he had that accident—you know his arm and leg. I could have sued but

I didn't know any better. I was too drunk. I don't know what I have with him but I can't sleep if he's not home. I don't know what I would do if he left me. He wants to, you know. But he knows I couldn't take it. I feel proud when I think about my kids. I know I have more than four but for me those are my only children because those are the ones I raised, so I'm proud they turned out good.

Study Questions

1. Do you think that Janette's translation is adequate in recreating authentic voice in a language other than the one in which the interview was conducted?
2. What do you think the children of Janette's interviewee felt when they read her life history? Is this a good use of the method do you think?
3. If you have reasonable familiarity with Spanish, comment on Janette's ability to transcribe the interview in the original language.
4. Does this life history portray Janette's interviewee in a good, bad, or neutral light? Explain your reasoning.
5. Compare this life history with the one recorded by Isadora Sahl. What are the points of resonance and dissimilarity?

Notes

1. Since I wrote this passage, I have lived in Buenos Aires for five years, reclaiming both my ethnic heritage and my command of the local dialect. As such, my linguistic sensitivities concerning Latin American Spanish varieties have changed substantially, but my original thoughts still apply.

8

Andrea Pernstich

By the time Andrea Pernstich took my fieldwork course, I had been teaching it annually for almost two decades. I was, therefore, fully aware of the capacity of the best students in the class to do superb work, and perhaps even getting a little blasé about it. So it came as something of a surprise to read Andrea's life history and feel the same amazement and excitement that I felt when I read Liz Jackson's at the end of my first year teaching the course. Andrea's documentation of Susanne's story moved me in so many ways.

Andrea and Susanne met at Purchase College and had an immediate affinity for each other. Both were a little older than the norm, being in their early twenties when they arrived at the college. Both took professional photography courses through the visual arts program, which meant not only that they had a common interest, but also that they spent a considerable amount of time using the same facilities (back in the days of film, chemicals, and darkrooms) and working for the same professors. But of paramount importance was the fact that both were adult immigrants from German-speaking countries: Andrea from Austria, and Susanne from the former East Germany.

Early in the friendship Andrea discovered that Susanne had had an extraordinary life as a teenager in East Germany, although she really knew only snatches of the whole story from bits and pieces dropped in conversation. She knew that Susanne had tried to escape to the West, several times, and had spent time in jail as a consequence before ultimately being exiled. Intrigued by the little she knew, she asked Susanne to be her subject for the life history project, and the most amazing tale of harrowing adventures full of courage, fortitude, and tribulation emerged.

At the most obvious level I was captivated to encounter a real-life story that read like an Arthur Koestler novel, and immensely impressed by Susanne's independence of spirit and personal bravery. But I was also intrigued by her personal quest for freedom and the many ironies that were woven into it. There is, for example, her paradoxical discovery that in prison she was free to say the things that on the outside she would have been threatened with prison for saying. What can they threaten you with when you are in prison? She seemed to be at her most free, as it were, when she had lost her freedom. Then there is the strange irony that her punishment for trying to escape East Germany was exile!

Balancing the gains that Susanne made at every step in her journey to freedom are the losses she incurred along the way. She escaped East Germany at the expense of leaving family, friends, and culture behind. It was this fact more than any other that attracted Andrea to Susanne (and probably what drew a strongly empathic response from me also). At age twenty-three it was very important for Andrea to leave Austria for the United States because she could see all too clearly the life that lay in front of her and wanted something different, something with more excitement in it. But she also recognized that this decision involved leaving her family and culture behind.

But for both, as for many, many immigrants, what they found in the United States left them ambivalent. It is indeed a land of opportunity. Andrea and Susanne could pursue an education and their professional aspirations in ways denied them in Europe. But the "land of the free" is not free in so many ways: not free in ways that most Europeans (even in the old Eastern bloc) take for granted. But there is no going back once the decision to emigrate has been taken. Both women have returned for visits to their home cultures and have found that they are now strangers in their own homes. Their sojourns in the United States have transformed them sufficiently that they have little in common with their former friends who stayed at home and did all the things that they ran away to avoid. That part of their inner worlds has not changed. But as the years go by, both are finding it hard to stay in the United States. They find themselves constantly weighing the positive and negative aspects of staying, and when the negatives gain the upper hand, they agonize over where to go that would resolve their inner conflict. As an adult immigrant to the United States myself (at the age of twenty-four), I find myself in deep sympathy with their plight (and I did eventually flee the United States).

Because of these conflicts, both Andrea and Susanne also turn over in their minds a number of "what if . . ." questions because of the dramatic changes in all parts of Europe. The fall of the Berlin Wall means that East Germany no longer exists. So, if Susanne had simply waited instead of trying to force her freedom, she would have attained her goal by default and would not have lost her ties to her home culture. Theirs is, therefore, a common but seldom told story of coming of age as an immigrant, a coming of age that involves losing one culture but not fully gaining a replacement. I do not suggest that this is a necessary outcome of immigration at a particular age—doubtless there are myriad possibilities—but I do believe that it is a recognizable and common outcome, and one that brought these two women together.

It is perhaps indicative of some of these sensitive cultural and personal issues that both women actually preferred to do the interviews in English without any promptings from me in either direction. Their voices in English symptomize their cultural dilemma. They are in the United States and are therefore willing to use the vernacular. Their comfort with the language and its culture can be seen in their speech patterns, which are idiomatically accurate with only sporadic hints of German syntax and phrasing. But they are not flawlessly fluent in English either. Apart from the occasional mistreatment of a verb or adjective, in discussion with each other they are sometimes forced to use a German word for an expression that has no English equivalent. They can manage in this country, but their alienation can send bubbles to the surface.

Andrea was as captivated by Susanne's story as I was, and she became an even more compassionate friend once she discovered the details. She continued interviewing Susanne long after my course had come to an end, and transcribed every word. This process has united them in ways that are difficult to describe. One might think of it as the touching of souls. This may be about as far away as one can get from objectified, scientized observation, yet the products are sociologically invaluable.

Life History

(Andrea chose to put her questions in parentheses.)

I can tell you that I grew up in a little village, more countryside village, right outside Berlin, right outside of West Berlin but in East Germany, and I basically can say that I had a beautiful childhood, because we had a huge garden with lots of trees around. We had a pond across the street. There was ice skating every day in the winter, and my parents were divorced. I grew up with my grandmother, with my mother and with my sister, in a big house, and, yes, everything seemed in a way, very nice, very beautiful. But it was always a little bit overcast because my mother got sick when I was, you know, 7, 8 years old, and she never, up to the day she died, she never really recovered. That doesn't mean that she was always permanently sick. But cancer came back, and so it was a little overcast by that. But basically I think we, we had a pretty, I had a pretty, great family, and I was more boy in the family than a girl. I was climbing trees, I was stealing apples from the neighbor's garden, I was stealing flowers out of other gardens to bring to my grandfather, my grandfather's grave. So I did like a lot of silly things, falling off the trees. I have, like, scars everywhere on my body and . . . but *ja* I had a, I really had a great childhood. But it got, you know, when my grandmother started getting sick, more often when I was about 10, 11. And this was also the time when my mother started getting really seriously sick again. My life became a little bit heavier than it was supposed to for a 10, 11 years old child. I mean I loved to take care, but, you know, you want to go outside and just play and be silly. But I was, like, cooking for my grandmother upstairs, and taking care of my mother downstairs, and, which I really loved to do. But I think nowadays I can see that what happened, because I was doing this, that sometimes I feel I have never really been a child, and now sometimes I really feel the need to be a child because there were just a couple of years which I totally missed out. So I was basically an adult when I was 12 which was also good I think. It is really because I was a very dream-like or dreamy child. I had always dreams. I was very introverted I was always out in the fields with my friends dreaming of something, dreaming for example of New York, America. When I was 8, I decided I am going to move to America to New York and get married to an American. This was a dream for a couple of years. So I was always a dreamer. I was very introverted I was, I think I was pretty far away from reality and because of everything what happened in my family I had to, to wake up pretty early, which probably was good for me, and I had to be responsible. I had to, like, I had to just be there for other people otherwise I would have been still a dreamer. I mean I am, but I am a dreamer who is living in reality, so, and *ja* my grandmother died when I was 13, and my father was living next town, like one town away from us. And my father . . . I have for myself, I have, like, really kind of interesting people in my family. My father was always, I think, when he came to visit us, and when he was with us, he was a very good father. But he was not a, you know, a typical father who always really takes care of his children. So basically he saw us every 3 or 4 weeks, like, for a day, or sometimes a weekend. And I really always missed him because he is,

I don't know how it sounds, he is crazy, but he is just very . . . he was just always very different than everybody else in my town, and he was a . . . just amazing person. Very smart, a lot of ideas, very much alive. And he was always a little bit, he was a dreamer as well. That is probably where I got my dreams from. But he was outrageous in terms of that. So he was . . . he had, like, a very, like, upright start in his career. And, and so, like, for people in my town, was what he was doing, what he was thinking, he was always a very strange and so for me he was always interesting and at one point, when I was very young, our family used to live in Sri Lanka, where he was working for the government. And, of course, for those people in that little town in East Germany, they just didn't understand, they didn't comprehend. And after we got back, of course, his views were even broader and wider. he learned a lot about East Germany. He was a pro-system person, or however you want to say, that he was a part of the party, a member of the party. But he learnt a lot, he found out a lot of truth, being in Sri Lanka, about East Germany, the whole communist system involvement of Russia in the civil war in Sri Lanka. So I guess he got very clear views after we returned. My father is a very fair person, a very honest person, and that's the reason that he got into a lot of trouble, because he just voiced his opinion in a way you should have not done. So this was another fact that he was considered weird because he was just too honest and too open. He lost his job and from, from a diplomat he actually ended up being unemployed in East Germany. He was a diplomat. He was working for the system, he was working for the government. He was an economical advisor of East Germany in Sri Lanka, and we were part there of the embassy. But there he found out a lot of facts, a lot of truths. There are letters existing, long letters, where he wrote everything down, sending back to East Germany, to my grandmother, telling her about everything. Even he knew that those letters were being read but, he just never could, *ja*, could put up with ah unfairness and dishonesty, and, I mean, he got many chances. He also got offered to be the major editor of a major newspaper in Germany. But after he got back and they, they basically interviewed him about all this and kicked him out, like, every possibility he had in East Germany was cut off. So he was, for a while, he was working in a factory, for a while he was, you know, driving people around for money. He was doing all kinds of work in order to survive. People like that did not exist too much in East Germany, in Berlin some, some in Dresden. But, so he was a little rebel, and then he started painting. He started writing scripts for theater. He was involved in children's theater, and he was painting little masks from Sri Lanka, in order to sell them on the street, and to stores. That's how he survived. He always would meet, like, with actors or artists. It was a kind of gloomy, you can imagine. People are drinking, smoking, talking about politics and art. My father was one of those, and that's always why he was considered as weird, and our family was kind of considered as weird as well. But my mother was totally different. My mother was very, I think there was a deep sadness sitting inside of her, which probably also created her illness. But she was a very good person, very big heart, and she was basically living for other people. So *ja* my grandmother died when I was 13. My grandmother was also very, very strong person, very strong headed person, very creative person, and she was an excellent cook, and everything that she did was very tasteful . . . the way she set the table, the way she dressed herself. My family was kind of the family that didn't have much but we made the nicest, the best out of what we had, even if we didn't have anything on the table, the few things we had on the table . . . She was a very dominating person, dominant person and, she had a lot of influence on my mother.

(Was your father supporting your family at that time?)

Ja he was always kind of like, you know, after he also was not working anymore. Sometimes he didn't have any money, sometimes he had a lot of money. He was supporting us as the money came in. So my mother was basically, in her own way, she wasn't like outspokenly strong, but she was very strong. She just didn't speak up to it, but she was very strong, because she handled our life, and she got us through everything, and she offered us so much. I mean we got as much as she could afford. We got, which was probably compared to especially American kids, nothing, but to us it was a lot, and she was a very strong person. She got us through by herself, basically, with her job that didn't pay much, and she did everything. My sister was, until she was 16, until I was 11, she was living at home. But then she *ja* . . . I don't know if they have something like that in America with that name, she was living in *ja* college probably *im Internat*. She was, she wanted to study medicine, but since just one out of each class could go to higher school, higher education, like *Matura*[1] and in her class she was the best out of her class. But there was another student whose father was very much involved in politics and he was very pro East Germany and our family not as much, so she got refused and she chose to take the harder way, the longer way to first be a nurse, get her *Matura* on a second, like continuing education level and then later on try to enter university. But this all didn't really happen because other things happened before. So my sister was, since I was 11, she was not permanently living with us anymore. She just came home for weekends and so for 3 years, until I was 14, she was 19, and, so, after my grandmother died, I think my mother . . . because my grandmother had so much influence on her, it was kind of, it was pretty hard on my mother, and, of course, her sickness advanced and she got *ja* basically each day she got sicker, and she had 3 operations altogether. And it was in the summer of '83, the year after my grandmother died, that I was by myself with my mother. Everybody was gone basically and it started that she, whatever she was eating, she threw up. She couldn't hold any food anymore, and so I called a friend of my aunt who was a doctor. My aunt was a doctor and so he told me to call the ambulance to get her into the hospital. So I got her into the hospital. She got the operation right away, the same day, but they opened her, they closed her right away because they saw there is nothing really they could have done for her anymore. So that was basically the time when it was going downhill, day by day, and my sister knew, my aunt knew everybody in my family knew, except me. I just felt something and, and then *ja* it was getting worse every day and, like, right after Christmas she . . . we had to put her into the hospital again and then she never left the hospital. It was it was kind of weird. I was telling Thomasina about it yesterday because she asked me about my mother and she asked me how I felt when she died, and it was something I never really know if people understand. People who went through that, like Julia. Do you know Julia? Julia understands because she had the same feeling. I think I could support her during this time and explaining this feeling to her, that it is fine. But you develop this feeling. I mean I went to visit her every second day. I took a train right after school in order to go to the hospital and visit her. But its somehow through all those years and always visiting all those years. I mean my mother was in the hospital, one month she was in the hospital, one month she was out, one month she was in. So she was constantly in there and there is something build up inside of you at this point. It was so strong because I saw that it was getting worse, and getting worse. So that every morning you wake up and there is fear there—is she still alive or not? Even you don't think that, but the fear is there. There is a weird feeling. And so I developed this, almost, this kind of thought which I was embarrassed for a lot of times, that I, that I almost was hoping that it would be over at one point because it seemed it seemed to be too heavy, that I can't carry anymore. But of course I didn't wish she would die *ja* it was something. So I don't know, I can't even really explain it. But it is almost that, you know, you are always like living on a not steady surface. You don't know if you fall off or you stay on, and then you sometimes wish either, or just let me fall down, or let me stay up here, but don't always have me like swing around like that. I don't know if this is an explanation, or a good metaphor for it, but this is almost what I sometimes felt. I remember a lot of times going home from school and having this thought, and I felt embarrassed for it, and because, I mean, I, I loved my mother. I mean, she was the most important in my life. I mean I love my father as well, but my mother and I had just a very strong connection, and *ja*, at this time I was basically, I was sleeping at my aunt's house. But I spent the afternoons at my house alone *ja* and, so and then the last time when I saw my mother was a Sunday, and she seemed doing very well, and she was actually sitting up and she made kind of jokes. She was sitting there and she looked good. Anyway she was beautiful, and she just looked so, so pure, I think almost like as pure as her nature was, and very, you know, just very pure and honest, and, I don't know . . . just the way she was. She looked and . . . so she was sitting there on the bed and then she said, like, "somehow I look like a child from India right?" She was getting so sick that, you know, you could see her joints coming out everywhere, and still she looked great, and something what I didn't know at this point, but my sister of course knew, is that, that right before somebody is going to die, it is almost like all their strength is collecting again, coming together, before they totally break down and die. Everything comes together, they are very much alive, and it happens a lot of times, and this was basically what happened to her, like, you know, everything was coming back . . . her strength and then, basically, two days later she died, and she died. We were on our way to the hospital again, and it was a kind of strange experience because we were coming from my sister's house, which was in Berlin. I stayed there for a couple of days, because I had vacation from school. I had off from school. I stayed at my sister's house, and her friend was there as well. So we all came down from Berlin to see my mother in the hospital, and we were so silly for no reason in the train, and it was getting so bad that we almost fell off our seat because we were laughing so hard about the dumbest stupidest, silliest, thing, and we didn't know how this all came up. And then we got to the hospital, and as soon as we entered the unit a nurse came towards us, and she was like just looking at us and we were just about to walk to the room, but she kept us back, and she brought us to this one room, and she told us that she had died an hour earlier, and, and again I was sitting there, and I first didn't say anything. I was just sitting there, and then again this weird thing happened, that I started crying for about a minute, maybe, but then I stopped crying, and again I had to laugh. I didn't know why, and then I started crying. I think somehow the whole time it was kind of very strange day, and, so I went outside, and I remember that I, I felt very . . . It was very cold and gray outside, and it felt very empty, like almost like a, you know, the . . . your body was aching inside, and everything was just so empty. The sky was empty. Everything was just so cold and empty. It just felt very strange, and, so, and then also at the funeral again. It was something. It didn't happen really to my sister that bad, and I don't know why it happened to me. But I can almost say, even I was very upset, I was in a good mood. I was prancing jokes all the time and was laughing, not during the ceremony. I didn't do or say anything during the ceremony. But afterwards, it's just I was in a very weird stage, and then, like, eventually a week later I kind of broke down, and I think it was the first time that I realized what happened, and then I changed over to the other side, and I started eating, and I was just eating. I don't know, I was just really, for a couple of weeks, I was in an eating mood, eating the whole day, and I gained a lot of weight. But somehow then I also had, like, this force in me, because my mother was always, always proud of . . . because we were good students, and she was also proud that I was a casual student when I was younger, you know, things came easy to me so I didn't really put any effort into it. I was more like on my trees out in the meadow. So I was an average B-student. But when she got sick I somehow had this goal. I wanted to make her happy, so I put more effort into it. So I was basically the top of my year, and, and then I decided that's what I want to give her. I want to still make her proud, even she is not there anymore. But I want to be the best because I know it made her happy. So I got myself together at this point. I was living on my own after my mother died because my aunt she met this one guy. She was also divorced, she met this one guy, like, two months before my mother died. And two months after my mother died she got married to this guy, and nobody liked him. And when my mother died he said, like, "well things like that happen in life." So, we really hated him, and he hated us, and, of course, this was not an option for me to go there. So, I was living, until I finished school, I was living for four months on my own. I mean my sister had to go for an interview because my sister applied for—what is the English word for it?—I don't even know the German one, hm, you know, she, whatever she applied to get like the right to take me and to substitute my mother. And I wanted to go to my sister because I didn't want to move to my father because actually you know you are 15, and my father was living in the woods somewhere. And, ah, as much as I admired him and his lifestyle, but it seemed inappropriate to me, like, you know, it just didn't seem exciting for me. I wanted to at least stay with my friends. I didn't want to move to the woods and to a different neighborhood, with different people and be with interesting, but at the same time, for a child, weird people, and somehow I was afraid I would become his house maid, or whatever, and, we never lived together, you know, and so I went to be with my sister, and, and, also my teacher offered to take me, which was very nice of her and her family, and so everybody was very supportive. My teacher was very supportive, my sister was very supportive. We were very close at this point, my sister and me, and I think from age 13 up to the point that we got split, because she had to stay in prison, and I was released, up to in this area, we were very close, in this period. So I was living on my own finishing up school, and I pretty much put everything aside. I mean, I really, I guess up to a couple of years ago I just pushed everything aside and I just tried to be bold and get through that, and I pretty much handled it very well, I think. I finished school. I was the second best student in school, and they offered me, I was able to go to higher education. They offered me that, and, of course, it was weird living in a big house by myself. My sister came as much as she could, but I closed as many rooms as I could. I just locked them. I never entered them. So I was just living in my room, the kitchen and the bathroom, and closed everything off, because it was just too empty too dark . . .

(Did you have to pay rent for the house?)

I did have to pay rent in East Germany. It was this two-family house, a very big house. But in East Germany you couldn't buy a two-family house because you might have been able to make money out of the second apartment, which was already like a capital way of thinking. So you couldn't buy a two-family house, but my family was living there since the 50s so it almost feels like, you know, I was living there 18 years of my life. And, so after my mother was dead, you know, my family was anyway kind of broken. My sister and me we decided that we would get, try to get, a visa for Hungary with some friends of ours, and use this possibility in order to get out of the country. And this is what we did. I mean, she was more. Everybody thought that she pushed me into that, but it was not true. They really didn't do right to her by saying that she pushed me to anything because it was actually my idea. But, of course, nobody thinks that, you know, the younger one would have this devastating idea. Three weeks later, or four weeks later, we went to Hungary. We got the visa and I prepared everything, like, all my papers, and I was ready not to return. Unfortunately, I was the only one who did return (laughs) *ja*. So, we went to Hungary, and as soon as we got there we decided we are not going to return. In Hungary we first spent, like, a week on our own there. I have never been in Hungary before and we decided to treat ourselves, but at the same time we were talking already before about it. When we met with my sister's two friends we kind of like worked out the whole thing, so, *ja,* we just, actually, we always had problems with East Germany, especially my sister, and me, because of my father, because we did look at things in a different way. We knew a lot of things which were happening. We had, like, open eyes about what's happening, and I told you before, our family was a lot of times, also, you know. We found bugs in my father's house, and so our family was always a little bit on the spot of everything. My sister was not able to do her education, and we just, anyway, never felt that we want to continue living there. But for me it was clear, it was always clear during the time my mother was sick. I said to myself I would never, I would never, leave her and do that. And something which also sounds kind of weird, but, in a way, sometimes I think that it almost seems like because she knew that, it's almost like, of her dying, she gave me my life, because I would have never left her alone, never, so sometimes I just wonder how things work out, and, and, of course, it's probably a totally silly thought but sometimes I wonder if she, you know, she gave me my life with that. Otherwise I would not be here. I would have not done anything. I would have been in East Germany in this little village, and I probably would, as much as I adored her, but, I probably would have been miserable for the rest of my life because, as I told you, I was a dreamer, big, big dreams always, and, but I would not have done anything with her being sick and being alive. So, and after she was gone, I was like, you know, now it is just, like, I don't have any need to stay here. My sister didn't have any need to stay there, so, ah, we decided that now is the time for us to do the step. So there was another friend, we were like five of us, but this fifth friend, she was going to come back, and, she didn't want to escape. So . . . and she was actually very nice, and because she knew everything, she was involved, which was very dangerous for her. She could have been put in prison right away for that, and, so, after, after actually she returned from vacation, she went to my sister's apartment in order to pick all the documents up, whatever we left there, we needed there. So she took it over to her house. I mean she was in total danger doing all this. So, anyway, we got there. We spent the first week on our own, just enjoying ourselves, and everybody was sure that we wouldn't return. As soon as our friends came, we informed them that we are going to do that, and two of them were like, "Oh my God." And there was one who was actually, was not that close of a friend, was, like, all right, my support. So and then like we spent another week with them and then we actually took the first step in packing a suitcase, packing all our belongings, the most basics we needed, and this was the time, you probably heard about it, when the embassies got occupied—Berlin Prague Budapest. And so we were, like, it was already high security there. But somehow, without smart little talk at the door, they opened it

Andrea Pernstich **177**

right away for us so it almost seemed to be too easy to be true, and it was too easy to be true. So they let us in and automatically you are on West German ground, and we were waiting there. We were talking to the ambassador and, but, basically what he told us—we were there for a couple of hours—what he told us was, like, he said "we can get you a passport but we can't get you a visa because the visa comes from a different place." So at the end it was almost like resigning, and a friend of mine she got up she said, "all right I've had it." She walked out and, of course, we all followed her. But he gave us a little tip, and he told us, or, he didn't tell us, because he was afraid as well, he wrote it down for us, that there was a little town on the southern border of Hungary. Grenzt, bordered to former Yugoslavia. There was a carnival coming up, but what he didn't understand, and he said like, "this would be a good time because there are a lot of things going on." But what he didn't understand was what we basically knew, it was intuition. We didn't know that but it was a right intuition we had, was, as soon as we entered the embassy the East Germans knew about it. This security system was so well developed, and it was true, we found out later, as soon as we entered, they knew, and they even knew who entered there. It's unbelievable. Or, maybe they didn't know right away who entered, but within a day they had the information, because otherwise they would have caught us right away. But we left the embassy and we knew all we had to do is, like, you know, not even waste a second. Go back to this little town we came from in the Balaton, and we went back and our friends were like "oh my God what happened?" So we told them about it. We told them about our plans. We prepared everything again. We packed our suitcases, we burnt all our documents, whatever we had, and put our black clothes on, like, very like criminals. So we basically were well prepared, and we took off at night, going down to this town. which was called Bartsch. And, so we got there, the car was filled with seven people. I was laying across of everybody, and somehow I fell asleep for a couple of hours on the way there. And the deal was that four girls plus this one guy, who said, "you get my support," he stayed with us. I mean he was so brave, because he actually wanted to escape with us. But he didn't need to. He was from West Germany. But just in order to make us feel more secure, and, so the deal was that us five would stay and try to find a way, and the two other guys would drive over to Yugoslavia wait there at a certain point. And if we wouldn't get there till 8 o'clock in the morning they would have to return, so we can try it again the next night. So we got out of the car. I fell asleep, and when I woke up and I got out of the car, everything felt kind of not right, just didn't feel right at all. So, and then what happened was basically like our travel through the woods, over fields, and the weirdest things happened there. It was a very strange experience, you know. First of all always, like, being in the dark. We didn't know the place. We had no orientation. We didn't have any information about this place, where we have to go, nothing. I mean you just really got there. We only knew that we had to do something, right away the same night, I mean, and so we got there without orientation. And we were actually . . . where we got out of the car was pretty close to the border. But there was a lot of military already around there so we knew where the border is, kind of. So we tried to sneak, like, our way *ja,* it felt like, you know, it was freezing, and I had a little bit of headache, and it just didn't feel right, you know. Sometimes you feel something might be right, but this just didn't feel right at all. Somehow I wished I could have just gone back and go to bed and just be somewhere, I don't know. So we tried to make our way through that area there without being seen. Every time we crossed a little bridge we thought we crossed the river. Of course we knew we didn't, but you know, you never know. We hope always. So, and then there was this kind of rural area, very country like. But there was this little town, and we made our way out of the town, and it was, like, probably also like in all the eastern countries. A lot of streets are sand streets, there is no concrete, and, so, a lot of fields, a lot of forest. And so we were basically crossing fields, and jumping across little rivers, and always we thought, like, "well maybe we somehow we are already there we just don't know." And we were always looking for, like, some kind of sign somewhere. And the first weird thing to happen was at one point *ja* we crossed through this cornfield. The corn was much higher than we were so it was like we were kind of trapped in there. We didn't really know where we were going, everything was wet and dark. We got out of the field and right into the woods and we crossed this, it was not big woods, maybe just 200 meters, and there was an open field, and there was a train track going through the field, and behind the train track, far away, about maybe 1,000 meters, like a 1 km, whatever, there was a little field, with this huge building, and it was totally lit. All the windows were lit, so, and this house was really like a ghost house, and it was very strange because we made our way over because we thought that there would be some kind of indication, a car or whatever, in order to let us know where we are. And so we walked over there, and then we got closer, and that's where we actually saw that all the windows were open. All the windows were open. There was light throughout the house, maybe three stories high, maybe seven, eight windows across. So it was a big house but we didn't see anybody in there, no person, nothing living, but just the sound of, like, like a couple of dryers *Schleudern Waescheschleudern ja.* So it was very strange in the middle of nowhere.

Then we saw a car, actually, and the car had the H in the back which means Hungary. So *ja* so we knew at least what we wanted to know. Then we kept walking and we walked for six hours, you know, left, right, back, forth, whatever, without real direction, just trying to find the proper spot, because all what we needed was to find the river to have the right conditions, and to just jump in, swim over, and that's all we were looking for. And then we got to those woods, and there was another weird thing, because in the middle of the woods, there were, like, a couple of cars, like construction cars, a couple of people. It was like 3 or 4 o'clock in the morning. So, and there was a fire, and somehow it seemed like a space shuttle is just going to go up. It seemed to be very weird. There was no reason for them to be there. I mean, there was probably a reason, but I didn't understand because it was just so out of place. And so we just walked by. Then we talked a couple of words with them, they were Hungarian but some fellow spoke a little bit of German, and, who knows, maybe those were the ones who, ah, turned us in, because somebody turned us in. But I don't think those were the ones because we kept going for an hour or an hour and a half, maybe two hours. I don't know. Actually we did find the perfect spot and there was an old man there. It was an old factory, like a little industrial area, and we saw the river right behind it. And there was, I don't know, like one of those people who take care, just to make sure that everything was fine *ja*. And there was this guy, an older man, he was sitting there. I think he saw us also because he tried to get, like, one friend of mine, and this guy tried to get closer in order to check out. If this was it, so I think this was the one who turned us in, because actually they came back. And we were just about to really make our way through there and do it, but suddenly, like, two military cars came, and the people, like the *Meliz*, just, like, jumped out of the car, with their rifles, and basically pushed us in there. So we never even got to the water. And so, and then, of course, at this point, being naive, without really knowing what to expect, we made up all kinds of stories, like, you know we were wandering, you know, we stayed close to the town and we made like a night wandering, or whatever, *Nachtwanderung*, you know. You just come up with whatever silliest idea at this moment, because it's like you are going to do something fast, otherwise it's too late. So then we drove to this, whatever station, police station, and they walked us in, each of us in a different room, totally wet clothes, tired and freezing, and we didn't even get like anything, you know, to cover ourselves, or to dry ourselves. So we were sitting there freezing. We didn't know what was going to happen. We were apart from each other and so we were sitting there for a couple of hours. And then, of course, naive as one can be I, was thinking: "God I would be never able to go to Hungary again or they probably don't let me be with my sister," instead of thinking, "well we will all going to end up in prison," as we knew before. But at this moment you don't realize that. I think you are just so overwhelmed by the sudden situation, and, so . . . But I don't know when it was, but it must have been 8 or 8:30, because we told our friends to return at 8, and for some reason they got checked at the border. I don't know if somebody said something, or if they just, I don't know what kind of indication they had. But they got the military checked them at the border, and they saw that they have like a lot of stuff there. Plus they found, I don't know exactly what they found, they found some kind of paper which had one of our names, but . . . So they got arrested as well, and I just saw them from a window that they got walked back from the military car to the headquarters, or whatever you would call it. So we were sitting, and this one guy, around 10 or 11, so this one guy was really scared, the one guy who returned also, he was really scared. And he gave like the first *wie sagt man dazu*[2] first *Gestaendnis*[3] *ja*. After he gave his speech of course it was like, you know, they asked one after another and said, "all right, this is what we have now write down your story." So this is how it all happened one story after another was written down and they put us again into cars, three separate cars, one my sister my two friends and those two guys were in, in one car, this one guy was in, and in another car was me. I never understood why they split us like that, and then they drove us to another prison, which was a real prison. And we got there at night, late at night, and again they took us in that room. This one guy got in separately, I got in separately, and again, waiting around, sitting in separate rooms, and waiting until you actually were asked to come out and give your speech. And so I guess by, I don't know, early in the morning, 2 or 3, it must have been very late, because I saw through the window that it was dark already for hours, and so at one point they assigned us to little cells, or cabins, or whatever *Kabienen*, or whatever, prison cells, and they gave us each a mattress, and this was like a real, I mean, I didn't even . . . This was all like a dream for me because I just didn't comprehend this whole thing at this point. It was almost like I got a kick out of it, but I had to laugh because, ah, I felt like in a strange movie. I was suddenly in the movie you know like what I was seeing on TV. I was part of it because they opened the door, this wooden door where they put me in, and suddenly I saw this cell with, like, four wooden benches, and here I had my mattress. I put it down and one blanket and I got a piece of bread and a cup of tea, and then the next morning I was there by myself in this empty room. It was just the strangest scene because I didn't really imagine that something like that would still exist, like a typical prison cell, and then my friend, my sister's friend, or also my friend, they put her in as well. So we were at least together. And the next morning at 5, like it was always, that we could keep the mattress for 6 hours, like from 11 to 5 in the morning. We stayed there couple of days and then had to give it back, so that there would not be any comfort anywhere. So the whole day you just basically sat on your wooden bench. But at least we were together, and we really, I have to say, probably it is also strange, but maybe it's not. We really had a good time. We really, like, supported each other. We were singing and we were talking and somehow we pretended it wasn't really true, and, somehow, we didn't really think that any . . . or we just tried to ignore the fact that it has consequences. I guess maybe that's something normal you do, and so my sister and her friend were together, and those guys were like way down there, so they couldn't really hear us. But we were like singing songs, and then a canon *Kanon* would start, and my sister and her friend would jump in there. And then it was actually the day where, when it was Aug. 13th, which is my father's birthday, and so we were sitting, you know, celebrating my father's birthday with a cup of water and bread you got in the morning. You got a chunk of bread and, with some jelly, like a piece of like very hard jelly. I mean, you had to take a bite out of it, and in the morning you got a cup of tea, but the rest of the day just water. I just didn't imagine that something like this still existed *ja*. The escape was Aug. 11th, and this was Aug. 13th, and by Aug. 17th they drove us over in a van all together, except the guys. The guys stayed there for three months. They had to stay in prison, and so they drove us to another Hungarian prison. We were like, you know, of course we had to go in *Verhoere*[4] and *ja*, and then they drove us. They drove us *ja* and in this prison you couldn't go outside. We were basically just sitting like in the cell all day long. The only thing you could do is smoke a cigarette *ja*. They gave us cigarettes, and couldn't shower there—nothing. It was kind of weird. It was a weird prison, and then they drove us over to Budapest and this is where we stayed 17 days. I just know it, I guess. I would have never known that if I wouldn't have been, like, searching through my cell to find like this little tiny piece of splinter—is it called splinter? Splinter in order to make like a mark in the wall so I would like keep track of the days. So they drove us over there and I think this was the first time that it became a little bit more serious, and we actually knew what was going to happen, because we kind of got introduced to this whole process, in prison, because they told us they had their experience with that . . . They told us what's going to happen to us and we got there again like hours of *Verhoere*, hearings, and separate, each was separate. So they put us into cells again, and I was in a cell with a Hungarian dancer. Her name was Eva. She was very, very nice person, a very sad person, very I guess, I don't know. Somehow there was something very typical about her, like something very dramatic about her, and the way she looked with this tiny little body. She was a dancer but she was in this closed space, for a dancer, which already is a kind of weird feeling. And she looked a little bit like Isabella Dunkin[5] the dancer, with this kind of sad happiness. She almost treated me like I could have been her daughter in there, but I kind of fucked up the situation, because I heard my sister, like, the next day. I heard my sister outside, you know, they always, like, took you out of the cells, to the room where the officer was sitting, always with another officer. You couldn't just walk around like you see in American movies. You couldn't see anything—nothing. You could just hear. So I heard my sister crying, so of course I was screaming through the door. I wanted to know if they did something to her. So she answered me, and so this guy got rude to her, and I just heard her saying, "leave me alone." Of course I was getting crazy. I thought they would do something to her, so I was banging at the door and screaming. And as a result of that they put me into like a single cell for the next 16 days. So I was there in this little cell all by myself not being able to talk to anybody, and *ja*, just by myself, 24 hours a day. And they had three books in German, which I all read, of course, like, within the shortest time. So I was sitting there basically every day for 24 hours. You were not supposed to lay down, but at least you had a mattress. So this was the first time that it kind of hit me in a strange way, what happened, and it's also, you know, back home my class was going on a trip, and just this feeling that they didn't know. Nobody at home probably knew what happened to us, and, and then the only contact to my outside world, which was not my contact, it was just that there were kids. I think it was also partly a children's prison because I heard young people, very young people. So it was interesting to me, to create this kind of picture. I didn't understand anything, but after a while I knew who everybody was just from their voices. That was comforting. I couldn't see anything because they had those, you know, glass bricks. I couldn't see anything but there was just like a little thing where air could come in, and at least I had some kind of story going on. I could make up my own stories, and one day, it was, I had a really bad day. I was crying a lot because of a stupid idea which came into my mind, but there was like a big firework outside, and, like, somehow it sounded like bombs were going off, and I didn't know that this was a major holiday in Hungary. So I didn't know what was going on. I couldn't ask somebody because nobody understood, and also I was, like, physically I was not in a good condition because I couldn't for the last I guess already 14 or 15 days, I wasn't able to go to the bathroom, so my stomach was getting bigger, and it hurt already—everything. I couldn't even sleep on the side anymore, and so I was physically not in a good stage, and mentally also, not really, and then this was going on outside, and there was still Cold War, you know. Any day it could have happened, who knows? and this is what I imagined I thought like now the war broke out and I was just sitting there, and I thought I would never see my sister anymore, and I was just really so afraid. I was sitting there and didn't know what was going on out there, so I was just crying all day. But then suddenly I was praying. Me, with no religion at all (laughs). But I was praying to God, and suddenly it stopped after a couple of hours. Maybe it was not a couple of hours, it just seemed to me a couple of hours. So there I had kind of on the edge day, and then it was the first time actually, at the end of this time, like the end of August beginning of September, that we actually got in contact with a *Stasi—Staatsicherheit*[6] which was always like, ah, invisible force in East Germany. You knew they were there, you knew that, ah, they did bad things. They were everywhere, but you didn't know where, so people were afraid. They had fear. That was also a reason why a lot of people didn't do anything, didn't dare to do anything, because out of fear. You never knew where is it, and it is weird of course, you know, that these are human beings as well, but you don't imagine them as human beings. You think that they are bigger and higher than that, more forceful. So at this point we were brought to this office, one after another. There was this guy from the *Stasi* sitting and asking questions and this was such a relief because it was the first time that we saw like, it's just a person. This is what the *Stasi* is all about and it was actually a very nice feeling. A lot of fear just fell off my shoulders, so, and then a couple of days later we got picked up by a bus, and also three other guys, and we were driven to the airport, somewhere, out far off. And there was this pathetic private plane standing and waiting for us seven people, and I was thinking how pathetic this whole thing was. We tiny little people, and they are so afraid of us. They have like a real plane just for us. I mean, who are we? It was strange. And then we were sitting on the plane, and we flew back to Berlin, and there we went into another prison, and, you know, checking up the body, there was this whole procedure, which nowadays they wouldn't do it to me anymore. But it was a little bit devastating at one point, because you had to take off all your clothes in front of male and female officers, and you had to do exercises you know where they saw your private parts, everything, and they actually grabbed into your private parts, if you smuggled anything. So it was, you know, one more of those things where you are just getting to the edge. But, of course, they want you to get you to the edge, and we tried not to get there, or not to show it. So, and then after all this they put us back in a little van, and I thought I would sit together with my sister and my friends there. It was a tiny little van, like a VW bus. There were six little cabins with little doors so each of us was sitting in one of those things. It was dark in there. You didn't know anything, and they were driving like maniacs, and, again, you are, like, so you have no direction. So, and then we were brought to this political prison *U-Haft* (detention pending trial), not a real prison. So we got there, and again the same procedure—you got in there, separated, one after another for a hearing, the whole story over and over again. Why? When we decided? How we decided? Who knew of it? Who was involved?—all those things, over and over again. Why did we leave?—and there was one wonderful thing, which was the first time that we could say whatever we wanted to. It didn't make any difference, and this was a wonderful feeling. I've never had, I mean nobody in East Germany had that. You always had to be careful when we wanted to talk about something political. My father and I went out for a walk just in order to make sure that nobody is going to listen to us. So, important things we could never discuss in the house or in, like, a set area. We had always to move around because you always had to watch what you were saying, always, constantly, always. And really after I came to West Germany I had to relearn how to voice your opinion. Not relearn, to learn, because I never knew what it means to just say what you have in your mind. But this was something in this prison that, you know, you couldn't lose anything else. We lost already everything, so we could just say it. It was a very nice feeling, even in this environment. But again it was a relief, so again we were put in different cells, everywhere, and they put me together with another woman, and, so, she was about mid-30s. She was a wreck when I entered the cell. I think she was just crying for days already, and so with me coming in there, it was kind of good for her. She was a mother and got split from her son, and they just picked her up from home, put her in prison, same as her husband, and she knew she is not going to see her son for probably a year, and her son was a teenager. He was like 13, so, and in that *ja*. In the first day we were just talking, talking way until midnight, and I stayed there for three weeks *ja*, until the end of September. And again, every day the same thing. I had to go to an officer for an hour or two, sometimes three, four, just to tell the same story over and over and over again. Of course we knew already what's going to happen because the people we were together in the cell, they were already advanced prisoners, they kind of knew what's going to happen. So we knew the whole procedure with a trial coming up, and after a trial being put into prison, and being probably there for a year. We knew all that but there was always the question: what happens to me because I was underage? So the next day I learned the prison language, and this was another experience. I never want to miss you actually start communicating with people you have never seen, you have never heard, and you probably will never see and will never hear. But that you can build a relationship with somebody. You don't know anything, you haven't seen nothing, I mean, because there is the wall and all you know is just the way they knock on the wall. But otherwise there is nothing. You cannot smell, you cannot use your senses, nothing, in order to figure those people out. But you can build a relationship, a very strong relationship. So after I learned this prison language, I started to talk with the guy next to me. For each letter it is like one knock like A.B.C.D.E.F.G. (knocks for each letter), and then second letter, usually after the third letter, this prisoner in the other room knocked twice and that means like, "I know" and we just started talking like crazy. And we just kept knocking, and, again, you can develop such a strong feeling for somebody you don't know anything except the words that get knocked through the walls. So we had like a very strong bond between us, and every time I heard something, I was so happy. If it was just like after lunch: "how was your lunch?" It was so strong and so that I really missed every second almost even with the women in my cell. We got along very well and, so . . . . And one time, you know, there were like two beds in there, a small walkway and a sink and a toilet. So you were going to the toilet in front of the other person and, you know, if you pee it is fine, but, you know, so you are already losing part of your dignity. But we were trying to make the other person comfortable, so we always would start smoking a cigarette and reading so we would not see and smell. But one time I remember an officer opened this little window and she was just sitting on the toilet there and he was just looking in. Afterwards she was just crying for hours because they just take everything from you, and, so, I got in trouble for knocking so much. They caught me a couple of times. I had to go to the prison director and so eventually it ended up that they took those two people out of the cell and put them somewhere else, and it was so again. It was almost like the feeling I had after my mother died again. This wall was getting so cold that I didn't really want to touch it with my arm because it was so cold so empty there. So I was very sad for a while.

. . .

This was the first time that we also had to wear prison clothes and *ja*, we wore sweat pants and sweaters of certain colors and a kind of military shirt, and we actually also wore, like, you know, miscellaneous underwear, and we had two pairs of underwear per week and 1 pair of socks. And every Wednesday was sock *sockentausch*, and the underwear was size 52 and sometimes 20. It was more or less luck if you got like a right size of underpants, plus you knew already how many people went through it. Anyway . . . this was another situation. Once a day we could go out, we were left out for a walk, and what happened was, was very much controlled. They would come in the morning and ask "who wants to go out, who doesn't?"—and so one couple left another went out. So what happened was they opened the door and by this time you always had to stand up. If the door was open there was no sitting down. So . . . and then you walked out, and everywhere there were red lights, around the whole building, going down the stairs. And it really looked like a prison, you know, as you know it from Alcatraz. You just see like a *Geruest*-like inside open *ja*, and . . . But it was just open on one side. But you could look downstairs. There was a metal staircase, but there were like red lights everywhere which meant that prisoners were out, and they were not supposed to see each other. So nobody else was out, just us, and another couple from another cell, and the officers, and then everywhere at every level there was another officer just waiting. Another officer went with us, so, and then we could go out there, there was another kind of like a cell-like or, like, house-like building, like a barn, basically, just four walls split up with more walls, so that there are little *Kabinen*. So there were three *Kabinen* on one side, and three on the other side. So you couldn't just go out in the yard, they put you right into another cell, and it was like a door and a fence on top. So the air came in and then you could just walk around in this little thing, so, and then on top in the middle of everything there was a walkway, and the officer was walking up and down, and up and down. And that was also the first time that we actually saw the prison from outside. We could see the windows and what they had in front of them, all those security things. So we could do that once a day, for 15 minutes. So, oh, everybody had a number. I was number 79 and my cell number was 89, and at one point they put me again in a single cell, which was 69. They put me in a single cell because at one point I was underage, and there was a problem what to do with me, and they decided that they would have to release me. And so right, before I got out, a week or five days before I got out, they put me into this single cell because they didn't want me. It was also before they told me that I am going to go because, ah, they didn't want me to carry any information or anything, somehow, out. So they put me, without me knowing about it, one day, they just came in said like: "OK five minutes to pack all your stuff, come with us." So, and then I just took all my belongings said goodbye and they put me into a single cell, and then soon after I heard that they release me from prison, which was at my point in my situation. I was not happy about it at all because in a way I felt comfort in there, because I knew that everybody else in there was in the same boat, everybody was thinking the same way. It is probably kind of silly but sometimes, like at night, we would just scream things like, "I hate this country," which, of course, you couldn't do outside. There is no way. I mean, people were thrown into prison for saying things like that. Of course, you cannot just go out and do that, but in there you could suddenly say whatever you wanted to say. It might not make that much sense to somebody. I mean, you probably understand. But it's like a very strong feeling that I could say, like, "I hate this country" and I just could say it and nothing would happen—nothing—because I was already in there. What else is going to happen? So this was kind of nice, and I felt that as soon as I would have to leave there it still had a certain freedom, compared to before, because it was known, my opinion was known: what I felt, what I thought. So I didn't have anything to hide, like before. But still I knew that I would meet a lot of enemies out there, which really was the case. When I was released my aunt and my father picked me up, and it was decided that I was living with my aunt, even I didn't like her husband, even that he didn't like me. But I told you before that I didn't want to live with my father, so I moved there, and my town, of course, it was kind of hard to go back there. And first of all I felt, I lost, and some people looked at me, saying, a lot of people said to me, "what do you think you are that you can leave?" and, so people were kind of happy that *wie wird man sagen auf Deutsch, Schadenfreude*, gloating that it didn't work out for us.[7] Other people were angry, other people were afraid, and just very few people didn't change their relationship towards me. One day I went to visit my best friend, relatively good friend, and she opened the door and her mother was just asking from behind, "who is it?" and she said my name, and her mother's respond was, "Oh my God." And that was basically what I always got to hear, or people would ignore me on the street. And so it was not easy. Plus, I mean, I was young. Even I have gone though some stuff already, but I was still young, and I still couldn't face reality so strongly, and, of course, it mattered to me. It hurt me and I wasn't strong enough to totally push it away. I did care, and then there was the next question, "what am I going to do?' I couldn't go to school anymore, they said, like, "no school for you," and in East Germany it was that nobody looked for their own apprenticeship or work, it was done by somebody else, it was done by the system. You said, "well I would like to do this and this" and they took care of everything. They said, "*ja* you can do it or no you can't," but you never went out there and were looking for a job. That's the reason that nowadays are a lot of problems, because nobody knows how to do, because it was not taught. We were taught to be very much dependent, so I didn't know what do to, and there was a thing called *Berufsberatung*[8] and my aunt and me went there, and this is where I got a job offer, which was working in a dry cleaner, having an apprenticeship as a dry cleaner, professional dry cleaner. And now I can smile about it, but at this point I was devastated. I started crying because I had hopes, I had hopes for my life, and I had dreams, and somebody telling me I should go to school for a year and a half to be a professional dry cleaner. So I started crying, like, right there, and this guy said, like, "well don't be so upset, there is a way to work your way up." And I asked him what he means by that, that I should become a super dry cleaner, or what else can you do? So we left there and I said to my aunt, "you cannot let me do that." So she said, like, "well, we will find something else for you." And one of my friends from school, she was my nature friend, so, and she started this apprenticeship as an industrial dress maker at this factory in my town, and she told me about it, because she just started doing that, and in the same night I saw in the West Berlin news that it was very fashionable to learn how to sew. And I was, like, "well, I want to go there, and if it is there very fashionable, that's what I am going to do, then." So I went over there and I asked, which was very unusual, never an individual would come and ask if they would take somebody. So they knew right away that something was wrong with me. Plus also, when I showed my papers, I had like my documents, where I had papers for a criminal, a passport, *Ausweiss*, and there was another thing called *Klappkarte*, which was called PM12, and everybody who was in trouble criminal or political, but mostly people think of you being a thief. So they knew right away something was wrong with me. So I told them my story and they said, "no, there is nothing that they could do for me." So I went home. I was very upset because I knew that there were still spaces available. So I told my aunt, and this was very lucky because the woman I talked to was actually a nurse, and my aunt was a doctor. So this woman once worked for my aunt and my aunt was a very respected doctor in my town. So we went there together and then I got this, I got in there, so I started working in a factory for a year and a half, and so I learned how to sew sitting on a *Fliessband*[9] I was sewing the first half a year zippers, for half a year sleeves, and for half a year *Bund*.[10] So, you know, it was quite a tough experience. Everybody knew about me, and it was always nice to pick on somebody, and, plus, I didn't fit in there at all. I didn't speak the same language because I came out of a more educated family, and I didn't look the same as everybody else. And then what happened again was a little bit of . . . I was a total outsider so it was kind of hard. I heard comments, you know, "what do you think you are?" and every day, basically, there was something going on. Somebody was, like, after me for being who I was, what I have done, and also what was . . . Also I still had to go once a month, I had to go to the *Staatssicherheits* station, and for an interview. And also two months after I got out we had the trial, of course. People knew about it, and it was also kind of interesting. It was kind of strange to see that my, sister my friends, came in in handcuffs, *Handschellen*. It's pathetic to think about, like real criminals. So the trial was going on for a couple of hours, and at the end they got convicted to 2½ years in prison, which is always the same procedure, about 2½ to 4 years. Usually you sit in prison for a year to one year and a half, and then they let you out, and for me it was *auf Bewaehrung*,[11] one year and four months *auf Bewaehrung*, and so this was basically it, and *ja*. I was just living my life there, going to the factory every day. In a way it was a harsh life because I hated this factory, and I still had problems with a lot of people, and, of course, a lot of people tried to influence me in those interviews at the *Stasi*. And twice also I had not a very pleasant experience with being *verhaftet*, arrested, again on the street because I had this document. It was nothing bad and they let me go after half an hour, but after something like that happened, the whole crowd of people, of course, staring at me. What has she done? Just because you had this stupid piece of paper in your hand. It is just so devastating because there is nothing you can do. But otherwise I was just living my life there, and about two weeks after my trial I met this guy and we were, like, involved for a couple of years. And I think he also helped me through a lot of this stuff. And then my education was over, my apprenticeship, and the same day I got my certificate I quit, and *ja* the first year, when my sister was still in prison, we had the permission to visit her once a month. So one month my father went, one month I went, and it was always, like, a six-hour travel on the train, and then . . . This was the first time I saw a real women's prison. It was an old castle on a hill, and it was always very disturbing to go there to see her because she was always very much on the edge. I mean she was strong and she handled it as good as she could, but I knew that it was not a pleasant experience for her. I mean what happened to her in prison was not to compare to anything I have experienced there, of course. Emotionally things were going on, but nobody mistreated me. But those women got mistreated in a very bad way a lot of times, also physically, and she looked very much down all the time, and not healthy at all. And then after 11 months she got released. Those were those *Mittwochsbusse* (Wednesday buses), and then she got out and she came to West Germany. So when I quit this job, you cannot just quit in East Germany because it is a hard procedure finding a new job, being politically correct. But again I was lucky because I saw a little ad of our nursery. There were very, very few private businesses in East Germany, but we had two private businesses in my town, and one was a nursery. And so since this nursery was on the same street where I grew up we have known each other since I was a baby. So I went over there and I talked to them. They were very nice, very open, people. So they said *ja* I can work there. So I started working in the nursery. I loved working in the greenhouse, out in the field. So for half a year I was working there. And so I had to leave . . . it was the time that I had to leave the house of my mother, because the apartment was needed for another family. I did live with my aunt but I kept the apartment of my mom as long as I could because mostly the weekends I would stay at my mom's apartment, and I would go there very often, you know, when we had problems or her husband was mean with me. So I spent there quite a lot of time, and then my 18th birthday came, and this was the day when I officially applied to leave the country, and then the interviews got more often. I had to go there every two weeks, and at one point, it was in September, they . . . I got a letter, no. I had to go to an interview again, and I went there. I got there and they just handed me over papers and were, like, "OK you have 24 hours." You have to got to go to all those stations, which was like, you know, the major, the electricity, the landlord, and the school. I had 8 different stations I had to go to, to get a signature. It was called *Laufzettel*[12] I got my *Laufzettel* and, so, but there was a holiday in those 24 hours, because they gave it to me in the afternoon, and the next day there was a holiday, and I was supposed to return it the same afternoon after the holiday. But I knew because of the holiday a lot of people were gone. So it was, like, really, I just really made it—barely. It was like running with the time to go everywhere, but still I made it, so, and this was basically the first step of leaving the county, and I was already sitting on my packed suitcases, and I just had one open where I changed my clothes from. Then they told me the procedure. They said everything needs to be listed. So I had six suitcases, and everything, even a tissue, had to be listed. So it was ready. So they said to me, call us every day at 1 o'clock from now on." So I called every day at 1 o'clock, every day I called, and they said, "no nothing nothing." I just waited for the point that they would say OK. By then, and then you have to leave the country. So this was going on for three weeks, and then, by Oct. 28, I called again. This was kind of strange day because my boyfriend was somewhere, my aunt was on a business trip for the day, and my father I couldn't get in touch with, which was fine. But then I called and then they told me, "OK come in today." It was 1 o'clock. It was in another city, so by 3, I was in the office. When I got to the office they gave me a document with my picture in it, and there was a time written down, and then they said, "by tonight 12 o'clock you have to leave the country." So I was like, "Oh my God." I went back. By 5:30 I was home, nobody was to find, and I had to leave in Berlin, which was another 1½[-hour] trip. So then I called my boyfriend. He wasn't there, and I called again, and then he was eventually there, and then he took the car of his mom, and he came out from Berlin. So I think by 7:30, or whatever, 8 o'clock, he got there. My father by accident stopped by. See, nobody really except my aunt, because she was a doctor, and other businesses, had a telephone, but nobody else. So, my father couldn't have called. So, by accident he stopped by. So, I told him, "well I am going to leave tonight, I don't know when I am going to see you again." And I was just waiting for my aunt and she just would not come home. And I was very nervous, tense, and everything, because I knew once I leave I don't know when I am going to see anybody again. And so eventually she showed up at 9:30, and it was just about time to really leave. Otherwise I wouldn't have made it. Of course she was very upset. She comes home, I had 5 minutes to spent with her, and I leave. We loaded the car with the suitcases, and we left, and I made it to the border, like, a quarter to 12, and I had, like, to call my sister in order to tell her to pick me up, because at this point she was already living in Berlin. And then, like, *ja* half a year after I applied to get out I got out, and it was kind of sad because at the border, I mean, my boyfriend dropped me off—and when are we going to see each other again? But in a way I was so happy, I was so overwhelmed, I couldn't believe that this dream of mine for so, so many years would come true, that I actually can pass this border. And the only freedom we had, we could choose where to pass the border, and, of course, I picked the place I have been so many times before, just always looking at this point, and just looking at the people who would go through, and I couldn't. I said, "that's where I want to cross the border." And so I walked the first time, and the last time, I walked through there *ja*. It was an amazing feeling, and then I got there. I suddenly, I totally was so out of my mind that I just, like, threw my suitcases at a couple of West German boys who just came back from their East Berlin trip, crossing the border. I was just like here, you take this one and then I was, like, with my list in my hand and I was just walking through there crying because I left him, happy because I was out of this, and I just walked right by the officers. And they came back and grabbed me and said: "hello." And then I had to go like through five or six different stations of the border, and then, suddenly, unexpectedly I was out of those controlling points. My sister and her friends were standing in front of me. This was amazing, and then out of there, right into the car, my first drive through West Berlin.

Study Questions

1. Having read Susanne's story, how would you define freedom? At what point in her life do you think she was most free?
2. Do you agree with Andrea's assessment that Susanne's life is defined by periods of apparent gain followed by loss?
3. Does the bonding of Susanne and Andrea come through in the interview materials? How do you think Susanne's story would be different if told to a different kind of person?
4. What lessons is Susanne teaching Andrea through her life story?

Notes

1. Secondary school diploma.
2. "As they say about this."
3. confession.
4. interrogation.
5. Isadora Duncan.
6. *Stasi* is the common German short form of Ministerium für Staatssicherheit, or Ministry for State Security, the secret police of East Germany.
7. Translated as "How would you say it in German? Schadenfreude."
8. career counseling.
9. production line.
10. waistband.
11. probation.
12. lit. "circular."

Conclusion

It should be evident from the foregoing chapters that good undergraduate fieldwork is both original and challenging for students and professionals in the field. That fact in itself should be enough incentive to teach field methods to undergraduates as a routine practice. Each of these students has become better at what they now do for having gained fieldwork skills, and, without trying to sound too sentimental, I think that each of the projects represented here has done something to make the world better.

What I should also point out is that these students did not produce powerful work because they were the cream of the crop of students in the conventional sense. It would be no surprise if I were to announce that the very best undergraduates can produce good work—I hope that is a truism. But these students represent a very wide range when it comes to academic abilities outside of fieldwork. At one end of the spectrum, one of these students graduated with high honors and took the most prestigious student prize that Purchase College has to offer at graduation (given in this case for a fieldwork-based senior project). But at the other end, three came to Purchase as "educationally disadvantaged" students through a special program, and about half graduated with no better than a low B average in general subjects. It was doing fieldwork that brought out the best in all of them, and in several cases it was the very fact of a "disadvantaged" background that gave them the ability to do the work that they did with their interviewees from that same background.

What these projects also teach us is that *what* we know in the world is in part contingent on *how* we go about seeking that knowledge. Historically, students have come to college without much awareness of the details of the data-collecting methods that are particular to the social sciences. Almost all of them have had some training in library research, and the majority of them have had some exposure to the controlled experimental method of the physical sciences. If they have had any experience with social scientific methodology at all, it is generally with survey research technique. That is, they may have some knowledge of quantitative methodology (from polls presented in the media if nothing else), but close to none have any idea of qualitative methods (or, worse, they confuse social science research methods with journalistic interviewing and the like).

In the years before I retired, I surveyed the members of large general anthropology classes I taught at Purchase College (65 to 110 students each) concerning their classroom experiences with various forms of research before they attended college. Obviously my sample (n = 658) is small and deeply skewed, so I am not willing to make too much of the results. Nonetheless, these data do provide hints of a potentially important state of affairs. At some point early in the semester I asked my students how many of them had done the following anywhere in grades K–12 (even if only once):

1. written a paper based on library research: 100 percent
2. conducted (or seen) a controlled experiment: 85 percent
3. interviewed someone: 3 percent
4. used a voice recorder to gather information: 3 percent
5. photographed people's daily activities: 0 percent
6. videotaped an interview or an event: 1 percent

Even after the echoes of my mea culpas for poor survey technique have died away, I think the results still speak plainly enough. The average student in my classes comes with little or no experience in some of the most rudimentary techniques of qualitative data collecting according to social scientific principles. It may be true that a large percentage of the polled students have used a voice recorder or camera outside of school, but that is not the point. Being able to operate a recorder or camera is not the same as being able to use them in the service of social scientific data gathering. The fact that the use of this kind of technology for data gathering, or the development of skills in any other qualitative field method, are omitted from many school curricula implicitly devalues them; and they are also devalued by the unspoken assumption that

Conclusion

such techniques can be picked up without any need for special training (which, in turn, reinforces the devaluing of the social sciences in general—as opposed to the "hard" sciences). It is most emphatically not true that field techniques can be picked up as you go (although, in the past, anthropology departments have been as much to blame for this erroneous perception as anyone else). These days it is well understood that good photo documentation, good interview technique, good observation skills, and similar qualitative methods must be taught as systematically as library research skills or experimental method (see Bernard 1998 and 2005; Wolcott 2005), and there is no pedagogic reason why such methods cannot be taught in basic form and with suitable controls in secondary or even elementary grades.[1]

If qualitative research methods are undervalued in this way, then the data gathered by these methods also get short shrift. But if we are going to be both sincere and genuine in our attempts to create an inclusive curriculum at all levels—that is, a curriculum that is open to hearing from and learning about the history and culture of people of color, women, LGBTQ+ individuals, immigrants, and the poor rather than hearing only from the male, White, straight, middle class—then we have to use research and pedagogic methods that will let us hear those voices directly.

My late wife, Deborah Blincoe, pioneered a highly successful fourth-grade curriculum module in rural New York State that did exactly what I am advocating here. The New York State elementary curriculum required fourth graders to work on local history as part of their social studies program, and one school district was looking for something new and exciting to fill the need. Working closely with teachers and administrators, she developed a series of presentations and exercises for the students to acclimate them to qualitative field methods and then had them prepare for tape-recorded interviews with a series of local interviewees. They worked in groups of four or five, dividing up the tasks of asking questions, taping, photographing, and transcribing.[2]

The children were highly engaged by the project, and many who were indifferent students in the traditional sense approached the project with energy and enthusiasm. It is well-known that such methods are highly successful for motivating students at all levels, as, for example, Eliot Wigginton's *Foxfire* project demonstrated (see Wigginton 1986). The problem is not the obvious success of such methods but the difficulty in insinuating them into schools. Teachers are already burdened with endless mandates from the administrative hierarchy, so that imposing one more—however well-meaning and salutary—seems almost cruel, and as I know from personal experience, such initiatives can be met with stout resistance. The solution that Blincoe found was to slot the teaching of these methods into an educational context that is consonant with curricular needs as they already exist (in her case, whole language learning and the state curriculum on local history).

We also have to face the problem of a vicious cycle in the arena of expertise. Very few schoolteachers are themselves trained in qualitative field methods, so before they can teach students, they have to be trained themselves, and they have to understand their value. One of my advisees wrote a senior thesis on anthropology in the high school curriculum in various locations in downstate New York. He was surprised to discover that where anthropology was an offering in the schools, not a single one of the teachers had any substantive or methodological background in anthropology at the college level (see Girard 2000).

This discussion all leads us back to Hymes's remarks quoted at the beginning of this book. One of the ways that anthropology can thrive as a discipline is by training undergraduates who then go out into the world, not as anthropologists but as lawyers, doctors, social workers, *and teachers*. The change, if it is to occur at all, therefore, must begin at the college level.[3] When college general education requirements are being discussed by curriculum committees and the inevitable (and perfectly justified) arguments for the inclusion of a writing component, computer skills, and lab methods come up, social scientists should be in there pitching for their methods as well.

Let me be perfectly plain here. I am not talking about *content* at all; I am talking strictly about *methods*. Anthropology departments usually have very little trouble convincing colleagues to include an introductory course or the like into a core curriculum on the grounds that it is good to know something about non-Western cultures. But this is a purely content-based argument and does not get at the issues I am dealing with here. I am saying that if we divide typical college core general education requirements into skills on the one hand and content on the other, social science content is almost always present, and social science methods are almost always absent. Yet the social sciences are no different from other fields where appreciation of the content is deepened by understanding of the methods behind the content.

It has also been frequently overlooked, and I hope this book stands as a suitable corrective, that the social sciences may be unique in that undergraduates with proper training and supervision are capable of producing data of real professional interest. I am almost drowning in good, new, original data produced by my undergraduate students. How many professors of physics or philosophy can say the same? This is the kind of work that can change lives.

Conclusion

This thought returns me to my own experiences with my students because their work has changed my life. The fact that students can create an empowered and authentic dialogue with their interviewees has itself been a powerful experience for me as their teacher. At the most basic level, I have been changed simply by being privy to these intense narratives. I cannot imagine ever having the opportunity to hear many of these stories except through the mediation of my students. They have brought worlds to me that I was not aware of. The sampling here is the merest tip of the iceberg. I examined and graded between twenty and thirty life histories each year, and did so for well over twenty years. I have glimpsed the world of immigrants from the four corners of the earth, vicariously experienced the lives of the homeless and privileged and everything in between, accompanied the dying on their journeys, visited Nazi death camps . . . and on and on.

Perhaps, if it has not been clear up to now, I should say here that I am immensely proud of my students' work—not proud in the conventional sense of a teacher seeing a student succeeding but a rare sense of joy that they have produced something that matters in the world at large. I had no idea when I first started teaching undergraduates over forty years ago that they were capable of such feats, but one at a time they have taught me their strengths, and in their doing so I have learned to expect worlds of them. Teachers can bring with them a great many unconscious biases concerning their students, and having limited expectations is certainly one of the more destructive, if not the most destructive. I know that I was guilty of this offense at one point, but I have been converted.

This thought, in turn, leads me to the recognition that while there are ways in which I have sought to empower my students, there are also ways in which they have empowered me. We too have our own dialectic of reciprocal empowerment. Actually, the whole process gets rather complicated, but I think it can be explained simply. It begins in the classroom with me attempting as best I can to treat my students with respect, and to encourage them as best I can. As I outlined in chapter 2, my first attempts always have varying success rates because of the basic facts of the power dynamic that exists between us. I set the tasks, I set the expectations, I assign the grades. No matter how much respect I show them, the power is very much in my hands, and they know it. I once asked one of my students whether sitting in a circle for classes made us feel more like equals. He replied, "yes, but we always knew who was in charge."

When they start on their life history projects, things between us start to shift, however. As they become empowered by the fieldwork process they start to treat *me* differently, and so our relationship changes. There is still a great asymmetry in the power each of us has by virtue of our respective places in the academic system, but the exercise of that power is quite different. We start to help each other to achieve our individual goals. A greater reciprocity opens up between us and continues beyond the class, and frequently beyond graduation.

One basis of this reciprocity is the same basis for the reciprocity between fieldworker and interviewee, namely, a strong sense of identification. I see in their struggles and personal issues my own struggles and issues. I see parts of myself in them, and they recognize those parts of themselves in me. Often I do not see those parts in myself, or I do not see them very clearly until I see them in my students, and, as such they are always teaching me something about myself. Life history method is, thus, an essentially humanizing experience for all concerned—student, interviewee, *and teacher*.

Isadora Sahl's difficulties growing up in poverty because her parents made certain choices perfectly reflects my own childhood. My parents made different choices, but I still grew up on the cusp of destitution, and I know the burden. I, like her, moved away to university as soon as I could and did not return for holidays or other breaks in school time once I had left: I had no desire to look back. Like Janette Yarwood I continue to struggle with my Spanish-speaking upbringing. Like her I can lay claim to a Hispanic background, but my day-to-day world while living in the United States was predominantly Anglo, and English was my primary language. I share Andrea Pernstich's ambivalence as an immigrant to the United States. She and I live in the strange limbo of first-generation adult arrivals in a new country who are no longer comfortable back "home" but not fully integrated in our new homes. Our old world still beckons us, but when we return there our new world calls us back. I am a widower and raised my son as a single parent in rural New York, and, thus, I can identify with Onalie Oakstar and her mother. Who could my son turn to when he and I were at odds?

I do not share all the details of my personal life with my students by any means, but when significant components of my world intersect with theirs I often open up. I feel the same tensions that Michael Avrut feels in coming out to his clients, and I often settle for revealing more rather than less, knowing that there is most likely going to be more good than harm done in the process. Like social work, teaching in the social sciences necessarily engages us in complex webs of relatedness and distancing. Not only can I convey certain social facts better when I draw on personal experience, I can also touch the lives of some, not all, of my students when I open myself up more to them. There is an inevitable dynamic push and pull, of course, and I have to maintain some boundaries as I would in any relationship, pedagogic or otherwise. But my personal life, and the lives of my students, are the stuff of social science. When we explore ourselves and each other in the context of our academic interests, our analysis is intrinsically deepened.

I chose the projects in this volume for a variety of reasons. Whether or not I had some personal sense of intersection with the students represented here, my relationship with each of them was special in some way. In virtually every case, that relationship began in the fieldwork class and was cemented through the life history process. By the same token I could have chosen any number of others instead of the ones before you. What I was aiming for in choosing examples was a sense of the general norm of what I expect from the students in each class who are putting in a dedicated effort. These are not the rare projects that floated to the top (although there are some in my files that are less worthy than these). What you have here is a fair and just sampling from my store of riches.

What I will say about these students, though, is that each in his or her own way has gone on to be a community activist, and activism is a thread that runs through the life history process and my fieldwork course in general. For many years I ran an advanced seminar in field methods that focused on the use of qualitative data to influence social action in the world at large—created originally at the request of a group of students who did not want the methods course to end. One of the earliest of these seminars took a series of campus problem areas (communications, student activities, off-campus transport, housing, food, registration) and used qualitative methods to define the problems and probe potential solutions. At the end of the semester the seminar students presented their findings to the college president's council, and every one of their recommendations was adopted and funded. They would not have succeeded had they not had both the motivation to solve the problems and, as important, the professional methodology to make a case for the changes they proposed.

Every one of the projects presented here implicitly argues for a change in the world. Most of the time the change begins with a broadening of outlook. These students are asking us through their life histories to expand our worldview and see beyond stereotypes and cultural norms. These life histories instruct us that single-parent families are not intrinsically better or worse than nuclear families, and a child can be raised by two lesbian mothers in a loving way; that homeless addicts can be caring parents; that being locked up in prison can free your mind; that having a disabling injury can unlock doors that were once closed and barred; that sometimes being poor is a choice, and under certain circumstances it is the right one no matter what the culture says. All these life histories show us alternatives to the mainstream. They also reveal all the attendant problems associated with these alternatives, certainly, but at the same time they uncover unexpected benefits as well.

Marginality is a common theme here for obvious reasons. The rich and powerful have voices that do not need our help; the marginalized require our ears. What strikes me quite forcibly, though, when rereading these life histories is both the ordinariness and the multifaceted nature of the marginal life. The marginal cover the waterfront of possibilities. Is marginality so widespread that we are all marginal in one way or another? Do we all feel marginalized in at least some aspects of our daily lives? These life histories tend to support such contentions, paradoxical though they sound (is it "normal" to be marginal?). My students most definitely feel themselves marginalized—sometimes by the college experience, sometimes by the wider culture, or both—and find strength in identifying with their interviewees' marginality and coping skills. Thereby life history method itself becomes a coping skill for the marginal.

I could spend a great deal of time exposing more of the common themes of these projects and analyzing their general and specific details. But that is not the point of this work. I have quite deliberately not analyzed them extensively in my introduction to each, or here. I leave that to readers to accomplish. This is raw data at your disposal. It has the potential to enrich and empower you too if you become actively engaged with it.

I always end every class I teach by thanking my students for being in class with me. Long ago I recognized the obvious fact that a teacher without students is not a teacher: I owe my identity as a teacher to them. If I enjoy that identity (which I do), it seems appropriate to give thanks to those who make it possible for me. Let me also, therefore, thank you the reader for coming this far with me. I need you, too, because a writer with no readers is not a writer. You are also helping to make me what I am and what I can become.

Study Questions

1. What common themes and issues in the life histories can you identify that the author has not discussed?
2. What is your reaction to the author's perceived relationship with his students? Do you sympathize with it (or not)?

Notes

1. There is a growing interest in teaching cultural anthropology in secondary schools supported by the American Anthropological Association. But student fieldwork is typically not part of the curriculum.
2. Both the methods and the results of this work were published in a school manual entitled *Tri-Valley Traditions*. She ran the program for two successive years and then adapted it for use in schools in both rural and urban settings.
3. Hymes himself was dean of the School of Education at the University of Pennsylvania and used this position to teach graduate students, who, in turn, influenced and taught teachers.

References

Angrosino, Michael V. 1989. *Documents of Interaction: Biography, Autobiography, and Life History in Social Science Perspective*. Gainesville: University of Florida Press.

Archer, Margaret S. 2012. *The Reflexive Imperative in Late Modernity*. New York: Cambridge University Press.

Bauman, Richard, and Joel Sherzer (eds.). 1974. *Explorations in the Ethnography of Speaking*. Cambridge: Cambridge University Press.

Behar, Ruth. 1990. "Rage and Redemption: Reading the Life Story of a Mexican Marketing Woman." *Feminist Studies* 16(2): 223–58.

———. 1993. *Translated Woman: Crossing the Border with Esperanza's Story*. Boston: Beacon Press.

Berg, Bruce L. 2006. *Qualitative Research Methods for the Social Sciences*. 6th ed. Boston: Allyn and Bacon.

Bernard, H. Russell (ed.). 1998. *Handbook of Methods in Cultural Anthropology*. Lanham, MD: Rowman and Littlefield.

———. 2005. *Research Methods in Anthropology: Qualitative and Quantitative Approaches*. 4th ed. Lanham, MD: Rowman and Littlefield.

Bertaux, Daniel. 1981. *Biography and Society: The Life History Approach in the Social Sciences*. Newbury Park, CA: Sage.

Blincoe, Deborah. 1988. *Dimensional Dreams: Constructed Scenes from a Brooklyn Childhood*. Exhibit catalog, Delaware Valley Arts Alliance.

Blincoe, Deborah, and John Forrest. 1993. "The Dangers of Authenticity." *New York Folklore* 19(1/2): 1–14.

Brooks, Jacqueline, and Martin Brooks. 1993. *In Search of Understanding: The Case for Constructivist Classrooms*. Association for Supervision and Curriculum Development.

Casagrande, Joseph B. (ed.) 1960. *In the Company of Man: Twenty Portraits of Anthropological Informants*. New York: Harper & Row.

Chamberlayne, Prue, Joanna Bornat, and Tom Wengraf (eds.). 2000. *The Turn to Biographical Methods in Social Sciences: Comparative Issues and Examples*. London: Routledge.

Clifford, James, and George E. Marcus (eds.). 1986. *Writing Culture: The Poetics and Politics of Ethnography*. Berkeley: University of California Press.

References

Crane, Julia G. 1987. *Saba Silhouettes: Life Stories from a Caribbean Island*. New York: Vantage Press.

Crane, Julia G. (ed.). 1999. *Statia Silhouettes*. New York: Vantage Press.

Crane, Julia G., and Michael V. Angrosino. 1984. *Field Projects in Anthropology*. 3rd ed. Long Grove, IL: Waveland Press.

Crapanzano, Vincent. 1984. "Life Histories: A Review Essay." *American Anthropologist* 86: 953–60.

Crotty, M. 1998. *The Foundations of Social Research: Meaning and Perspective in the Research Process*. London: Sage.

Davies, Charlotte. 1999. *Reflexive Ethnography: A Guide to Researching Selves and Others*. New York: Routledge.

Diamond, Stanley. 1972. "Anthropology in Question." In *Reinventing Anthropology*, edited by Dell Hymes, 401–29. New York: Pantheon Books.

Dilthey, Wilhelm. 1961. *Pattern and Meaning in History: Thoughts on History and Society*. Edited by H. P. Rickman. New York: Harper Torchbooks.

Dwyer, Kevin. 1999. *Moroccan Dialogues: Anthropology in Question*. Baltimore, MD: Johns Hopkins University Press.

Dyk, Walter. 1938. *Son of Old Man Hat: A Navaho Autobiography*. New York: Harcourt, Brace, and Co.

Ellis, Carolyn, and Arthur P. Bochner (eds.). 1996. *Composing Ethnography: Alternative Forms of Qualitative Writing*. Lanham, MD: AltaMira Press.

Forrest, John. 1988. *Lord I'm Coming Home: Everyday Aesthetics in Tidewater North Carolina*. Ithaca, NY: Cornell University Press.

———. 1999. *The History of Morris Dancing (1458–1750)*. Toronto: University of Toronto Press.

———. 2022. *Doing Field Projects: Methods and Practice for Social and Anthropological Research*. New York: Wiley-Blackwell.

Forrest, John, and Deborah Blincoe. 1995. *The Natural History of the Traditional Quilt*. Austin: University of Texas Press.

Forrest, John, and Elisabeth Jackson. 1990. "Get Real: Empowering the Student through Oral History." *Oral History Review* 18(1): 29–44.

Freeman, James. 1979. *Untouchable: An Indian Life History*. Stanford, CA: Stanford University Press.

Frisch, Michael. 1990. *A Shared Authority: Essays on the Craft and Meaning of Oral and Public History*. Albany, NY: SUNY Press.

Gaudio, Rudi. 1994. "Sounding Gay: Speech Properties in the Speech of Gay and Straight Men." *American Speech* 69(1): 30–57.

Geertz, Clifford. 1990. *Works and Lives: The Anthropologist as Author*. Stanford, CA: Stanford University Press.

Giglioli, Pier Paolo (ed.). 1972. *Language and Social Context*. Harmondsworth: Penguin.

Girard, Tim. 2000. "Anthropology in the High School Curriculum." BA thesis, Purchase College, SUNY.

Goodall, H. L. 2000. *Writing the New Ethnography*. Lanham, MD: AltaMira Press.

Gumperz, John J., and Dell Hymes. 1972. *Directions in Sociolinguistics*. New York: Holt, Rinehart and Winston.

Hertz, Rosanna (ed.). 1997. *Reflexivity and Voice*. Thousand Oaks, CA: Sage.

Hurston, Zora Neale. 2018. *Barracoon: The Story of the Last "Black Cargo."* New York: Amistad.

Hymes, Dell. 1972a. "The Use of Anthropology: Critical, Political, Personal." In *Reinventing Anthropology*, edited by Dell Hymes, 3–79. New York: Pantheon Books.

———— (ed.) 1972b. *Reinventing Anthropology*. New York: Pantheon Books.

————. 1974. *Foundations in Sociolinguistics: An Ethnographic Approach*. Philadelphia: University of Pennsylvania Press.

————. 1981. *"In Vain I Tried to Tell You": Essays in Native American Ethnopoetics*. Philadelphia: University of Pennsylvania Press.

Ingold, Tim. 1991. "Fieldwork Projects in Undergraduate Anthropology." *Anthropology Today* 7(2): 22–23.

Ives, Edward D. 1974. *The Tape Recorded Interview: A Manual for Field Workers in Folklore and Oral History*. Knoxville: University of Tennessee Press.

Jay, Robert. 1972. "Personal and Extrapersonal Vision in Anthropology." In *Reinventing Anthropology*, edited by Dell Hymes, 367–81. New York: Pantheon Books.

Jenike, Mark R. 2005. "Cross-Field Collaboration in Undergraduate Education: Nutritional Anthropology and Discovery-Based Learning." *Anthropology News* 46(1): 32.

Jolly, Margaretta (ed.). 2001. *Encyclopedia of Life Writing: Autobiographical and Biographical Forms*. New York: Routledge.

Kemmis, S., and R. McTaggert (eds.). 1988. *The Action Research Reader* 3rd ed. Geelong: Deakin University Press.

Kratz, Corrine. 2001. "Conversations and Lives." In *African Words, African Voices: Critical Practices in Oral History*, edited by Luise White, Stephan Miescher and David William Cohen, 127–61. Bloomington: Indiana University Press.

Kukla, Andre. 2000. *Social Constructivism and the Philosophy of Science*. New York: Routledge.

Kumoll, Karsten. 2010. *Beyond Writing Culture: Current Intersections of Epistemologies and Representational Practices*. Oxford: Berghahn Books.

Lancy, David F. 2003. "What One Faculty Member Does to Promote Undergraduate Research." *New Directions for Teaching and Learning* 93: 87–92.

Langness, L. L. 1965. *The Life History in Anthropological Science*. New York: Holt, Rinehart and Winston.

Langness, L. L., and Gelya Frank. 1981. *Lives: An Anthropological Approach to Biography*. Novato, CA: Chandler and Sharp.

Linde, Charlotte. 1993. *Life Stories: The Creation of Coherence*. Oxford: Oxford University Press.

Livia, A., and K. Hall (eds.). 1997. *Queerly Phrased: Language, Gender and Sexuality*. Oxford: Oxford University Press.

McCutcheon, G., and B. Jurg. 1990. "Alternative Perspectives on Action Research." *Theory into Practice* 24(3): 144–51.

McKernan, J. 1991. *Curriculum Action Research: A Handbook of Methods and Resources for the Reflective Practitioner.* London: St. Martin's Press.

Marcus, George E. 1998. *Ethnography through Thick and Thin*. Princeton, NJ: Princeton University Press.

Middleton, Alexandra. 2018. "Beyond the Fieldwork Imaginary: Cultivating Undergraduate Exposure." In *Attending to Undergraduate Desire: A Collection of Papers on Making Anthropology Legible to Students, University Administrators, and the Public*, edited by Carolyn Rouse and Richard Handler. Washington, DC: American Anthropological Association.

Mishler, E. G. 1991. "Representing Discourse: The Rhetoric of Transcription." *Journal of Narrative and Life History* 1(1): 255–80.

————. 1995. "Models of Narrative Analysis: A Typology." *Journal of Narrative and Life History* 5(2): 87–123.

Neihardt, John G. 1932. *Black Elk Speaks*. New York.

Ochs, Elinor, and Lisa Capps. 1996. "Narrating the Self." *Annual Review of Anthropology* 25: 19–43.

References

Orwell, George. 1946. "Politics and the English Language." In *Shooting an Elephant and Other Essays*. London: Secker and Warburg.

Peacock, James, and Dorothy Holland. 1993. "The Narrated Self: Life Stories in Process." *Ethos* 21(4): 367–83.

Peacock, James L., and Ruel W. Tyson. 1989. *Pilgrims of Paradox: Calvinism and Experience among Primitive Baptists of the Blue Ridge*. Chapel Hill: University of North Carolina Press.

Piot, Charles (ed.). 2016. *Doing Development in West Africa: A Reader by and for Undergraduates*. Durham, NC: Duke University Press.

Prawat, R. S., and R. E. Floden 1994. "Philosophical Perspectives on Constructivist Views of Learning." *Educational Psychologist* 29(1): 37–48.

Radin, Paul. 1920. "The Autobiography of a Winnebago Indian." *University of California Publications in Archeology and Ethnology* 16: 381–473.

Rau, W., and B. S. Heyl. 1990. "Humanizing the College Classroom: Collaborative Learning and Social Organization among Students." *Teaching Sociology* 18: 141–55.

Richardson, Miles. 1990. *Cry Lonesome and Other Accounts of the Anthropologist's Project*. Albany, NY: SUNY Press.

Riessman, C. K. 1987. "When Gender Is Not Enough: Women Interviewing Women." *Gender and Society* 1: 172–207.

———. 1990. "Strategic Uses of Narrative in the Presentation of Self and Illness." *Social Science and Medicine* 30: 1195–1200.

———. 1993. *Narrative Analysis*. Qualitative Research Methods Series Vol. 30. Newbury Park, CA: Sage.

Rosengarten, Theodore. 1974. *All God's Dangers: The Life of Nate Shaw*. New York: Alfred A. Knopf.

Rosenwald, George C., and Richard L. Ochberg (eds.). 1992. *Storied Lives: The Cultural Politics of Self-Understanding*. New Haven, CT: Yale University Press.

Sanjek, Roger. 1990. *Fieldnotes: The Makings of Anthropology*. Ithaca, NY: Cornell University Press.

Scholte, Bob. 1972. "Toward a Reflexive and Critical Anthropology." In *Reinventing Anthropology*, edited by Dell Hymes, 430–57. New York: Pantheon Books.

Sharma, U. 1989. "Fieldwork in the Undergraduate Curriculum: Its Merits." *British Association for Social Anthropology in Policy and Practice* 3: 3–4.

———. 1991. "Field Research in the Undergraduate Curriculum." *Anthropology in Action* 10: 8–11.

Sharma, U., and S. Wright. 1989. "Practical Relevance of Undergraduate Courses." *British Association for Social Anthropology in Policy and Practice* 2: 7–9.

Shostak, Marjorie. 1981. *Nisa: The Life and Words of a !Kung Woman*. Cambridge, MA: Harvard University Press.

Simmons, Leo W. 1942. *Sun Chief: The Autobiography of a Hopi Indian*. New Haven, CT: Yale University Press.

Slavin, R. E. 1989. "Research on Cooperative Learning: An International Perspective." *Scandinavian Journal of Educational Research* 33(4): 231–43.

Spradley, James P., and David W. McCurdy. 1972. *The Cultural Experience: Ethnography in Complex Society*. Long Grove, IL: Waveland Press.

Thorn, R., and S. Wright. 1990. "Projects and Placements in Undergraduate Anthropology." *British Association for Social Anthropology in Policy and Practice* 7: 4–5.

Titon, Jeff Todd. 1988. *Powerhouse for God*. Austin: University of Texas Press.

Totten, S., T. Sills, A. Digby, and P. Russ. 1991. *Cooperative Learning: A Guide to Research*. New York: Garland Science.

Turnbull, Colin M. 1972. *The Mountain People*. New York: Touchstone.

Urban, Greg. 1989. "The 'I' of discourse." In *Semiotics, Self and Society*, edited by B. Lee and G. Urban, 27–52. Berlin: Mouton.

Watson, C. W. 1995. "Case Study: Fieldwork in Undergraduate Anthropology—For and Against." *Innovations in Education and Training International* 32(2): 153–61.

Wigginton, Eliot. 1986. *Sometimes a Shining Moment: The Foxfire Experience*. New York: Anchor.

Windeatt, B. A. (trans.). 1985. *The Book of Margery Kempe*. London: Penguin.

Wolcott, Harry. 2005. *The Art of Fieldwork*. Lanham, MD: Rowman and Littlefield.

Index

AA, 18, 19, 27, 80. *See also* Alcoholics Anonymous.
Abraham Lincoln, 47
activism, 199
AIDS, 78, 83, 91, 99, 117–18, 163. *See also* HIV
alcoholic, 18, 161
Alcoholics Anonymous, 18, 27. *See also* AA
anti-objective, 11
asthma, 95, 105, 106, 107, 108
Attica, 42
Austria, 166, 167
authentic voice, 2, 10, 14, 20, 22, 35, 41–44, 78, 79, 92, 150, 165
autobiography, 2, 13, 14–15, 20

Bank Street College, 102
Bartsch, 177
bathhouse, 81
Berlin, 168, 170, 173, 176, 183, 188, 191
Berlin Wall, 168
Black Elk Speaks, 16
black plague, 45
Blincoe, Deborah, 63, 195, 203
bookstore, 79, 80, 86
Boston, 96, 202
Boy's Club, 118, 119, 120

Brooklyn, 41, 53, 97, 160, 202
Budapest, 176, 181

C. S. Lewis, 121
Camden, SC, 44
cancer, 101
Carnegie Library, 74–75
coal, 65, 66, 67, 70
Columbia University, 45, 69, 101–3, 125, 127
CORE, 104
Crane, Stephen, 2

Dilthey, Wilhelm, 14
disabled, 21, 64
drugs, 84, 111, 112, 113, 114, 129–31, 153, 157, 159–64

East Germany, 166–68, 170–71, 175–76, 183–84, 189, 190, 192
embassy, 170, 177
ethnopoetics, 20

family, 11, 18, 38, 42, 43, 46–47, 51–52, 55, 65–66, 68, 70–71, 78, 98–99, 100, 109, 112, 114–15, 128, 133, 135–136, 144, 148, 151–53, 161, 167, 169, 170–72, 175, 176, 188, 190

farmer, 65, 66
football, 138

gonorrhea, 45–47
HIP, 104–5, 109
HIV, 152–53, 164. *See also* AIDS
Hollywood, 140
Hungarian, 179, 181
Hymes, Dell, 3–6, 9–10, 20, 26, 196

intimacy, 15, 25, 85, 86–87
Ithaca, 143–44, 203, 205

jail, 131, 153, 155, 158–59, 163, 166.
   See also prison
Jenkintown, 137, 141, 142, 143, 144

kinship, 6–7, 135

lacrosse, 138
Larry Kramer, 91

Manhattan, 96–97, 100
Margery Kempe, 14, 206
marginalized, 200
marriage, 12, 68, 82, 87
Mine Shaft, 82–83, 91
Monroeville, PA, 67–69, 73, 74
Montour Falls, 143–44
mule, 50, 67

New Jersey, 80, 144
New York, 2, 49, 51, 52, 54–56, 61,
   63, 77, 78, 81, 97, 100, 160, 169,
   195–96, 198
New York Folklore, 63
North Carolina, 11, 13, 111

objectivity, 10–11, 14, 78
Orwell, George, 19

poverty, 94–96, 100, 198
Prague, 176
prison, 32, 33, 34, 35, 167, 175, 176,
   180–87, 189, 199. *See also* jail
   clothes, 185
   language, 185
Prohibition., 72
publication, 36, 37
Puerto Rico, 150, 151, 154–57, 160, 163
Puritan, 65

recorder, 15, 16, 25, 29–30, 44, 134,194
reflexivity, 10, 16

sexuality, 78, 87–88
sharecropping, 49–50
slave, 47
Spanish, 150–54, 165, 198
Sri Lanka, 170
Stasi, 183, 189, 192

tea, 180–81
testimony, 17–19
transcription, 13, 23, 26, 31–38, 43, 66,
   76, 79, 92, 136, 148, 150, 152

Verstehen, 14, 15
video, 6, 137
videotape, 136, 148
Vietnam, 2, 125
Village (Greenwich), 80

Washington Heights, 96
Weber, Max, 14
Wigginton, Eliot, 195
Wilkinsburg, PA, 68
WPA, 72

Yale University, 153
Yauco, 159

www.ingramcontent.com/pod-product-compliance
Ingram Content Group UK Ltd.
Pitfield, Milton Keynes, MK11 3LW, UK
UKHW020719180125
453877UK00007BA/90